CHILD and YOUTH CARE
across SECTORS

CHILD and YOUTH CARE across SECTORS

Canadian Perspectives | Volume 1

Edited by Kiaras Gharabaghi and Grant Charles

CANADIAN
SCHOLARS

Toronto | Vancouver

Child and Youth Care across Sectors: Canadian Perspectives, Volume 1
Edited by Kiaras Gharabaghi and Grant Charles

First published in 2019 by
Canadian Scholars, an imprint of CSP Books Inc.
425 Adelaide Street West, Suite 200
Toronto, Ontario
M5V 3C1

www.canadianscholars.ca

Library and Archives Canada Cataloguing in Publication

Title: Child and youth care across sectors : Canadian perspectives / edited by Kiaras Gharabaghi and Grant Charles.
Names: Gharabaghi, Kiaras, editor. | Charles, Grant, 1953- editor.
Description: Includes bibliographical references and index.
Identifiers: Canadiana (print) 20190055383 | Canadiana (ebook) 20190055448 |
    ISBN 9781773381039 (v. 1 ; softcover) | ISBN 9781773381046 (v. 1 ; PDF) |
    ISBN 9781773381053 (v. 1 ; EPUB)
Subjects: LCSH: Child care—Canada. | LCSH: Child care services—Canada. | LCSH:
    Children—Institutional care—Canada.
Classification: LCC HQ778.7.C3 C55 2019 | DDC 362.70971—dc23

Text and cover design by Elisabeth Springate

Printed and bound in Ontario, Canada

Canadä

CONTENTS

INTRODUCTION

A Profession on the Move

Kiaras Gharabaghi and Grant Charles

Child and youth care is not unique to North America. Quite to the contrary, much longer and deeper traditions of being with young people, their families, and their communities exist in other parts of the world, especially in southern Africa and Europe, but also in Asia, South America, and Indigenous communities around the world. While the professions involved in child and youth care may go by different names, the idea of being with young people where their lives unfold is certainly not a uniquely Canadian or North American idea. Nevertheless, there has been for quite some time now a uniquely North American, and especially Canadian, approach to building a profession based on a particular way of being in the world. This way of being centres relational practice (Garfat, 2008), life-space intervention (Gharabaghi & Stuart, 2013), strength-based approaches (Oliver & Charles, 2014, 2015, 2016), and reflective, ethical praxis (White, 2008).

We are very proud to be presenting this two-volume series about child and youth care practice in Canada. We believe that it is in and of itself noteworthy that this field we have been building collectively for the past 50 years or so can now be found, in some form, across many different sectors and contexts that involve young people, their families, and their communities. We have come a long way from our institutional beginnings. While not everything in our field is cause for celebration, the fact that we need two volumes in order to describe where we work, how we work, and how we might further evolve as a collective enterprise is quite something! We offer this two-volume series not as an analysis of what child and youth care is or how to practise child and youth care most effectively, but instead as a way of capturing the rich, expansive, hopeful, and sometimes problematic ways in which our professional identity appears across service settings, child and youth spaces, communities, institutions, identities, and geographic regions. As we will discuss later in this introduction, there is not currently a book or series of books that explores our field, for better or for worse, in the context of its traditional sectors, such as residential care, foster care, school-based practice, and hospital-based practice; emerging sectors such as immigration and settlement programs, in-home support services, autism communities, Deaf communities, and Trans people's communities; or cutting-edge sectors such as digital life-space and post-secondary education as practice settings. At the same time, we want to engage in contexts in which our field has largely been silent and, through that silence, complicit in chronic and deeply embedded structures of oppression. To this end, we present our field also in the context of Black Youth,[1] gendered practice, and youth justice. And of course we will dedicate considerable space and attention to the Indigenous contexts of our field, including those the field has largely neglected as well as those the field has meaningfully engaged. Finally, this two-volume series will do something that has never been done before in the Canadian child and youth care field—it will include discussions of geographies that virtually never appear alongside discussions of Canada's child and youth service systems. To this end, we are also drawing attention to child and youth care in the North and in Quebec, knowing that these geographic and cultural contexts are largely foreign to most child and youth care students and practitioners. But let us not get ahead of ourselves. We want to first provide some context about how we understand our field and its evolution over time. We believe a lot has happened over the years, and a lot more is about to happen as we move forward.

TRACING CHILD AND YOUTH CARE IN CANADA

There was a time, not so long ago, when child and youth care was more of an idea than a profession. While much of the field today owes a great debt to 20th-century pioneers such as August Aichhorn (1951), Fritz Redl (1957), and Urie Bronfenbrenner (1979), it wasn't really until the late 1960s and into the 1970s that we came to know a "field" called child and youth care. Perhaps one of the stranger aspects of this field is that the more we move ahead, the more we attribute our field further into the past. Today, it is not unusual for some people in our field to cite Janus Korczak (1991 [1925]) and Jane Addams (1910) as early 20th-century child and youth care pioneers (the former because of his heroic commitment to children before and during the Nazi era, and the latter for her work in the settlement sector in Chicago, captured beautifully in the book *Hull House*), despite the fact that Korczak was a pediatrician and Addams was a social worker. Accounts of the history of child and youth care frequently reference developments during the 19th century and the period of rapid industrialization and accompanying urbanization as the starting point of values, practices, and ideas that ultimately gave rise to child and youth care a century later (Charles & Gabor, 2006; Charles & Garfat, 2009). Indeed, when it comes to the active practice of being with young people, engaging young people, and sharing their life-space, one might, without sounding too far off, even cite the Platonic dialogues, and in particular the representation of Socrates, as antique roots for the field; Socrates was, after all, ultimately sentenced to death for "corrupting the minds of youth," presumably with radical thoughts on justice, rationality, and enlightenment.

We don't want to provide a complete history of child and youth care for several reasons. First, it is likely impossible to do so in a way that would capture all of the possible individuals and historical scenarios that may have contributed to the idea of child and youth care as we know it today, not to mention that any such attempt would inevitably represent very strong Eurocentric biases. We in North America know very little about historical accounts of being with young people in other cultural and geographic contexts, perhaps with some exceptions (such as the context of South Africa, which has a rather well-documented history of child care practices and, today, one of the most developed child and youth care infrastructures in the world). Secondly, any such history, even if one accepts the Eurocentric biases, would require a multi-volume work in order to do justice to both the highlights and the lowlights of historical features of our field. Indeed, even in Canada, the lowlights sometimes are startling; the history of residential schools, featuring the very public and both state- and church-sponsored attempts to "civilize" Indigenous peoples, could easily be seen as a historical manifestation of one sort of child and youth care practice (Charles, 2015). Thirdly and perhaps most importantly, our goal in this book is not so much to represent or reinterpret the past as it is to consider the present and deliberate on the future of what now is, without any doubt, a field of practice in its own right, complete with practitioners who are far more professionalized than ever before, a post-secondary education system that is expansive and still growing, and a multitude of contexts and service sectors in which our practices unfold. We want to do this specifically from a Canadian perspective, citing Canadian examples, and using largely, but not exclusively, the latest and strongest Canadian scholarship and practice leadership as our guide.

Interestingly, our goal of describing, critically engaging, and ultimately saying something meaningful about the future of child and youth care across service sectors in Canada is not without precedent. In fact, at least three books come to mind, which were all published within short succession of one another about 25 years ago. The first of these is an edited collection by Denholm, Ferguson, and Pence originally published in 1987 and then re-issued as a second edition in 1993. Right in the middle of the years between the two editions came another volume (1990), edited by the same three in addition to James Anglin, that had a slightly different focus but included chapters that similarly sought to speculate on the future of the field. And a third book, published in 1988, is an edited collection by Charles and Gabor that focuses on child and youth care practice across service sectors in Alberta, and that, much like this volume, includes contributors from academia and from practice.

The 1980s and early 1990s were a time of very rapid expansion of writing, academic and practice gatherings, and professional development of the field of child and youth care in Canada. The *Journal of Child and Youth Care* started its run of 15 volumes in the mid-1980s (led by founding editors Gerry Fewster and Thom Garfat), ultimately becoming transformed into *Relational Child and Youth Care Practice* in 2003 (under the leadership of then-Managing Editor Carol Stuart). The first national child and youth care conference was held in Victoria in 1981, and Canada (Vancouver) hosted the first international gathering of child and youth care academics and practitioners in 1985. Provincial child and youth care associations were formed or resuscitated from the ashes of previous attempts *en masse*, with especially strong movements in Alberta and Ontario during the 1980s. And during this time, the conceptual and research-based writing in the field really took off; Gerry Fewster, for example, gave us *Being in Child Care: Journey into Self* in 1990. Thom Garfat started on a tear of publications during this time, ultimately leading to the development of the International Child and Youth Care Network (CYC-Net) in collaboration with friends in South Africa. Perhaps most importantly, and with transformative consequence, cross-border connections in the child and youth care community resulted in a North

American whirlwind of discussion, gatherings, and publications involving the likes of Mark Krueger, Karen VanderVen, Martha Mattingly, and Lorraine Fox, all of whom became regular attendees at Canadian child and youth care events and gatherings.

By the 1990s, the profession of child and youth care practice clearly was on the move across North America, with Canadian and American contributors closely connected. Concepts and theoretical frameworks were being developed faster than these could be absorbed in practice settings. Much of the substantive content of the field was framed around several key approaches to being with young people, building on the work of Bronfenbrenner (ecological perspectives); Lewin and Redl (life-space intervention); Maier (therapeutic relationships); and the emerging work of Fewster (self), Garfat (relational practice), VanderVen (engagement and activity-based approaches), Fox (trauma-informed care), Krueger (teamwork and working in the moment), and Brendtro, Durrant, and many others (strength-based work). As much as these theoretical and conceptual formulations were gaining strength, perhaps the more significant development during the 1990s and into the 21st century related to the field itself, and specifically the kind of work settings where child and youth care practitioners found themselves engaged and employed.

It is important to point out that in spite of the very significant and rapid growth of thought, ideas, and approaches in child and youth care described above, much of the field and indeed much of the infrastructure developing around the field was still focused on the residential care, or the milieu, context. In Canada, group care was (and in some provinces still is) by far the largest employer of child and youth care practitioners, although it is notable that the nature of residential group care also evolved into myriad forms and contexts. These ranged from privately owned group homes that housed young people often without much oversight or accountability (and often in rural and isolated areas) to treatment-oriented facilities as part of children's mental health service systems and agencies. The role of child and youth care practitioners reflected this differentiation in group care settings; in some organizations, child and youth care practitioners were presumed to be little more than security guards, tasked with behaviour containment duties and offered virtually no training or supervision. In other contexts, the practitioners became highly trained and skilled professionals with responsibilities that ranged from the everyday provision of care to case coordination, family work, and treatment provision, usually in multi-disciplinary teams that also included psychologists, psychiatric consultation, and clinical social workers.

The 1990s also featured increasingly dialectical trends across Canada. In British Columbia, residential group care started to decline significantly, and remains a relatively small component of the child and youth service system today. In Ontario, by contrast, the 1990s were a time of massive expansion of the group care system, both in the private sector and also in the public child protection sector. Especially after some legislative changes in child protection that incorporated "abandonment" as a protection criterion, a massive influx of young teenagers quickly overwhelmed the system and group homes suddenly emerged everywhere. Even Children's Aid Societies (CASs) joined the build-up of this sector, and at its height roughly between 2000 and 2005, CASs in Ontario were operating just over 40 group homes themselves, in addition to more than 300 group homes operated by the private sector. Other provinces largely stayed the course, with Alberta and Nova Scotia in particular maintaining quite steady numbers of programs over this period.

In spite of the overwhelming focus on group care across much of the country, other service sectors started to incorporate child and youth care practitioners, or, in many cases, at least the values and approaches of child and youth care practice, in the hope that these could be implemented by individuals with all kinds of different pre-service backgrounds ranging from university degrees in psychology and sociology to high school diplomas; college certificates in social service work, human development, addictions, or developmental services; and even work backgrounds in farming, industry, or general labour. In some of the poorly funded sectors, such as youth homelessness, street-involved youth, or neighbourhood services, child and youth care emerged as an idea but without trained professionals. In the better-funded sectors, such as education, hospitals, children's mental health services, and foster care, much greater emphasis on proper credentials and higher levels of training was evident.

Over the course of the past 15 years or so, something dramatic happened in the field of child and youth care. Although the beginnings of child and youth care practice across sectors are located much earlier in the field's development, the "normalization" of child and youth care deployment across sectors really took off, quite abruptly and with considerable consequence. In fact, it is increasingly difficult to identify any social sector in Canadian society, across provinces (but a little less so across territories), that has not been impacted by child and youth care in some shape or form. Today, we find child and youth care practitioners still deeply embedded in residential group care, but we also find them in day treatment settings; working to support foster care placements; providing interventions in family homes; participating as team members in in-patient eating disorder units, psychiatric units, and paediatric units in hospitals engaged with social groups often long neglected in terms of supportive or therapeutic services such as the LGBTQ2S+ community, newcomers, specific cultural groups, and First Nations, Métis, and Inuit urban communities. In British Columbia, a combination of growth and development in the School of Child and Youth Care at the University of Victoria and significant shortages of qualified human resources resulted in the acceptance of child and youth care-degreed individuals as eligible for child protection jobs. In Ontario, the rapidly growing autism service sector is increasingly incorporating child and youth care approaches and practitioners, and in Newfoundland, the entire child protection system is shifting towards a progressive form of foster care led by a child and youth care professional.

One area of child and youth care activity that is perhaps still somewhat underestimated in terms of its growth is the policy and advocacy sector. With the rapid proliferation of university degrees in child and youth care, even at the graduate level at the University of Victoria, at Concordia University in Montreal, and at Ryerson University in Toronto, child and youth care practitioners are increasingly emerging in municipal and provincial policy circles. At the municipal level, we find them in particular in social policy, housing, and recreation departments, and at the provincial level, they are well represented in provincial advocacy offices and in corporate or regional ministry offices, charged with developing child welfare and children's mental health policy and regulation. Furthermore, the past decade has seen enormous growth of private-sector activity among child and youth care practitioners. They are leading private, often for-profit agencies that provide residential care, therapeutic foster care, counselling and outreach services, insurance-funded rehabilitation services, as well as adventure-based and outdoor therapeutic activity, camps, and back-country trips.

A PROFESSION ON THE MOVE

Child and youth care is clearly a profession on the move. For many, this is exciting and undoubtedly a positive development. It is important, however, not to overlook the challenges and less positive aspects of the rapid growth of this profession. Although pre-service training through colleges and universities has become the norm, curriculum has improved, professionalization has made progress, and even issues of compensation and professional recognition have shown encouraging improvements, the quality of practice, the ethical foundations of many practice approaches, the level of supervision, and the commitment to excellence are not to be taken for granted. To state it more succinctly, there have always been and there continue to be many examples of bad practice. Many young people in very vulnerable situations are not receiving particularly good services from child and youth care practitioners. Feedback from young people who lived in group care and also foster care continues to be overwhelmingly negative. Re-traumatization of wounded young people due to insensitivity or incompetence is not at all uncommon.

In addition, the service sectors that have in fact incorporated child and youth care practitioners, or that have adopted child and youth care approaches, have not necessarily shifted their service cultures, their operational procedures, or even their organizational styles and rhythms to reflect the profession's values. Congruence within agencies and across service sectors remains a major problem. In spite of the recognition that such congruence, focused on relational practice, on well-articulated approaches to caring, and on ensuring young people's participation and empowerment in their own treatment, service, or goal setting, is an essential feature to excellence (Anglin, 2002), it is often not present. Stories about institutional abuse, neglect, or simply inadequate service are ubiquitous across the country.

The outcomes of services that feature child and youth care practitioners in significant numbers are ambiguous. Young people living in group homes are still far more likely to be criminally charged for their behaviour than young people living at home (Finlay, 2007). The percentage of homeless youth with a history of foster or group care is still far greater than it should be. Graduation rates from high school for young people growing up in care are far below those for the general population, even if one factors in learning disabilities and other adversities (Gharabaghi, 2010, 2011). Young people involved in any service system are far more likely to be suspended from school. Indigenous youth in urban settings and Black Youth are overrepresented in custody settings, school suspension programs, and the homelessness sector. Notwithstanding significant improvements in some agencies, service sectors continue to struggle with their approaches to serving members of the LGBTQ2S+ community, and issues of cultural competence, identity politics, and other oppressive dynamics are alive and well across sectors.

It becomes clear, then, that as the field of child and youth care continues to grow and expand or becomes consolidated in service sectors and settings that are quite different than the milieu-based residential care sector of its origins, much work needs to be done. This includes work to ensure that practitioners who identify with the field are competent; understand their roles, their capacity, and also their limitations; and contribute to the development of congruent structures, organizational cultures, and everyday practices that are centred around the principles of care and relational practice.

One important component of doing this work is to ensure the field creates opportunities for a holistic self-reflection—a way of exploring itself in its totality, across all of the service sectors where it is present, and also across jurisdictions or contexts that offer specific or unique circumstances and approaches to practices pursuant to such circumstances. This is what this two-volume series aims to do; it is a broad survey across service sectors and contexts that explores the role of child and youth care in each of these, with a view of describing current trends in each sector, exploring prospects and challenges for the field currently and in the near future, and providing hard-hitting analysis of how the field in one sector might interface with the field in other sectors. The two-volume series presents a conversation amongst individuals, academics, and practitioners who have long been involved in this field of child and youth care, and who have observed changing patterns, trends, and dynamics over the years.

THE TWO-VOLUME SERIES

This two-volume series is centred around Canadian perspectives and experiences. Nevertheless, we recognize that the field of child and youth care has also evolved significantly in other jurisdictions, similarly to the Canadian experience in some cases, but also quite differently in other cases. Each of the chapters, therefore, will make an effort to provide some global context. This is especially appropriate given the many connections of Canadian child and youth care practitioners, commentators, and scholars with their peer communities in especially the US, the UK, Ireland, South Africa, Israel, Australia, and Europe (especially Germany, the Netherlands, and Denmark). Each of the contributors was asked to incorporate a series of objectives into the writing of their chapter; this is different than providing a rigid structure for each chapter from the outset, and appropriate given that each contributor's experience within a particular sector is premised on their particular context, situation, and professional pathway. The objectives common to all the chapters include a description of the evolution of child and youth care involvement in the sector/region/context; an analysis of the current status of child and youth care in the sector/region/context, including pressures and challenges, and prospects and opportunities; exploring the connections between the sector/region/context and other sectors/regions/contexts— cross-referenced to other chapters in the book; discussing the prospects of the sector/region/context as an employment sector for CYC practitioners; and finally, looking forward, and anticipating and/or recommending directions for child and youth care within the sector/region/context.

The first volume of the series covers a range of traditional CYC sectors and contexts, as well as long-neglected or newly emerging contexts such as Trans communities, the Deaf communities, and digital life-space. We are also pleased to have chapters on the post-secondary education context as a site of practice, as well as outdoor and adventure-based settings. What is missing from this first volume is a focus on Indigenous communities. This is not an oversight, but instead a decision we made as editors of this series to group the three chapters on Indigenous contexts together in the second volume. Volume 2 of the series will also have a chapter on Black Youth, which is particularly significant in the contexts of Ontario and Nova Scotia, but elsewhere too.

Between the two volumes, we have tried very hard to represent virtually every practice context of the field of child and youth care in Canada today. We have no doubt that additional contexts will emerge with time. We have also made a conscious effort to recruit writers for the chapters that reflect diversity in the context of not only identity, but also professional location. To this end, we are delighted to have some of the most prolific writers and thought leaders in the field in Canada represented while also being able to introduce emerging scholars. In many instances, our writers are both scholars and practitioners, which, uniquely in the field of child and youth care, is not uncommon. Our hope is that this mix of writers presents you, the reader, with perspectives that reflect on decades of involvement in the field on the one hand, and on the other hand, the optimism, hopefulness, and sharp and sometimes edgy perspectives of those much earlier in their practice and/or scholarly careers.

We will start this volume with what are arguably the two most traditional and embedded sectors in the field of child and youth care—residential care and foster care. From there, we will journey along with our writers to the community, into the outdoors, through the halls of post-secondary institutions, right into the homes of families and beyond.

NOTE

1. Throughout this book, we (the editors of this volume) decided to use capital *B* and capital *Y* when using the term *Black Youth*. We did so because on more than one occasion when meeting with groups of African Canadian young people, one of us (Gharabaghi) has been told that they prefer the term *Black Youth* so long as it is capitalized and specifically refers to young people involved with child welfare or other child and youth services. One particular young person explained that the term *Black Youth* is similar to the designation as Canadian; it provides for a common experience and context but appreciates that there is diversity within the group. We also decided to capitalize the word *Indigenous* throughout the book, but not the word *youth* when referencing Indigenous youth; this is because Indigenous young people have explained to one of us (Gharabaghi) that they see themselves as part of communities, and capitalizing the word *youth* would suggest a division between the communities and the young people within that community. Note that our decisions in this respect are responsive only to the young people who have spoken to us about these issues; we do not claim that these decisions are in any way representative of the preferences of all African Canadian or Indigenous youth. Furthermore, these decisions were made by us as the editors of this volume, not by the authors of the individual chapters, who may or may not have made the same choice.

REFERENCES

Addams, J. (1910). *Twenty years at Hull-House: With autobiographical notes.* New York: Macmillan.

Aichhorn, A. (1951). *Wayward youth.* London, UK: Vivago.

Anglin, J. (2002). *Normality and the struggle for congruence: Reinterpreting residential care for children and youth.* Binghampton, NY: Haworth Press.

Anglin, J., Denholm, C., Ferguson, R., & Pence, A. (1990). *Perspectives in professional child & youth care.* Binghampton, NY: Haworth Press.

Bronfenbrenner, U. (1979). *The ecology of human development.* Cambridge, MA: Harvard University Press.

Charles, G. (2015). Doomed to repeat it: The selective and collective ignorance of the shadowy historical foundations of child and youth care. *International Child and Youth Care, 200,* 52–58.

Charles, G., & Gabor, P. (Eds.). (1988). *Issues in child and youth care practice in Alberta.* Lethbridge, AB: Lethbridge Community College.

Charles, G., & Gabor, P. (2006). An historical perspective on residential services for troubled and troubling youth in Canada revisited. *Relational Child and Youth Care Practice*, *19*(4), 17–26.

Charles, G., & Garfat, T. (2009). Child and youth care practice in North America: Historical roots and current challenges. *Relational Child and Youth Care Practice, 22*(2), 17–28.

Denholm, C., Ferguson, R., & Pence, A. (1987). *Professional child and youth care.* Vancouver: UBC Press.

Denholm, C., Ferguson, R., & Pence, A. (1993). *Professional child and youth care* (2nd ed.). Vancouver: UBC Press.

Fewster, G. (1990). *Being in child care: Journey into self.* London, UK: Haworth Press.

Finlay, J. (2007). *Keeping kids safe in custody: Youths' perception of safety while incarcerated in Canada*. Waterloo, ON: Wilfrid Laurier University.

Garfat, T. (2008). Gestures and moments that change our lives. *Relational Child & Youth Care Practice, 21*(2), 75–76.

Gharabaghi, K. (2010). In-service training and professional development in residential child and youth care settings: A three sector comparison in Ontario. *Residential Treatment for Children & Youth, 27*(2), 92–114.

Gharabaghi, K. (2011). A child & youth care approach to residential care management. *Relational Child & Youth Care Practice, 24*(1/2), 133–141.

Gharabaghi, K., & Stuart, C. (2013). *Right here, right now: Exploring life-space interventions for children and youth.* Toronto: Pearson.

Korczak, J. (1991 [1925]). *When I am little again / The child's right to respect.* Lanham, MD: University Press of America.

Oliver, C., & Charles, G. (2014). *Strengths-based practice in child protection.* Victoria, BC: British Columbia Ministry of Children and Family Development.

Oliver, C., & Charles, G. (2015). Which strengths-based practice? Reconciling strengths-based practice and mandated authority in child protection work. *Social Work, 60*(2), 135–143.

Oliver, C., & Charles, G. (2016). Enacting firm, fair and friendly practice: A model for strengths-based child protection relationships? *British Journal of Social Work, 46*(4), 1009–1026.

Redl, F., & Wineman D. (1957). *The aggressive child.* New York: The Free Press.

White, J. (2008). The knowing, doing, and being in context: A praxis-oriented approach to child and youth care. In G. Bellefeuille & F. Ricks (Eds.), *Standing on the precipice: Inquiry into the creative potential of child and youth care practice* (pp. 109–134). Edmonton, AB: MacEwan Press.

CHAPTER 1

The Classic Setting: Residential Care
and Treatment

Kiaras Gharabaghi and Grant Charles

HISTORICAL CONTEXT

No sector or setting is more closely associated with child and youth care practice than residential care and treatment. Indeed, the field of child and youth care evolved from within residential group care settings. While the earliest examples of residential care go back to at least the orphanages of ancient Rome (Miller, 2003), the modern institutions within which child and youth care eventually grew from appeared in the mid-1800s (Charles, 2015; Charles & Garfat, 2009). The earliest examples of formal residential care in Canada were religious-based orphanages and the "condition"-based institutions. These included "institutions for idiots" and "institutions for the feeble-minded," "homes for incorrigible girls," "schools for the deaf and dumb," as well as "receiving houses" for the Home Children (Charles, 2015). This last group was poor children brought over from the United Kingdom to serve as farm hands and domestic servants (Charles, 2015, 2018). The Indian Residential School System was also set up during this period (Truth and Reconciliation Commission [TRC], 2015).

The original institutions were set up during what has been labelled the child-saving era (Charles & Gabor, 2006). While the stated objective of the time was to help children, intervention was based upon a self-righteous sense of moral, racial, gender, ability, and class superiority that manifested an obligation to help those who were deemed inferior while at the same time dehumanizing and de-personalizing them (Charles, 2015). Later stages in the development of residential services moved away from a stance of moral superiority to one of professional superiority where there was still a hierarchical orientation that exposed a belief that the people receiving the services were somehow lesser beings who needed the direction of those who knew better. It is only in recent years that there have been beginning attempts at *joining with* rather than lording over service recipients. The previous philosophies, though, have not fully disappeared from residential services (Charles & Gabor, 1991).

Residential programs are a reflection of the values of the times in which they were established (Charles & Gabor, 2006). While these values can change over time, there are often residual influences from earlier times that linger below the surface in programs even if the current philosophies said to be used in the setting are described in contemporary terms. This is important to remember as these hidden values can still drive how staff interact with young people and families.

CURRENT CONTEXT

There is wide variation within the residential care landscapes both across the country and within local jurisdictions. On the one hand, there are service providers with clearly identifiable standards around hiring practices, quality of care, training and professional development, and outcomes-focused strategies, and on the other hand, there are service providers who are still operating based on the intuition and accumulated wisdom of the program founders. This holds true across the public, profit, and non-profit arenas (Gharabaghi, 2011). This variation is in part a result of the sector developing with minimal regulation and standards. This only began to change in the 1980s when a number of jurisdictions developed basic standards of care that went beyond focusing almost solely on the programs' physical environment, in response to a number of institutional abuse scandals (Harris, 1991; Taylor, 2015; TRC, 2015; Wheatley, 2013). This has led to a current emphasis upon higher standards of care predicated on evidence-based practices (Charles, Ernst, & Ponzetti, 2003; Charles & White, 2008; Hiebert & Charles, 2008), although a great deal of work remains to be done before there is a consistent and high-quality residential service system (Gharabaghi, Trocmé, & Newman, 2016).

There are also significant differences in the theoretical groundings of the sector depending upon the jurisdiction. For example, in Quebec, both residential care and the field of child and youth care more generally (psychoeducation) has developed according to norms and conceptual models much more akin to some European, and particularly French, jurisdictions (see Mann-Feder, this volume).

Group care service provision also varies in a number of other ways across the country. These include the size of the organization, which can range from multi-service, multi-site, and multi-disciplinary large organizations with multi-million dollar budgets to a house somewhere in a rural setting operating on a shoestring budget in near-total isolation. Some group care is operated on campus-like properties on the edges of cities; other group care is operated in regular homes in suburban or downtown neighbourhoods; and still other group care is operated in rural isolation far from any community or urban life. There is also uncertainty about what kinds of services are to be included when discussing group care. Minimally, we include staffed group care programs for child welfare–involved young people, but additionally, we sometimes include child and youth mental health treatment centres, hospital-based in-patient psychiatric units or eating disorder clinics, homeless youth shelters, youth custody programs, and potentially even private boarding schools that may specialize in serving young people facing adversities.

In short, discussing child and youth care practice in the residential care and treatment sector is no easy task; inevitably, a single chapter cannot capture the nuances of all of these variations, nor can it do justice to all the excellent innovations and practices that unfold in this sector. But it can, perhaps, capture the core elements and principles of child and youth care practice as they relate to group care, and it can also outline the landscape of professional opportunities embedded within this sector.

CHILD AND YOUTH CARE PRINCIPLES OF RESIDENTIAL CARE AND TREATMENT

It should be said at the outset that child and youth care thinking about group care and child and youth care practice in group care are often, but not always, worlds apart. In a positive scenario, we can identify specific agencies and organizations across Canada that operate their programs in accordance with core child and youth care principles (Charles, 2016; Gharabaghi, Charles, & Kavanagh, 2016). This means that they are fundamentally oriented towards a caring and sometimes even loving environment (or milieu), in which staff and young people are relationally engaged and where practice is reflective in nature. Staff supervision occurs consistently and in myriad forms; staff are trained and have meaningful pre-service qualifications; and issues of child and youth participation, community involvement, family involvement, and participation, as well as varied and meaningful therapeutic programming, are readily identifiable. These programs do exist, even if much of the current attention paid to group care does not reference them. Instead, between professional commentators, grey literature such as government reports, expert reviews, and scholarly explorations of residential service systems, as well as media reports, the focus is often squarely on the less-than-desirable conditions in group care. It is true that one can readily identify these scenarios as well: programs based on control, conformity, and compliance, where young people are subject to near-total surveillance at all times, where relationships are commodified as things one "has," and where child and youth participation is rejected on the basis that the young people are far too damaged to meaningfully contribute to their own care. Even in usually public, multi-disciplinary, and often very expensive residential treatment settings that explicitly emphasize their work with families from systemic perspectives, one often struggles to find any meaningful forms of family involvement, participation, and engagement.

In this chapter, we don't want to focus on the problems of residential group care in practice. Instead, we want to highlight some of the ideas and innovations that the field of child and youth care has contributed and continues to contribute to residential group care. Specifically, we want to speak to the central idea of relational practices, the focus on strength-based practices, the development of new and much deeper forms of child and youth participation, and new ideas and approaches to working with families in the context of residential group care.

Relational Practice

For many years, the field of child and youth care has focused on the role of relationships in being with young people in residential settings (and also in non-residential settings; see, for example, chapters by Newbury & Vachon; Shaw; Modlin & Leggett; as well as Marshall, this volume). The thinking has evolved from a focus on having relationships to relationship-based practice to the current idea of relational practices. The movement in nomenclature is not just a matter of semantics; the idea of *having* relationships attributes ownership over the way in which we are with young people, and given the inherent power differential between youth and staff, clearly such ownership is not a shared concept. Furthermore, as hinted at above, ownership implies property, and property ultimately is little more than a type of commodity. Discomfort with this formulation led the field to speak of relationship-based practice, with the central idea that anything therapeutic in our practices unfolds through *the medium of* relationship (Gharabaghi, 2010). In an everyday context, this meant the structure and routines of residential group care settings were adjusted to create opportunities for being with young people in contexts that promote interaction, communication, and joint activities. Within this context, the field developed endless examples of activity-centered ways of being with young people, from phrases such as "hanging out" (Garfat, 2008a) to more concrete descriptions of doing therapeutic work through sports, travel, adventure, board games, and other social contexts.

The idea of relational practices pushes these ideas further and perhaps changes the focus of the role of relationship. Instead of understanding relationship as an "object," that is, as a noun describing something in particular, relational practices transform the idea of relationship to the adjective form, thus describing not an object but the nature (or the process) of sharing moments (Garfat, 2008a). In this formulation, the practice itself is focused on the relationship instead of the parties to the relationship. Relational practices seek to generate a way of being together in which change (or learning, personal growth, human development) is contingent on the experience of being together. That experience, in turn described as the space in between the self of the practitioner and that of the youth (Garfat, 2008b), relies very substantially on the use of self in everyday practice. It includes "relationship check-in," in which practitioner and young person regularly and explicitly reflect on their relationship, or the way they are together, together.

The idea of relational practice pushes our thinking about residential care, and in particular the role of child and youth care practitioners, far beyond the traditional focus on behaviour. Instead, this role shifts from one of imposing change through behaviour management techniques to one of engendering change based on the cumulative experience of the relationship itself. The practitioner focuses on guiding the young person to use reflective, inquisitive, and curiosity-based approaches to uncovering new possibilities, to developing a sense of relational safety (a child and youth care version of trauma-informed care) (Garfat, 2008b), and to understanding their relationship to others and the world around them.

Strength-Based Practice

Whereas in the past, the purpose of residential group care was often seen as addressing deficits in young people, our thinking has shifted over the past few years to a focus on the strengths of young people in their everyday lives. This means that we construct the role of the practitioner very differently. Rather than thinking of that role as one of intervention (in the deficits of the young person), we think of it as one of exploration (Oliver & Charles, 2014, 2015, 2016). Practitioners are tasked with building confidence, self-efficacy, and self-respect for the young person in an effort to uncover and then build on existing strengths. Within this process, behavioural challenges, relationship difficulties, and emotional crises are seen not as targets of treatment interventions but instead as barriers for the young people to experience themselves as competent, strong, and able subjects in charge of their own lives.

Strength-based practices are not limited to psychotherapeutic activities. In other words, the practitioner is not tasked to explore potential or latent strengths using counselling or psychotherapy. Instead, it is the everyday moments, even when mundane and seemingly trivial, that provide the opportunities for practising decision-making, taking action, and reflecting on meaning (Krueger, 2004). Working through daily life events provides opportunities for young people to see themselves differently, to explore new strategies for managing adversity, and to observe themselves succeed in various kinds of tasks and activities (Garfat, Fulcher, & Digney, 2013). Complementing a strength-based approach is a focus on community involvement and recreational activity. Child and youth care practitioners in residential settings ideally see their work not as limited to the setting itself, but as extending into the community where young people are encouraged and supported to participate in organized and also informal activities, including sports, arts, and culture-based activities.

One additional element of strength-based practice, although not extensively covered in the field's literature, is a focus on identity and the intersections of multiple identities. Child and youth care is moving from traditional articulations of cultural competence and diversity to a much more complex position on intersectionality. Within this context, the role of child and youth care practice in residential settings (and also in other settings; see, for example, Newbury & Vachon, this volume) extends to acknowledging and naming multiple identities, and to shaping a milieu that allows space for such identities and the way in which they may intersect to express themselves.

Child and Youth Participation

It is perhaps not surprising that young people's participation in their own treatment was not at the forefront of residential care practices in the past. Given the strong focus on control and externally imposed behaviour management measures, participation was secondary to conformity and compliance (Fox, 2001), often to the serious detriment of young people. Indeed, young people who retrospectively speak to their experiences in residential care and treatment frequently say that they felt largely insignificant, voiceless, and powerless in these settings (Gharabaghi, Trocmé, & Newman, 2016). More recently, in Canada and also across many international jurisdictions, the importance of participation, both as a therapeutic method and as a fundamental right, has been rediscovered. As a result, in many residential settings, measures are being taken to re-evaluate program elements and practitioner roles through the lens of child and youth participation. At an everyday practice level, common tasks such as menu planning, deciding on which activity to engage in on any given day, and even the rules and expectations of the program are now often discussed with young people. In some instances, complex decision-making processes have been developed to give young people not only a voice in such matters but in fact reduce the power and control of practitioners to unilaterally impose rules and activities on young people.

One way of articulating the rediscovery of the importance of child and youth participation is through the lens of "mattering," a concept long at the periphery of human service settings but more recently reinvigorated in the writing of Grant Charles and colleagues (Charles & Alexander, 2014a; Charles & Garfat, 2016). The core of this orientation to practice is that young people need to know they matter to others and they need to have people in their lives that matter to them. This concept is central to understanding the meaning of human interaction. Additionally, while Charles talks about mattering as a different way of thinking about attachment and trauma-informed care, it is entirely possible to understand this concept in relation to participation. Through their active participation in the things that impact on them, young people can learn to believe they matter; their ideas, their decisions, their identities play a substantive part in how they experience themselves.

Of course this creates new challenges for practitioners, who now must reassess their long-held perspectives on expertise, knowledge, and knowing what is right. Through the lens of mattering, one of the core processes of residential care and treatment is particularly impacted—the process of planning, or what in

Canada is conventionally referred to as the plan of care or the treatment plan. Participation cannot be limited to the routines and structures of residential programs, but must also be reflected in the individual planning processes and the substantive plan developed with a young person. This means that conversations between practitioners and young people must move much more substantially into the realm of the young person's life-space, including the relational, mental, and virtual dimensions of that life-space (Gharabaghi & Stuart, 2014). Plans generated through participatory processes must reflect not merely the concrete and measurable outcomes often promoted by service providers at the clinical level but also the dreams, aspirations, hopes, and what may appear as unrealistic expectations of the young person. For young people to matter, they must be able to set, or at least negotiate, the agenda for their care, including what the hoped-for outcomes might look like.

Family Involvement

Child and youth care practitioners in residential settings see themselves as primarily engaged with young people. Family involvement in this setting is often translated as family contact (Gharabaghi, Trocmé, & Newman, 2016). It is common for young people in residential care and treatment settings to have ongoing contact with their families, to go on home visits, and in some instances to be involved in family therapy outside of the residential setting but as part of the overall plan for family reunification. The child and youth care practitioner role in these activities is frequently limited to observing young people before and after such family contact and to monitoring the interactions between family and the young person that unfold at time of pick-up and drop-off or through phone calls. Many of these dynamics are remnants of older modes of residential care in which family was often seen as the problem or a barrier to young people developing as autonomous and self-sufficient individuals (Charles & Gabor, 2006; Garfat & Charles, 2013). Indeed, the idea of "growing up" in residential care was, until at least the 1990s, a central idea and one that in fact resulted in young people moving towards emerging adulthood on the strength of their experiences in their relationships with practitioners and the residential programs as a whole. This has shifted considerably in the past 20 years.

Today, we recognize that young people are always connected in some way to their families. Whether such connections involve physical contact with family members or not, young people think and dream about family, have visions of their birth family and the family they may one day create themselves, and are steadily engaged with their own concept of family mentally, relationally, and virtually. This means that child and youth care practitioners in residential care and treatment settings have a responsibility to expand their focus from the individual young person to the young person in the context of family, recognizing that each young person may construct the idea of family in a very specific and individualized manner. Relational practices, as articulated earlier in this chapter, must integrate not only the space between practitioner self and young person self, but also the dimension of family within which this space exists, develops, and is shaped.

At a practical level, child and youth care practitioners often do have opportunities to encounter and engage with family members; this may include parents, siblings, or other individuals who appear as family to the young person. In contemporary residential care and treatment, practitioners must accomplish much more in those moments than merely recording descriptively the young person's interactions with such family members and then passing such recording on to the family therapist. The role of the practitioner now includes, and perhaps is defined by, his, her, or their engagement of family members, which includes inviting family members into the residential setting figuratively and literally. It is no longer sufficient to think of the residential setting apart from the family setting; these settings are inherently linked, and practitioners can no longer exercise the kind of ownership over the physical setting and by extension its culture, its routines, and its processes independently from family cultures, processes, and routines (Garfat & Charles, 2013).

THE GROUP WORK TENSIONS

So far, this chapter has considered residential care and treatment settings primarily in the context of practitioner engagement with young people individually. In practice, much of the work in residential care and treatment is not individual work but group work. Over the past 10 to 15 years, there has been an overwhelming trend in residential care and treatment to speak to the need for individualization of care and treatment (Stuart & Gharabaghi, 2013). Intuitively, this orientation towards individualization appears meaningful and appropriate. After all, every young person is in fact an individual, and no two young people face identical circumstances in their lives. On the other hand, young people experience their time in residential settings primarily as a group experience. They live with other young people; they share bedrooms, bathrooms, kitchens, and living spaces; they eat together, often go to school together, and follow common routines. They also share adult relationships. Every young person in a residential setting has access to the same adults for relational engagement as every other young person living there. In this way, child and youth care practitioners cannot ignore the group context of group care and must recognize that this group context provides a mediating platform through which interpersonal exchanges with young people unfold. Moreover, practitioners are not the only ones contributing to the developmental growth and learning of the young people in residential care and treatment settings. One might argue that the peer group may well be a much more significant source of knowledge, experiential learning, and identity formation for every individual young person living in this setting. For this reason, there have been attempts to develop program structures and processes that explicitly tackle the group dynamics of residential care and treatment settings. Perhaps best known amongst these is positive peer culture (PPC), cited as an evidence-based practice that focuses on the social interactions among peers in residential settings and tries to guide these towards a supportive and caring culture (Brendtro, 1988). Another model that explicitly recognizes the social/community dimension of residential care and treatment is the sanctuary model that emerged out of the trauma-informed care movement present primarily in the United States (Byrson et al., 2017). While the focus of this model is not specifically on peer culture, it does take into account the congruence of cultural dynamics at all levels of organization, including managerial and professional practitioner levels, but also including the "client" level.

Group dynamics are not, of course, limited to the young people. Team dynamics among practitioners have long been recognized as a core element of residential care and treatment settings. Discussions of these dynamics have appeared through the years in, among others, the works of Redl and Wineman (1952), Krueger (2004), and Maier (2001). Practitioners have to recognize that in residential care, they are members of a team of practitioners and their ability to practice according to their principles and based on their strengths is very much dependent on the perspectives and the support of their team members. In the past 20 years or so, the concept of team has been further complicated by the focus on multi-disciplinary teams, which in many settings have proven to be associated with both opportunities and challenges. Multi-disciplinary teams provide, on the one hand, opportunities for intersecting, enriching, and complementary perspectives, while on the other hand also opening the door for hierarchies, power structures among professional orientations, and deep misgivings and conflict, sometimes reflected in passive-aggressive responses, across disciplinary and professional groups (Salhani & Charles, 2007).

While there is a great deal of variance in the quality of multi-disciplinary team dynamics and practices across service systems in Canada and elsewhere, we can say with some confidence that these dynamics have increasingly introduced both personal and professional adult issues into the process of being with young people in residential settings. This has not always been positive. There has been a tendency among some child and youth care practitioners, especially in residential centres, to see themselves as being owners of relational practice and to see themselves as being somehow in the only profession that is able to truly understand and connect with the young people in their care (Charles & Alexander, 2014b). This has served to create "us vs. them" interactional scenarios that minimize the contribution of other professions. Part of this appears to be created as a response to power imbalances between some professions, although much of it is simply a lack of understanding of the roles and responsibilities of the other professions by CYC practitioners (Charles & Alexander, 2014b). Regardless of the root causes, the people who are hurt most by interprofessional conflict are the people being served by the programs. Residential services are complex and only work effectively when all concerned parties, including all of the professions and the young people and their families, are working together with common goals and desired outcomes.

MOVING FORWARD IN RESIDENTIAL CARE AND TREATMENT

A lot is changing in how we think about residential care and treatment these days. On the one hand, we have, as a human service field, become quite apprehensive about this form of being with young people. Our apprehension is driven in part by specific events that have exposed the vulnerabilities of residential care and treatment from a safety and well-being perspective (such as multiple deaths of young people and caregivers; sexual abuse scandals; and emerging evidence that in some services, young people are subject to cruel and unusual punishment, insufficient food, and cultural oppression; Bombay, Matheson, & Anisman, 2011, 2014; Charles & Degagné, 2013; Harris, 1991; Taylor, 2015). But it is also driven by at best ambiguous outcomes (Bryson et al., 2017). Young people themselves have told us repeatedly and consistently that their experience in these settings is often negative and sometimes traumatic (Gharabaghi, Trocmé, & Newman, 2016). We have learned that transitioning out of residential care and treatment can be enormously difficult, perhaps because the tight structure and control exercised within the setting cannot be replicated outside of it (Charles & Oliver, 2012). And we have learned that, at least in Canada, specific identity groups, such as Indigenous young people, Black Youth, and young people identifying as LGBTQ2S+, often experience this form of care as particularly oppressive and unhelpful. In spite of these challenges and an increasing rejection of this form of care, we have also maintained a belief that one can operate a residential care setting well; recent writings have suggested that the problems of residential care are not inherent but constructed. Smith, Fulcher, and Doran (2013), for example, have argued compellingly that residential care can and should be considered a positive form of life-space for young people, but needs to recommit to some core principles, including an infusion of "love" as a central component of being with young people.

In response to challenges and negative perceptions, one very strong trend in residential care and treatment is the focus on evidence-based practices (Bryson et al., 2017). Tired of unmeasurable and often unsubstantiated program structures and routines, methods of intervention, and claims of success, governments and regulators are increasingly demanding that the practices in residential settings be based on well-researched methods that have produced reliable and valid evidence of positive outcomes. As a result, we can now witness approaches to residential care and treatment that simply did not exist 20 years ago. In Canada, we can see various translations of dialectical behavioural therapy (DBT) appearing in residential settings as an overarching service delivery model, shaping not only the theoretical orientation of the program but the everyday actions and interventions of practitioners. In some settings, we observe other manualized evidence-based practices such as Stop Now and Plan (Augimeri, Walsh, Levene, Sewell, & Rajca, 2014) and Collaborative Problem Solving (Greene, Ablon, & Martin, 2006). Even crisis intervention approaches have moved towards an evidence orientation. Therapeutic crisis intervention, said to be an evidence-based practice, has overtaken some of the long-standing approaches in the field (crisis prevention/intervention—CPI; understanding and managing aggressive behaviour—UMAP; Shechory Bitton, 2015). Other manualized approaches are increasingly marketing themselves as evidence-based practices, including for example, life-space crisis intervention (Fecser, 2014), Wrap Around (Painter, 2012), and the Circle of Courage (Brendtro, Brokenleg, & Van Bockern, 1990).

The move towards evidence-based practices has had an enormous impact on the professional context of child and youth care practice. On the one hand, manualized interventions generate some consistency and predictability in the way practitioners respond to the challenges presented by young people. On the other hand, many of the concepts and ideas that are central in child and youth care practice are rendered secondary to the implementation of manualized approaches. As a result, relational practices, working in the moment, "hanging in and hanging out," and even the idea of mattering as discussed above are not part of the package of competencies or skills that employers are looking for. Clinical meetings about young people focus on the responsiveness of the young person to the manualized interventions much more so than the observations and interpretations of child and youth care practitioners in the context of foundational child and youth care practices. None of the recording tools in residential care ask about those foundational practices, and the judgment about success does not take account of these. To be fair, some evidence-based practices such as sanctuary do have some focus on the everyday experiences of young people within the program structures and routines, and generally hold up concepts such as empathy and nurture as key components of a trauma-informed approach to care (Bryson et al., 2017).

Perhaps a particularly obvious context in which evidence-based practices are overshadowing child and youth care concepts is residential care focused on autistic children and youth. The prevalence of applied behavioural analysis (ABA) and intensive behavioural intervention (IBI) has reintroduced many of the control-oriented features of residential care that were largely discredited some time ago, including token economies, point and level systems, and an explicit demand for compliance and conformity (see also Marshall, this volume). The 25 characteristics of child and youth care practice articulated by Garfat and Fulcher (2013) stand in sharp contrast to the requirements of ABA and IBI.

Nevertheless, we have today perhaps a better sense than ever before of what high-quality residential care might entail. We can say with some confidence, in part because young people have repeatedly told us so, that relational practices are foundational to creating an environment in which young people feel safe, comfortable, and able to grow. We can also say that child and youth participation at many different levels of their care experience is a critical factor in quality of care. And finally, we must take seriously the identity dimension of young people (and of practitioners) and recognize that an approach that takes account of intersectionality as well as anti-racism and that is able to operationalize such intersectional and anti-racist elements of care is now, more than ever, foundational to high-quality care as well.

CHILD AND YOUTH CARE CAREERS IN RESIDENTIAL CARE

In Canada, notwithstanding apprehensions related to residential care and treatment, this sector continues to be the largest employment sector for child and youth care practitioners in most provinces. Unlike some other sectors, however, working in residential care and treatment is associated with some clear challenges. These include what is often a difficult shift schedule, involving working hours overnight and on weekends and holidays. The pay is often insufficient, and particularly where private, for-profit residential care is ubiquitous, the pay often barely exceeds minimum wage standards in the province. Basic features of support for front-line practitioners are sometimes missing entirely or are inadequately represented; of particular importance here is the process of supervision in whatever form, as well as opportunities for professional development (Gharabaghi, Trocmé, & Newman, 2016).

In spite of shortcomings and challenges, employment in residential care and treatment settings also has advantages. There are few other settings where practitioners can be with young people in as intensive and all-encompassing a manner than in residential care. The nature of relational engagement, given the life-space context of this form of care, is challenging to the self and to one's professional capacity for making meaning of the virtually infinite circumstances and happenings one encounters. It is also a setting where, given the power and intensity of individual and group interactions, it is possible to be open to the bidirectional nature of relationships. There can be a richness in relationships between staff and young people that contributes to the well-being of both, rather than just a re-creation of the traditional one-way expression of most professional interactions (Alexander & Charles, 2009). It is not a coincidence that almost all of the most prolific contributors to the field of child and youth care over the years have entered through residential care settings. The work is rewarding and eye-opening, and as a practitioner, it is difficult to find better opportunities to grow within the field than through practising in residential care.

Beyond the richness of the experience, careers in residential care and treatment offer many professional pathways worth considering. These include entering the ranks of supervisors, trainers, and knowledge disseminators; moving towards residential care system design positions either through senior leadership roles in agencies and organizations or through policy roles in government; and of course entering the world of post-secondary education as a teacher of new and emerging practitioners for the field (see Stuart, Snell, & Magnuson, this volume). In addition, residential care and treatment settings offer opportunities to work across sectors, including all of the sectors described in this book. From outdoor adventure therapy to community practice, and from in-home family support work to specialized practices with particular communities such as the Deaf community or the autism community, residential child and youth care practitioners can find ways of expanding the experiences in their specific settings to incorporate program elements or specific professional expertise that transcend the walls of the setting. While many other sectors offer rewarding and meaningful opportunities to develop child and youth care careers, it is probably still fair to say that residential care and treatment is a gateway sector to virtually all that the field of child and youth care has to offer.

REFERENCES

Alexander, C., & Charles, G. (2009). Caring, mutuality and reciprocity in social worker-client relationships: Rethinking principles of practice. *Journal of Social Work, 9*(1), 5–22.

Augimeri, L. K., Walsh, M., Levene, K., Sewell, K., & Rajca, E. (2014). Stop Now And Plan (SNAP) Model. In *Encyclopedia of criminology and criminal justice* (pp. 5053–5063). New York: Springer Science—Business Media.

Bombay, A., Matheson, K., & Anisman, H. (2011). The impact of stressors on second generation Indian residential school survivors. *Transcultural Psychiatry, 48*(4), 367–391.

Bombay, A., Matheson, K., & Anisman, H. (2014). *Origins of lateral violence in Aboriginal communities: A preliminary study of student-to-student abuse in Indian Residential Schools.* Ottawa: Aboriginal Healing Foundation.

Brendtro, L. K. (1988). Two studies of positive peer culture: A response. *Child & Youth Care Quarterly, 17*, 156–158.

Brendtro, L. K., Brokenleg, M., & Van Bockern, S. (1990). *Reclaiming youth at risk: Our hope for the future.* Bloomington, IN: National Educational Service.

Bryson, S. A., Gauvin, E., Jamieson, A., Rathgeber, M., Faulkner-Gibson, L., Bell, S., … & Burke, S. (2017). What are effective strategies for implementing trauma-informed care in youth inpatient psychiatric and residential treatment settings? A realist systematic review. *International Journal of Mental Health Systems, 11*(36), 1–16.

Charles, G. (2015). Doomed to repeat it: The selective and collective ignorance of the shadowy historical foundations of child and youth care. *International Child and Youth Care, 200*, 52–58.

Charles, G. (2016). *Secure care summary report (part two): Secure care as a component of an integrated service network model.* Vancouver: School of Social Work and Division of Adolescent Health and Medicine, Department of Pediatrics, Faculty of Medicine, University of British Columbia.

Charles, G. (2018). Worrying about reconciliation: Building upon our commonalities and our differences as a way to move forward. In G. Charles, S. Rodgers, M. Degagné, & G. Lowry (Eds.), *Speaking my truth: The journey to reconciliation* (pp. 203–212). Ottawa: Aboriginal Healing Foundation.

Charles, G., & Alexander, C. (2014a). Beyond attachment: Mattering and the development of meaningful moments. *Relational Child and Youth Care Practice, 27*(3), 26–30.

Charles, G., & Alexander, C. (2014b). An introduction to interprofessional practice in social and health care settings. *Relational Child and Youth Care Practice, 27*(3), 51–55.

Charles, G., & Degagné, M. (2013). Student to student abuse in the Indian residential schools in Canada. *Journal of Child and Youth Services, 34*(4), 343–359.

Charles, G., Ernst, K., & Ponzetti, J. (2003). Ethics and outcome measures. *Canada's Children, Canada's Future: The Journal of the Child Welfare League of Canada, 10*(2), 5–11.

Charles, G., & Gabor, P. (1991). An historical perspective of residential services for troubled and troubling young people in Canada. In G. Charles & S. McIntyre (Eds.), *The best in care: Recommendations for the future of residential services for troubled young people in Canada.* Ottawa: Canadian Child Welfare Association.

Charles, G., & Gabor, P. (2006). An historical perspective on residential services for troubled and troubling youth in Canada revisited. *Relational Child and Youth Care Practice, 19*(4), 17–26.

Charles, G., & Garfat, T. (2009). The practice of child and youth care in North America. In P. Share & K. Lalor (Eds.), *Applied social care: An introduction for students in Ireland* (pp. 34–45). Dublin: Gill & Macmillan.

Charles, G., & Garfat, T. (2016). Supervision: A matter of mattering. In G. Charles, J. Freeman, & T. Garfat (Eds.), *Supervision in child and youth care practice* (pp. 23–28). Cape Town, South Africa: CYC-Net Press.

Charles, G., & Oliver, C. (2012). *Transitioning young people out of care in Canadian jurisdictions: A review of the issues and supports.* Ottawa: Child Welfare League of Canada.

Charles, G., & White, J. (2008). Outcome research, best practices and the limits of evidence. *Canadian Social Work Review, 25*(1), 71–85.

Fecser, F. A. (2014). LSCI in trauma-informed care. *Reclaiming Children and Youth, 22*(4), 42–45.

Fox, L. (2001). The catastrophe of compliance. *CYC-Online, 31*(8), 1–5.

Garfat, T. (2008a). Gestures and moments that change our lives. *Relational Child & Youth Care Practice, 21*(2), 75–76.

Garfat, T. (2008b). Wonderings about being a competent practitioner. *Relational Child & Youth Care Practice, 21*(3), 72–75.

Garfat, T., & Charles, G. (2013). *A guide to developing effective child and youth care practice with families* (2nd ed.). Cape Town, South Africa: Pretext Publications.

Garfat, T., & Fulcher, L. (2013). The therapeutic use of Daily Life Events with families. *Relational Child & Youth Care Practice, 26*(4), 50–51.

Garfat, T., Fulcher, L., & Digney, J. (2013). Potential life changing moments. *Relational Child & Youth Care Practice, 26*(2), 3–5.

Gharabaghi, K. (2010). In-service training and professional development in residential child and youth care settings: A three sector comparison in Ontario. *Residential Treatment for Children & Youth, 27*(2), 92–114.

Gharabaghi, K. (2011). A child & youth care approach to residential care management. *Relational Child & Youth Care Practice, 24*(1/2), 133–141.

Gharabaghi, K., Charles, G., & Kavanagh, H. (2016). *Alternative care strategy— International services project*. Toronto: School of Child & Youth Care, Ryerson University.

Gharabaghi, K., & Stuart, C. (2014). Life space intervention: Implications for caregiving. *Relational Child & Youth Care Practice, 27*(3), 6–9.

Gharabaghi, K., Trocmé, N., & Newman, D. (2016). *Because young people matter: Report of the residential services review panel*. Toronto: Ministry of Children and Youth Services.

Greene, R., Ablon, J., & Martin, A. (2006). Innovations: Child and adolescent psychiatry: Use of collaborative problem solving to reduce seclusion and restraint in child and adolescent inpatient units. *Psychiatric Services, 57*, 610–612.

Harris, M. (1991). *Unholy orders: Tragedy at Mount Cashel*. Toronto: Penguin Books.

Hiebert, B., & Charles, G. (2008). *Accountability and outcomes in health and human services: Changing perspectives for changing times*. Calgary, AB: Canadian Outcomes Research Institute.

Krueger, M. (2004). Youthwork as modern dance. *Child & Youth Services, 26*(1), 3–24.

Maier, H. W. (2001). Pioneer house: Reflections on working with Redl and Wineman in 1947. *Reclaiming Child Youth, 10*(2), 71–74.

Miller, T. S. (2003). *The orphans of Byzantium: Child welfare in the Christian empire*. Washington, DC: The Catholic University of America Press.

Oliver, C., & Charles, G. (2014). *Strengths-based practice in child protection*. Victoria, BC: British Columbia Ministry of Children and Family Development.

Oliver, C., & Charles, G. (2015). Which strengths-based practice? Reconciling strengths based practice and mandated authority in child protection work. *Social Work, 60*(2), 135–143.

Oliver, C., & Charles, G. (2016). Enacting firm, fair and friendly practice: A model for strengths-based child protection relationships? *British Journal of Social Work, 46*(4), 1009–1026.

Painter, K. (2012). Outcomes for youth with severe emotional disturbance: A repeated measures longitudinal study of a wraparound approach of service delivery in systems of care. *Child Youth Care Forum, 41*, 407–425.

Redl, F., & Wineman, D. (1952). *Controls from within: Techniques for the treatment of the aggressive child.* New York: The Free Press.

Salhani, D., & Charles, G. (2007). The dynamics of an interprofessional team: The interplay of child and youth care with other professions within a residential treatment milieu. *Relational Child and Youth Care Practice, 20*(4), 12–20.

Shechory Bitton, M. (2015). Therapeutic crisis intervention system in residential care for children and youth: Staff knowledge, attitudes, and coping styles. *Children and Youth Services Review, 56*, 1–6.

Smith, M., Fulcher, L., & Doran, P. (2013). *Residential child care in practice: Making a difference.* Bristol, UK: Policy Press.

Stuart, C., & Gharabaghi, K. (2013). Personalized service delivery: Exploring the supports and challenges to collaboration. *Relational Child & Youth Care Practice, 26*(1), 48–58.

Taylor, W. L. (2015). *The Nova Scotia Home for Colored Children: The hurt, the hope and the healing.* Halifax: Nimbus Publishing.

Truth and Reconciliation Commission (TRC). (2015). *Honouring the truth, reconciling for the future: Summary of the final report of the Truth and Reconciliation Commission of Canada.* Ottawa: Author.

Wheatley, T. (2013). *"And neither do I have wings to fly": Labeled and locked up in Canada's oldest institution.* Toronto: INANNA Publications.

CHAPTER 2

The Role of Child and Youth Care in Foster Care

Heather Modlin and Andy Leggett

Given the pressures and generally negative governmental and societal perspective on institutional care, child and youth care activity in foster care settings has increased dramatically over the past ten years. This chapter will provide insight into the evolution of child and youth care practice in the rapidly expanding foster care sector and highlight current trends and future developments from the perspective of organizations offering fostering services in Canada and elsewhere.

A BRIEF OVERVIEW OF THE FOSTER CARE SYSTEM IN CANADA

In Canada, children historically ended up in out-of-home care because their parents died or were unable to provide adequate care for them due to illness or poverty (Charles & Garfat, 2009). In the late 19th century this began to change as governments recognized that they had a role to play in the protection of children, and corresponding child protection laws were created (Commission to Promote Sustainable Child Welfare, 2010).

Until the mid-1800s, the majority of displaced children were housed in orphanages run by religious orders (Charles & Gabor, 2006). Over the next several decades, as child welfare services in Canada expanded, these large institutions were gradually phased out in favour of foster homes, smaller group homes, or residential care facilities. Eventually, foster homes began to replace residential care as the preferred placement option (Burnside, 2012).

Since the 1990s, the number of children in Canada in need of protection—and those taken into care—has increased significantly (Mulcahy & Trocmé, 2010). In 1997, there were a reported 36,080 children in care (HRDC, 1997). In 2013, that number had jumped to 62,400 (Jones, Sinha, & Trocmé, 2015). The increase in numbers, coupled with an increase in the complexity of children's needs and length of stay in care, has contributed to a significant strain on foster care systems across the country.

In Canada, child welfare services fall under the jurisdiction of provincial and territorial governments. This results in differences in service design and delivery. Despite these differences, all Canadian provinces and territories have experienced similar difficulties in the provision of foster care. Most jurisdictions have reported losing foster homes in the last several years. This has been attributed to problems with recruitment and retention of foster families (Farris-Manning & Zandstra, 2003). The declining number of foster homes coupled with the increased number of children in care has resulted in a situation described by many as a crisis (Canadian Press, 2012; *Globe & Mail*, 2016; *Huffington Post*, 2015).

WHAT HAPPENS WHEN THERE AREN'T ENOUGH FOSTER HOMES?

The shortage of foster homes has resulted in many children, who would best be served in a family, being inappropriately placed in group care or other forms of residential care. In some provinces, the lack of suitable placement resources has resulted in children being temporarily placed in hotels or other ad hoc living arrangements. As stated by Gough, Shlonsky, and Dudding (2009), "the service response to children and youth with disabilities, youth with complex behavioural and mental health problems, and youth transitioning out of care, is often not sufficient to meet their needs" (p. 367).

There was a 58 percent increase in the number of young people placed in residential care in Canada from 1990 to 2001 (Barbell & Freundlich, 2001), and the number has continued to climb in many provinces. In Newfoundland and Labrador, for example, there were approximately 900 children in care in 2008, and over 90 percent of these were placed in families (Fowler, 2008). By 2015, that number had swelled to over 1,200 and the percentage of young people placed in families had decreased to approximately 85 percent (Department of Child, Youth and Family Services, 2016). Alternatively, in some provinces, most notably Ontario, the number of young people placed in group care has declined over the course of the past five years. This is perhaps reflective of the larger number of specialized foster care options available in Ontario in comparison to the rest of the country.

While residential care can be a valuable resource for young people needing this level of care, it is not suitable for all young people. Young people themselves have expressed concern about being inappropriately placed in group care (Haire, 2009).

In an informal survey conducted by the authors, colleagues were asked to comment on the state of foster care in their province or territory. Some of the comments are presented below.

We are broken. (BC)

Extremely variable; 47 individual systems operating, varying from excellent to abysmal. Definitely in crisis. (ON)

Foster care continues to be the program of choice for children and youth coming into care but there continues to be a shortage of foster home placements. (ON)

I would describe there being a shortage of foster care homes in Nova Scotia. I do not know of the frequency of breakdown. I do not know about a "state of crisis" as the adjective but there is certainly room for improvement.

In Manitoba there is a shortage of Aboriginal foster homes. There has been a new "campaign" by one of the authorities to attempt to recruit more Aboriginal caregivers. Placements break down on a regular basis.

Too many children placed in staffed arrangements, we have gone beyond crisis to this being the norm for the past ten years. Recently, however, government seems to have recognized the role that child and youth care workers can play in providing and supporting family placements and we are hopeful that we have turned a corner. Creativity and innovation is now being embraced. (NL)

CHILDREN WITH CHALLENGING BEHAVIOURS AND COMPLEX NEEDS

Factors associated with foster care breakdown include the complex needs of children placed in care, and lack of adequate supports to foster families to meet those needs (Brown & Bednar, 2006; MacGregor, Rodger, Cummings, & Lescheid, 2006). In the past decade, reference to children and youth with "complex needs" has become commonplace across Canada and beyond. While the meaning of this term may vary across jurisdictions, it generally refers to young people who are dealing with a multitude of issues that require assistance from multiple service sectors (Child Welfare League of America, 2007). These young people are often in receipt of specialized services from child welfare, mental health, education, and other government departments. Children and youth with complex needs may exhibit challenging or high-risk behaviour that repeatedly puts themselves and/or others at serious risk of harm. They may also experience multiple developmental and/or mental health issues that impact their decision-making and problem-solving abilities and capacity to participate in "regular" daily life events. Ultimately, young people with complex needs are those for whom all available resources in the child welfare system have been exhausted and/or deemed inadequate to meet their needs (Burnside, 2012).

To define complex needs in a way that puts the responsibility on the system rather than the child, one can view the exacerbation of a young person's developmental, medical, social, and mental health problems as resulting from the interaction between the young people and a system that is ill-equipped to meet their needs (Child Welfare Information Gateway, 2006). It is the system itself, and the challenge in effectively coordinating service provision across multiple sectors, that creates the complexity (Burnside, 2012). In some ways, complexity is "in the eye of the beholder" (Rich, 2009) and relative to the skill level of those providing care. The following example from one of the authors illustrates this notion.

Larry was referred to our organization at the age of eight, having experienced 17 placement breakdowns in the prior two years. The breakdowns were attributed to Larry's "complex needs" and challenging, aggressive behaviours. Larry was placed in a home by himself, with a team of child and youth care workers providing 24-hour care.

When Larry moved in, it was clear that (1) Larry did not feel safe, and (2) Larry was expecting another rejection. Our intervention in the first few months focused on these areas. This was easier said than done, however, as Larry had developed many strategies to push people away and there was no line he would not cross. He regularly hit, kicked, bit, and spit on the child and youth care staff. He also damaged property—our organization paid thousands of dollars in vehicle repairs in those first few months. There were many nights when the staff left their shift covered in bruises, drenched in spit, driving a car with a cracked windshield, dented roof and no rearview mirrors.

But they kept coming back.

Through a child and youth care and trauma-informed framework, the staff team was able to understand Larry's behaviours and, more importantly, develop and implement strategies that would meet his needs. Within a few months, the aggressive behaviours had all but subsided, Larry (and the team) felt safe, and the therapeutic focus shifted to other areas.

Larry now lives in a family with one of the child and youth care workers on his original team. He presents as a "normal" 14-year-old boy. He attends school full-time, plays sports, goes to camp, has friends in the neighbourhood, and resolves conflict with words rather than fists.

The label of complex needs no longer applies to Larry.

In addition to illustrating how the behaviours of children and youth in care are often more reflective of the context in which they have been embedded than any internal dysfunction (Larry's behaviours were very functional in relation to the situations he encountered), this example also highlights the value of a child and youth care approach to foster care. The authors are familiar with a number of situations in which young people have been transitioned from residential care to family-based care, with foster parents (or "carers" as they are called in some organizations) who are experienced child and youth care practitioners. The benefits of a child and youth care approach in these situations have been evident. Child and youth care workers providing family-based care are able to skilfully use the life-space, taking advantage of moments throughout the day to provide therapeutic intervention and promote development. A slammed door, a refusal to go to school, and a hurled insult are viewed as bids for connection. Child and youth care workers, as therapeutic carers, perform a professional role suffused with the nurturing, caring, and attachment opportunities that are associated with family life. The absence of shift changes that occur regularly throughout the day in a residential program decreases the anxiety associated with transitions for the majority of children and youth in care, particularly those with complex needs.

INDIGENOUS CHILDREN AND YOUTH IN FOSTER CARE

Any discussion of foster care in Canada must acknowledge the overrepresentation of Indigenous children in the child welfare system. In 2011, 30,000, or 48 percent, of children and youth in foster care across Canada were Indigenous children, even though Indigenous peoples comprise only 4.3 percent of the population (Aboriginal Children in Care Working Group, 2015). While the reasons for this are complex, there is evidence to suggest that the prevalence of Indigenous children in care can partly be attributed to the presence of multiple risk factors such as oppression; poverty; the legacy of residential schools and intergenerational trauma on parenting capacity; and other cultural, economic, and social variables (Burnside, 2012).

The following example illustrates the way in which child and youth care workers may be engaged to work with Indigenous children in care and to assist with capacity building in the community.

Ben was 11 when a referral was made to a treatment foster care program in Ontario from an isolated fly-in community in Northern Canada. Ben presented with a complex clinical profile involving trauma/abuse, parental abandonment, and multiple caregivers and placements. The grandmother, now the "caregiver," and the elders in the community were all supporting the need for Ben to receive specialized treatment outside of their community.

The referral was taken by phone by the program's resource worker, a child and youth care worker, whose responsibilities within the program included referral/intake, coordination of placement, and the screening, approval, and ongoing evaluation of foster parents. Once an information package was received, the resource worker conferred with a program clinical manager, also a child and youth care worker, about a potential placement.

The role of the clinical manager was to supervise a number of foster homes and develop and implement the treatment plans, in consultation with the treatment team. The clinical manager got in touch with the referring child welfare agency in the Northern community and visits were arranged for the clinical manager to fly into the community to meet Ben, his family, community Elders, and child welfare personnel.

Following the second visit to the community, and a number of meetings with all involved in the community, the decision was jointly made to have Ben placed in a treatment foster home in Ontario. Conditions of the placement included regular visits back to the community, regular visits to Ontario by the grandmother and Elders if requested, participation by family members and Elders in planning meetings, and a clear plan to have Ben return to the community to live upon completion of his treatment and any supports necessary within the community to be developed.

Ben's first month in the foster home was difficult for him and he required around the clock support by the clinical support team, made up of a roster of child and youth care workers and the emergency response team, comprising the senior members of the clinical support team.

After the first month, it was determined that the amount of child and youth care worker support could be cut back, and over the next three months, the amount of support decreased from around the clock to about 60 hours per week.

A particular area of difficulty for Ben was school as his attendance in his home community had been sporadic. So a child and youth care worker from the clinical support team, who had worked with Ben from his placement onward, was selected to work with Ben in the school.

Initially, Ben could only manage to stay for about a quarter of the day, but by the end of his first year, he was attending school full time, still requiring support from a child and youth care worker while he was there.

Ben began visiting home after three months and was accompanied by a child and youth care worker who helped support him and his family during visits. Visits occurred minimally every three months with his grandmother visiting him in Ontario in between.

Ben is now 15. He is attending school on his own. He has worked through most of the trauma-related issues that were so significantly impacting him. The number and length of his visits home have increased and he is now able to return home and visit with his grandmother without a child and youth care worker attending with him.

Ben, with the support of his grandmother, has asked to stay in Ontario to complete high school, including a small engine repair co-op that he is taking that he hopes will become an apprenticeship. He is back in his home community virtually the whole summer and most vacation breaks. The treatment program is working with the home community in the hopes of training mentors to assist Ben when he returns home after he graduates high school.

FOSTER CARE AS THE PREFERRED PLACEMENT OPTION

In response to the recognition that the service delivery model for "high risk" children and youth is less than adequate, many provinces and territories in the past decade have commissioned studies on the placement needs of young people with complex needs (see, for example, Burnside, 2012; Fowler, 2008; Richard, 2008). The need for a continuum of residential services is a common recommendation arising from these studies. In particular, the lack of adequate resources in the area of specialized treatment foster care has been identified as "the most glaring gap in the continuum of options" (Haire, 2009, p. 16).

In spite of the nationwide shortages of foster homes, family-based care is still commonly identified as the preferred placement option for children in the child welfare system (Farris-Manning & Zandstra, 2003; Kluger, Alexander, & Curtis, 2000). For young people with emotional and behavioural issues and special needs, treatment foster care is often preferred over group care (MacDonald & Turner, 2007).

THERAPEUTIC FOSTER CARE

Therapeutic or treatment foster care is a form of specialized foster care designed specifically for children and youth with high needs whose difficulties place them at risk of multiple foster home breakdowns or placement in a more restrictive environment. This includes young people who have experienced trauma, abuse, neglect, and abandonment and those with mental health issues (MacDonald & Turner, 2007).

Although programs can vary, in general treatment, foster parents are highly trained and skilled, and supports are wrapped around them and the young people to create a team approach to treatment. A significant amount of evidence has been gathered on the effectiveness of treatment foster care in comparison to other placement and treatment options. Placement breakdown occurs less frequently in treatment foster care placements (Chamberlain et al., 2008; Lipscombe & Farmer, 2007). This corresponds with improved placement stability (Chamberlain, 1990), which has been repeatedly linked with more positive outcomes for children and youth (Perry, 2009; Roberts, 2007). It has been found that children and youth in treatment foster care are better regulated emotionally (Verso Consulting, 2011) and less likely to develop anti-social behaviours (Smith, Chamberlain, & Eddy, 2010). They are also more engaged in community (Frederico, Long, McNamara, McPherson & Rose, 2017) and educational activities (Verso Consulting, 2011).

Because treatment foster care is a community-based service, it also minimizes the challenge of reintegrating young people back into the community (Twigg, 2006) and is less costly than institutional and group home alternatives (Barth, 2002; MacDonald & Turner, 2007). Most treatment foster care is provided through private agencies or public-private partnerships, and exists alongside a range of free-standing programs to those that are part of a larger continuum of services (Twigg, 2006).

FOSTER CARE AS A CHILD AND YOUTH CARE PRACTICE SETTING

As problems in the foster care system have worsened, governments have had to explore alternative options to caring for children and youth, particularly those deemed to have complex needs. In many provinces and territories, this has opened doors for child and youth care workers to be involved in new and creative ways.

In the survey conducted by the authors, respondents from across the country were asked about the role of child and youth care workers in the foster care system. It was reported that when child and youth care workers are involved in the foster care system, it is primarily in relation to treatment foster care. This is most common in Ontario, where treatment foster care, usually run by non-governmental agencies, has been a regular component of the continuum of care for many years. It is perhaps not a coincidence that the formal education of child and youth care workers has been going on for much longer in Ontario than in any other jurisdiction in Canada. Child and youth care workers are more commonly recognized in this province by other professionals and the general public, and tend to fill a wider variety of roles.

As stated by one respondent, "we use CYWs to work with the children in the foster homes and this can include spending time with the child in the home, out of the home and in the community or through group work within our office or at a location off site. The children and youth are connected with their worker and they are also connected to their peers through on-going group work and drop in activity nights with the CYWs. Our kids feel as though they belong and despite their trauma or quirky ways they have a peer group that accepts them" (K. Rock, personal correspondence, January 15, 2016).

Treatment foster care is also available in British Columbia, Saskatchewan, and Manitoba, although it is limited and varies across regions. It is not readily available in Alberta, Nova Scotia, Prince Edward Island, New Brunswick, or the territories. In Newfoundland and Labrador, the Department of Children, Seniors and Social Development recently entered into an agreement with a community-based, non-profit organization to provide family-based care across the province. This is quite similar to treatment foster care, and marks a significant departure for the NL government, which previously restricted the provision of family-based care to foster homes contracted directly through government.

UNDERSTANDING THE ROLE

Before the role of child and youth care workers in foster care can be properly understood, it is important to understand the ways in which child and youth care workers and foster parents share a common connection that is likely unique from other supporting professions.

The child and youth care profession originated in residential care for children and youth. Historically, child and youth care workers were hired to work in group homes and residential treatment centres, and their job was to assist children and youth who were placed in these programs to navigate through their days. Child and youth care workers got the "residents" up, cooked and ate with them, took them to school, often stayed at school to support them, helped them with their various recreation activities, and prepared them for bed. Child and youth care workers were there during the nights when children and youth would wake up with nightmares and night terrors.

Child and youth care workers hung out and celebrated with the young people during good times and hung in and endured with the young people during bad times. Child and youth care workers were on the receiving end of the young people's displaced anger and rage that would flare up at virtually any moment of the day and were often the first people to hear the heart-wrenching stories that prompted the anger and rage.

A significant part of the child and youth care culture became not only knowing how to support children and youth to get through the day, but to support children and youth whose lives had been forever impacted by trauma and abuse, whose cognitive functioning had been damaged or altered, and who were left to try to somehow function in a world in which they were ill equipped to do so, a world that had failed them. Child and youth care workers were asked to be, for all intents and purposes, the "surrogate parents" to children and youth who, for whatever reasons, could not cope with living in traditional families.

Foster parents are asked to do exactly the same thing, except that there is no "next shift" of parents coming in a few hours to relieve them. This common foundational piece positions child and youth care workers to truly understand the challenges facing foster parents from an experiential perspective. They have "lived it" too. When we discuss the various roles that child and youth care workers play in the foster care system, we can do so from a framework of a common and shared perspective and experience.

As foster parents and their families are being asked and expected to take children and youth with increasingly challenging and complex needs into their homes, the manner in which foster parents are supported has been evolving. Treatment foster care programs have emerged with the intent to provide foster parents with the clinical supports they need to meet the needs of these children and youth in the foster family's home. Meeting the needs of these young people "where they live and where they are at" in a family setting is quite different than more traditional modes of therapy. Doing so successfully requires a degree of affinity and sensitivity to what the foster parents and family face.

Traditional thinking would have the child and youth care workers interacting with the children and youth independent from the foster parents. The workers would take the youth on outings or interact and deal with the youth when in crisis. But more and more child and youth care workers are working in tandem with foster parents. Many of the characteristics of child and youth care practice (Garfat & Fulcher, 2011) serve as important skills to assist the foster parents to make the necessary adjustments in their interactions with the children and youth. For example, child and youth care workers "hang in" alongside the foster parents through the tough times, providing support and helping them to maintain perspective. They spend time with the family, in the life-space, using everyday events as opportunities to promote growth and change. This could occur while preparing and eating meals together, helping with homework, playing basketball in the driveway, going on an outing to the beach, or any number of activities. "Meeting them where they're at" applies to foster parents as well as young people. This means "responding appropriately to their developmental capabilities, accepting their fears and hesitations, celebrating their joys and hesitations, and enabling them—without pressure—to be who they are in interactions with them" (Garfat & Fulcher, 2011, p. 9). Child and youth care workers can provide practical supports, such as transporting children to school or appointments, supervising visits with birth family, and assisting with the bedtime routine, to help foster parents manage their day-to-day responsibilities and prevent them from becoming overwhelmed. They can also provide support and guidance in areas such as managing behaviours, dealing with challenging situations, and meeting the needs of the young people. Child and youth care workers engage in relational practice with foster families. They work alongside the foster parents, doing "with," not "to" or "for," as integral members of the family. Their approach is strength-based and needs-focused.

As child and youth care workers take more active roles in working with foster parents to meet the needs of the children placed in their homes, they are also beginning to take on an increased role in supervising foster care systems or programs. The fact that undergraduate and even graduate degrees in child and youth care are becoming increasingly common provides the field with the necessary academic qualifications to assume roles within the system that were previously the domain of social workers or psychologists.

Perhaps the most intriguing role, as mentioned previously, that child and youth care workers are taking on in the foster care system is being foster parents themselves. The development of clinically "sophisticated" and well-supported treatment foster care systems provides child and youth care workers an opportunity to pursue their profession within the confines of their own home. In specialized family-based care, young people with complex needs can receive an individualized placement underpinned by a child-centered and needs-led model of in-home and wraparound supports. The goal of such an intensive service is to enable young people to safely and successfully settle into a stable family environment, as well as to prevent children who have experienced multiple placement breakdowns from experiencing another placement failure. Family-based carers are well compensated to reflect the demanding and professional nature of their role. This is particularly timely considering the trend internationally for more family-based placements and the difficulty and challenges in finding foster parents through traditional means.

CHILD AND YOUTH CARE WORKERS IN THE TRADITIONAL FOSTER CARE SYSTEM

In the regular foster care system, the involvement of child and youth care workers varies across regions. They can be used to provide respite for foster parents, to supervise visits between young people and their parents, or to support challenging placements. They may provide direct care and intervention to young people living in foster homes. In Newfoundland and Labrador, for example, the Department of Children, Seniors and Social Development contracted a community-based organization to expand their family support program, previously focused exclusively on birth families, to service foster families. In this new pilot project, family support workers (all child and youth care workers) provide training and support, including 24-hour on-call support, to foster parents throughout the province.

In one organization that provides specialized foster care in Canada, child and youth care workers permeate the organization in multiple roles. The provincial directors in each province are child and youth care workers. Many program supervisors, who provide intensive oversight to between four and six families, are child and youth care workers. Several of the families who provide care comprise child and youth care workers. Families receive wraparound support from professionals in multiple disciplines, including education, social work, psychiatry, and counselling, and child and youth care workers are integral members of these teams. Most front-line support to carers and young people is provided by child and youth care workers.

As highlighted in the above example, a tangential benefit of child and youth care involvement in foster care is that it increases opportunities for interdisciplinary practice.

HELPING YOUNG PEOPLE TO TRANSITION OUT OF FOSTER CARE

Transition planning is another key area in which child and youth care workers can be involved in the foster care system. Outcomes for youth after they "age out" of care are consistently poor. In comparison to their peers, youth aging out of care are at higher risk for mental health and substance abuse problems, homelessness, involvement with the criminal justice system, unemployment, and dependence on social assistance. They are also more likely to leave school without graduating and become a parent at a young age (Charles & Oliver, 2012).

Young people leaving care have identified the importance of ongoing, supportive relationships to ensure a successful transition to adulthood.

> Young people said they felt much better about the transition into independence when they were connected to professionals beyond their caseworker … support from a community agency was seen by youth as being a better match to their needs, since they were able to access ongoing support to check in, ask for advice, or celebrate successes even after the youth's program had ended. They also liked that agencies provided programs and supports on evenings and weekends, made decisions based on their personal knowledge of them and had the freedom to "think outside the box" when it came to meeting their needs. When young people developed a strong connection to community agency staff, the community agency became the youth's surrogate family. (Office of the Child and Youth Advocate Alberta, 2013, p. 12)

Some former youth in care have recommended that all young people in care should have a child and youth care worker assigned to them, in addition to their social worker (Charles & Oliver, 2012). There are, in many jurisdictions, community-based programs that provide supports to young people transitioning out of care, and these supports are often provided by child and youth care workers.

SUMMARY

Child and youth care workers specialize in the therapeutic use of daily life events (Garfat & Fulcher, 2011). They are trained to work with children and youth who have experienced difficulties in their lives; this includes those with complex needs and challenging behaviours. For children and youth in foster care, placement stability is key to promoting positive outcomes. There are many situations in which the strategic use of child and youth care workers in foster care could enhance the therapeutic potential of a placement or prevent placement breakdown. Child and youth care workers can help to promote placement stability by:

- Providing direct care in the role of treatment foster parents
- Supporting and/or supervising foster parents
- Providing intervention and support to young people who are placed in foster homes
- Supporting young people as they "step down" from residential care to foster care
- Bridging the connection between foster families and birth families
- Supporting young people as they transition out of the foster care system

While there are many examples of child and youth care practitioners working in foster care, there is plenty of room for expansion. In most jurisdictions, child and youth care workers are still underutilized in the child welfare system. In some provinces, this may be due to a lack of consistency in the education and qualifications of those employed as child and youth care workers. In other provinces, where child and youth care education is more prevalent, it may be due to a lack of regulation of the field, a lack of understanding of what child and youth care workers can do, or a lack of self-advocacy on the part of child and youth care workers. Regardless of the contributing factors, it is clear that child and youth care workers can have an important role to play in strengthening the foster care system for children and youth in Canada.

REFERENCES

Aboriginal Children in Care Working Group. (2015). *Aboriginal children in care: Report to Canada's premiers.* Retrieved from http://canadaspremiers.ca/phocadownload/publications/aboriginal_children_in_care_report_july2015.pdf

Barbell, K., & Freundlich, M. (2001). *Foster care today, Casey family programs.* Washington, DC: Casey Foundation.

Barth, R. P. (2002). *Institutions vs. foster homes: The empirical base for the second century of debate.* Chapel Hill, NC: University of North Carolina, School of Social Work, Jordan Institute for Families.

Brown, J. D., & Bednar, L. M. (2006). Foster parent perceptions of placement breakdown. *Child and Youth Services Review, 28,* 1497–1511.

Burnside, L. (2012). *Youth in care with complex needs: Special report for the Office of the Children's Advocate in Manitoba.* Retrieved from http://www.childrensadvocate.mb.ca/wp-content/uploads/Youth-with-Complex-Needs-Report-final.pdf

Canadian Press. (2012). Canadian foster in crisis, experts say: Some children placed in homes before safety checks made. *CBC News.* Retrieved from http://www.cbc.ca/news/canada/canadian-foster-care-in-crisis-experts-say-1.1250543

Chamberlain, P. (1990). Comparative evaluation of specialized foster care for seriously delinquent youths: A first step. *Community Alternatives, 2*(2), 21–36.

Chamberlain, P., Price, J., Leve, L. D., Laurent, H., Landsverk, J. A., & Reid, J. B. (2008). Prevention of behavior problems for children in foster care: Outcomes and mediation effects. *Prevention Science, 9*(1), 17–27.

Charles, G., & Gabor, P. (2006). An historical perspective on residential services for troubled and troubling youth in Canada revisited. *Relational Child & Youth Care Practice, 19*(4), 17–25.

Charles, G., & Garfat, T. (2009). Child and youth care practice in North America: Historical roots and current challenges. *Relational Child & Youth Care Practice, 22*(2), 17–28.

Charles, G., & Oliver, C., (2012). *Transitioning young people out of care in Canadian jurisdictions: A review of the issues and supports.* Ottawa: Child Welfare League of Canada.

Child Welfare Information Gateway. (2006). *Child abuse and neglect fatalities: Statistics and interventions.* Retrieved from www.childwelfare.gov/pubs/factsheets/fatality.cfm

Child Welfare League of America. (2007). *Facilitator's guide: Supervising the care of youth with complex needs.* Retrieved from http://www.uiowa.edu/~nrcfcp/training/documents/Youth%20with%20Complex%20Needs%20Facilitators'%20Guide.pdf

Commission to Promote Sustainable Child Welfare. (2010). *Jurisdictional comparisons of child welfare system design: Working paper no 2.* Toronto: Government of Ontario.

Department of Child, Youth and Family Services. (2016). *Transition binder 2015.* St. John's: Government of Newfoundland and Labrador. Retrieved January 29, 2016, from http://atipp-search.gov.nl.ca/public/atipp/Search/?show_all=1

Farris-Manning, C., & Zandstra, M. (2003). *Children in care in Canada: A summary of current issues and trends with recommendations for future research.* Ottawa: Child Welfare League of Canada.

Fowler, K. (2008). *Children in care in Newfoundland and Labrador: A review of issues and trends with recommendations for programs and services.* St. John's: Department of Health and Community Services, Government of Newfoundland and Labrador. Retrieved from http://www.gov.nl.ca/cyfs/publications/childcare/InCareReport.pdf

Frederico, M., Long, M., McNamara, P., McPherson, L., & Rose, R. (2017). Improving outcomes for children in out-of-home care: The role of therapeutic foster care. *Child and Family Social Work, 22,* 1064–1074.

Garfat, T., & Fulcher, L. (2011). Characteristics of a child and youth care approach. *Relational Child & Youth Care Practice, 24*(1/2), 7–19.

Globe & Mail. (2016, June 21). Foster-parent shortage across Canada reaching a crisis point. Retrieved from https://www.theglobeandmail.com/news/national/declining-number-of-foster-parents-across-canada-becoming-a-crisis/article30538343/

Gough, P., Shlonsky, A., & Dudding, P. (2009). An overview of the child welfare systems in Canada. *International Journal of Child Health and Human Development, 2*(3), 357–372.

Haire, B. (2009). *Residential services review.* Charlottetown: Department of Social Services and Seniors, Child and Family Services Division, Government of Prince Edward Island. Retrieved from http://www.gov.pe.ca/photos/original/ResidentialServ.pdf

Huffington Post. (2015). Why does Canada have so many kids in foster care? Retrieved from http://www.huffingtonpost.ca/marni-brownell/foster-care-in-canada_b_8491318.html

Human Resources Development Canada (HRDC). (1997). *Number of children in care of provincial and territorial child welfare authorities, by province and for Canada, as of March 31, 1997,* Table 437. Retrieved from www.hrdc-drhc.gc.ca/sp-ps/socialppsociale/reports/reports.shtml

Jones, A., Sinha, V., & Trocmé, N. (2015). *Children and youth in out-of-home care in the Canadian provinces.* CWRP Information Sheet #167E. Montreal: Centre for Research on Children and Families, McGill University.

Kluger, M. P., Alexander, G., & Curtis, A. P. (2000). *What works in child welfare.* Washington, DC: Child Welfare League of America.

Lipscombe, J., & Farmer, E. (2007). What matters in fostering adolescents? *Social Work and Social Sciences Review, 13*(1), 41–58.

MacDonald, G., & Turner, W. (2007). Treatment foster care for improving outcomes in children and young people. *Cochrane Database Systematic Review, 23*(1). Retrieved from http://library.college.police.uk/docs/Treatment-foster-care-2007.pdf

MacGregor, T. E., Rodger, S., Cummings, A. L., & Leschied, A. W. (2006). The needs of foster parents: A qualitative study of motivation, support, and retention. *Qualitative Social Work, 5*(3), 351–368.

Mulcahy, M., & Trocmé, N. (2010). CECW Information Sheet #78. *Children and youth in out-of-home care in Canada.* Montreal: Centre for Research on Children and Families, McGill University.

Office of the Child and Youth Advocate Alberta. (2013). *Where do we go from here? Youth aging out of care: Special report.* Edmonton: Government of Alberta.

Perry, B. (2009). Examining child maltreatment through a neurodevelopmental lens. *Journal of Loss and Trauma, 14,* 240–255.

Rich, J. (2009). *Labels that disable: Meeting the complex needs of children in residential care.* Retrieved from http://www.nice.org.uk/nicemedia/live/11879/47438/47438.pdf

Richard, B. (2008). *Connecting the dots: A report on the condition of youth-at-risk and youth with very complex needs in New Brunswick.* Fredericton: Office of the Ombudsman and Child and Youth Advocate.

Roberts, R. (2007). *A new approach to meeting the needs of looked after children experiencing difficulties: The multidimensional treatment foster care in England project.* AMACH Occasional Papers, 26, 59–68. Retrieved from http://wearelumos.org/sites/default/files/research/ACAMH_MTFCE_2007.pdf

Smith, D., Chamberlain, P., & Eddy, J. (2010). Preliminary support for multidimensional treatment foster care in reducing substance abuse in delinquent boys. *Journal of Child and Adolescent Substance Abuse, 19,* 343–358.

Twigg, R. (2006). *Withstanding the test of time: What we know about treatment foster care.* Monograph prepared for the Foster Family-based Treatment Association. Retrieved May 15, 2010, from www.ffta.org/members/publications/monograph.pdf

Verso Consulting. (2011). Evaluation of the therapeutic care residential pilot programs: Final summary and technical report. Retrieved from http://www.dhs.vic.gov.au/__data/assets/pdf_file/0005/712868/therapeutic-residential-mecare-report.pdf

CHAPTER 3

Child and Youth Care Practice with Families

Kelly C. Shaw

Research, writing, and exploration on child and youth care (CYC) practice with families has increased steadily over the past few decades, arguably faster than this practice area has grown. It is now recognized that there is a CYC approach to working with families (Garfat, 2003). Child and youth care practitioners who work with families have myriad resources to support them as they engage in this unique practice arena.

Canadian practitioners have shared extensively the range of their experiences as it relates to family work. This foundation of experience has been built on by other authors to create a collection of articles that practitioners can access as they move into this area of practice. In Canada, implementation of CYC family-based practice, while underutilized, occurs primarily in out-of-home preventative services with families struggling to live together effectively. Practice with families specifically as it juxtaposes with residential, school, and foster care practice has room for growth (see Modlin & Leggett, this volume). The more practitioners are grounded in the skill set needed for family-based practice (e.g., be confident in their practice and decision-making skills, able to monitor without direct supervision, possess the ability to self-supervise, and be confident in their judgment and decision-making without other team members directly present), the more there are practitioners positioned to advocate for this method of intervention supporting children, youth, and families to live together well.

THE CANADIAN PRACTICE COMPLEXITY

One cannot engage in a discussion about Canadian CYC practice with families without first being explicit about some of the elements that make this discussion a challenging task. Canada is geographically, ethnically, and culturally diverse. Child protection, health, and education are government departments, systems, or services that each province maintains legislatively and structurally, controlling the legislative agenda and policy development that determines program delivery. As such, actualizing the scope of practice (as established by the Canadian Council of Child and Youth Care Associations) for CYC practitioners varies from province to province. Further complexity is added when one explores the numerous job titles with which CYC workers may be identified (McElwee & Garfat, 2003). This means that as we try to examine where and how CYC practitioners work with families, it is difficult to articulate with confidence the nature of the practice occurring.

In general, child and youth care practice occurs contextually (Garfat & Fulcher, 2012), and therefore every CYC practitioner works with family, although how each individual practitioner constitutes family can be quite different. In CYC practice, we enter every relationship with the understanding that each specific interaction occurs within a certain context. Part of that context is the family or families that each child (and each practitioner) has grown up within (Garfat & Fulcher, 2012). The family relationship shapes the way the child conceptualizes relationships, including the relationship with the CYC practitioner, and therefore family is always present (Minuchin, 1985).

WHAT WORKING WITH FAMILY *MEANS* IN CANADA

In preparation for this chapter, provincial associations were asked to seek input from their membership in response to the following question: Do you work with families? Usually practitioners respond in the positive only if they are working with entire family units with the intention of family preservation or family reunification. Practitioners who work in community and school-based programs recognize that family is included in the work they do, yet they do not necessarily identify that they work with family, nor identify the family as the focus of their work.

Practitioners who work in group care with youngsters in the permanent care of the state often indicate they do not work with family (see Gharabaghi & Charles, this volume). In my experience they sometimes even indicate the young people they care for and about do not have family. This is an interesting but unfortunate perspective. It has been advocated that residential/group treatment programs be seen as resources for families, and they are also the best places to spend time if you want to learn about working with families (Garfat, 2007). Practitioners in this practice arena do not seem to mirror this perspective.

In many provinces, individuals who identify as CYC practitioners working with family also indicate there are many other jobs in supporting family wellness that could be done by CYC practitioners but are instead filled by members of other professions such as social work or psychology. Often, the reasons given for not hiring CYC practitioners into these roles are about regulation, registration, and licensing—they are not concerns specifically about skill set or education.

CYC practitioners work with families in a multitude of capacities, not un-like the laundry list of titles identified by McElwee and Garfat (2003). They are employed as family support workers, family access facilitators, in-home sup-port for foster parents, and community navigators (those who support families in navigating complex systems). This list is not exhaustive, yet it does illustrate the various ways that Canadian CYC practitioners identify they work with families.

CANADIAN CYC PRACTICE CONTEXT

Child and youth care in North America traces its history back about 150 years (Charles & Garfat, 2009). Its roots are firmly planted in residential care (Charles & Garfat, 2009; Charles & Gabor, 2006), although Canadian CYC practice has been evolving since at least the 1970s to engage in work in hospitals, community centres, streets, schools, and family homes (Denholm, Ferguson, & Pence, 1987; Gharabaghi & Charles, this volume).

In the early days of CYC practice, children living in residential programs were cared for by house parents (Maier, 1987), who often cared for large num-bers of youth in the same household. Their role was clearly that of substitute parent (Charles & Gabor, 2006). These house parents were described as "partly qualified, basically friendly, but clearly professionally naïve, laymen" (Redl & Wineman, 1952, pp. 65–66). Children were placed in these settings as a result of parental absence or issues related to abuse or neglect (Charles & Gabor, 2006). Families were seen as the cause of the problem and were usually excluded from continued involvement with their child. If CYC practitioners were involved at all, they generally focused their work only on the child. They saw their role as having to protect the youngster from the negative influences of the parents (Garfat, 2007). CYC practitioners who adopted this position with families identified their role as one of being available to negotiate *for* the youngster *against* the parents and being available should these young people need rescuing from their "evil" parents (Shaw & Garfat, 2003). When I began working in residential care in 1992, parents and families were seen as the cause of the problems of the youngsters with whom we worked (Fewster & Garfat, 1993; Garfat, 2008; Shaw & Garfat, 2003), and residential programs and child welfare systems still positioned themselves on the youngster's side often against the parents (Fewster & Garfat, 1993).

This position regarding families has continued to shift and has often been accompanied by a change of intent. As a result, skills and knowledge typically used within the residential environment have been transferred to the family context (Garfat, 2007). Child and youth care pre-service education programs across the country now include courses on family in their curricula, further supporting this change in practice focus. It is now common to hear CYC practitioners say they work with families, in whatever form this work might take (see Anderson-Nathe, this volume).

CYC practitioners who work with families use a way of being that incorporates characteristics of a CYC approach (Garfat & Fulcher, 2012). These characteristics are applied within the context of a therapeutic relationship with a family. For example, when CYC practitioners work with a family, they engage in the family's life-space—in their home. They use daily life events like bedtime and mealtime, mowing the lawn, and birthday parties as opportunities for intervention. Jones (2007) has built on these characteristics and explored the CYC family work literature, identifying that one of the specific elements that makes the CYC way of working with families unique is the *relational* aspect of our work.

FAMILY PRACTICE IN CANADA

Services are scarce for families who have children in care (Modlin, 2015). Typically, without child welfare involvement, accessing intervention is financially prohibitive and most often involves formal clinical intervention and not specifically CYC intervention. Some jurisdictions have delivery systems in place that make access to external CYC practice difficult and restrict funding dollars to clinicians unless service is provided within government programs. In Eastern Canada, for example, there is little access to family intervention outside of the child welfare system, and clinically educated individuals facilitate most of the family intervention done within the health care sector. In some provinces, there has been recent change in recognizing family support as an important step to implement. The intention is to decrease the need for more intrusive child welfare involvement.

In Central and Western Canada there are many large organizations with a spectrum of programs, including in-home family support. "Family support" is the language Canadian CYC practitioners often use when they say they are working with families. Phelan (2004) has differentiated this from other professionals' way of working with families. He suggests that CYC practice with families happens in a "natural place," perhaps their home or their yard or their church. He goes on to state that "boundaries in life-space work are more intimate" (Phelan, 2004), which places demands on an individual practitioner's self-awareness. He further suggests that there is significant opportunity for reciprocal generosity reflective of the relational element of CYC practice.

PREPARING FOR IN-HOME FAMILY-BASED PRACTICE

CYC practice is recognized as complex, dynamic, relational work (Anglin, 2002; Bellefeuille & Ricks, 2008; Fewster, 2001; Garfat, 2008). Families are fascinating systems, and working with a family is complicated because of the requirement to navigate the myriad of roles and relationships (Shaw, 2015). Working with family in the home is not a milieu for a new or inexperienced practitioner.

Numerous authors (Fulcher & Garfat, 2015; Garfat, 2000, 2003; Hill & Garfat, 2003; Jones, 2007; Phelan, 2004) have suggested that CYC practitioners need education specifically related to working with families. Practitioners should have grounding in residential CYC practice before they engage with family because working within the context of the family's life-space is more complicated than working residentially (Hill & Garfat, 2003).

CYC practitioners who have worked residentially and then change roles or jobs to work in family preservation, support, or reunification express that they are doing new work (Shaw, 2009). They recognize the characteristics of CYC practice; however, the *actual* work is brand new (Shaw, 2015). Without the learning they experienced during their time working in residential or group care, they would not know how to make meaning of their internal experience (Shaw, 2009). They stressed that although they were disconnected from the usual and predictable cues of the residential practice environment, now that they were working in the family home, they were able to use their observation skills, their ability to remain calm and present in interactions with individuals who are in crisis, and their knack for recognizing multiple complicated relational dynamics at once. These are all things they honed while working in residential group practice, and they use these skills to make sense of, or to structure, their new encounters (Shaw, 2009). They iterated that without their residential practice experience, they would not have been able to feel as effective working with families as they did (Shaw, 2009). With that previous knowledge and confidence, they were able to share their internal understanding appropriately with parents in order to support parents to structure their own experience of the intervention.

Even experienced CYC practitioners who work in-home with families identify a tremendous sense of responsibility, in part because both the family and the practitioner are disconnected from residential group care (Shaw, 2009). This feeling of immense responsibility is always framed from their professional perspective and often linked to other emotions. For example, they express a feeling of the privilege to be intimately working within a family system as a feeling of responsibility (Shaw, 2009). They feel the responsibility to be prepared, trained, and confident in their practice in order to represent themselves professionally and competently with the family and within multi-disciplinary teams. CYC practitioners identify that their practice with families is serious work that involves being with families as they live their lives and utilizing daily life events as they are unfolding in order to support families to live together with less stress and (perhaps) more feelings of efficacy as parents and children (Shaw, 2009).

Even if practitioners are part of multi-disciplinary teams, the work they do is often done solo with parents and children and not in tandem with other professionals. They may be present in the life of a family as the mother tucks her young child into bed, as a parent argues with his teenage son, as they fold laundry or cook supper beside Dad while his children are doing homework at the kitchen table. This isolation has influenced practitioners to notice that they sometimes feel anxious with the responsibility they have been offered in this type of work (Shaw, 2009), which led them to be differently aware of their self than they remembered being when they worked residentially, where they were typically alongside numerous other CYC practitioners (Shaw, 2009). Now they are alone to make decisions with the family with whom they were working. Often, they are the only CYC practitioner who has intimate knowledge of the family, placing further demand and responsibility on the practitioner in situations requiring advocacy (Shaw, 2009).

The intricacy of family systems increases the opportunity for us, as practitioners, to be challenged by having our own histories and experiences evoked. Working with a family in isolation leaves us alone to address these issues of self.

If our self-awareness is not well developed, we will not be able to distinguish between self and other (Fewster, 1991), and supervisors (because they are not present) will not have our practice as a context to support our development of self.

Krueger (1999), in his exploration of presence as a theme of CYC work, suggested that as CYC practitioners gain confidence, they increase their ability to be present in the moment with a child, youth, or parent and that this presence is based in self-awareness. This presence is like a dancer using their awareness, skill, and knowledge to engage creatively, all the while maintaining an openness to what may occur next—and sensing the myriad possibilities (Krueger, 1999). CYC practitioners who work in the family's home also notice things differently than when they worked residentially. For example, they notice self differently and they notice the work that they do differently. They express that they felt less safe and more anxious than when they were working residentially. They highlighted the lack of teammate support when they were in the family home, and indicated this influenced feelings of isolation and autonomy. They identified that when working within family homes, there are increased opportunities for situations to arise that evoke reflection. Being immersed in the family dynamic, they were also confronted with new learning about self—which has been identified as an outcome of relational practice (Garfat, 2008).

Knowing self is a way of being, an awareness, or a presence (Garfat & Charles, 2007) and it is essential to relational CYC practice. If we do not know self and have an awareness of self, we cannot know or understand other (Fewster, 1991; Krueger, 1999; Lundy, 2008; Ricks, 2001), and in order to enter into a relationship with another and to work relationally, we have to be able to identify our own experiences, separate from the experiences of other, since it is only our own experiences we can know (Fewster, 1991). If we do not know ourselves and understand that we are showing up when we respond in interaction to another, then we cannot engage therapeutically (Fewster, 1991).

Given these experiences of CYC practitioners who are working in-home with family, it is essential that CYC practitioners who work in an in-home practice environment with families be supervised in a way that ensures they have the support they need to effectively navigate the challenges of this work. The individual working with the family is often the only one who has specific knowledge of the family, and this requires that the practitioner has adequate support for assisted self-reflection in this independent environment.

Jones (2007) states that when working with families, the change process is "dynamic and inter-related" and that the process of change is not only about the parent changing and growing; it is also about the personal and professional growth of the CYC practitioner. Regardless of the tremendous responsibility, the anxiety, the ability to be present or to notice the layers of complexity in their practice, CYC practitioners who work with families recognize the growth that they experience as a consequence of the engagement in relationship with parents (Shaw, 2009). Kelly (2004) has identified that because of the active self-awareness that is required by our profession, we cannot remain unchanged by our work with families: "active self-awareness facilitates change."

AN ARENA OF POSSIBILITY

As in Canada, CYC intervention with family varies globally, perhaps linked to the socio-cultural view of family. Research suggests that effective group care or residential programs require partnership between parents and the professionals supporting the children and young people involved in the program, yet in the United States, they are seldom included as members of the treatment team (Brendtro & Mitchell, 2011).

Several countries have developed models that fit within their particular legislation. These models are fairer and more focused on ensuring that the rights of children are at the centre of intervention than most approaches currently used in Canada.

In the Netherlands, legislation allowing children, youth, and families to seek the support they need to match their own circumstance has been implemented (Metselaar, Knorth, & Van den Berg, 2007). The intention of this approach is to offer a framework to allow child welfare intervention to be client focused. By offering individuals the right to access the intervention that is best for them, service delivery can be democratized. Evaluation of this approach has shown that family involvement when children are placed in out-of-home care positively influences reunification (Geurts, Knorth, & Noom, 2007).

Foster parents and caseworkers have identified that children who spend time with their parents return to placement struggling to be emotionally regulated and requiring additional staff support during their transition back to placement (Jones & Kruk, 2005). This perspective perpetuates parents as problematic and shows the value and importance of engaging in supporting children's relationship with their family of origin to support placement—and avoid placement breakdown.

When youngsters run away from a group care or residential treatment program, they often run to their family (Jones & Kruk, 2005). When their care agreement terminates, when they encounter discharge from a program, or when they age out of care, they usually return to their family (Jones & Kruk, 2005). It is therefore important that when a youngster resides in a residential or group treatment program there also be support for them within their family relationships. This will offer opportunities for them to continue to feel a sense of belonging in their family and to negotiate changes in relationships long before they make the choice to return home when they are emancipated from public care (Nickerson, Colby, Brooks, Rickert, & Salamone, 2007). These recommendations reinforce the argument made by Charles and Garfat (2010) that a comprehensive and integrated strategy of youth and family service delivery be developed at a national level in Canada, perhaps mirroring what has been done in the Netherlands.

Isibindi is a social franchise model developed by the National Association of Child Care Workers in South Africa (Thumbadoo, 2011). This is a model designed to be adapted to meet the needs of an individual community and culture. This program utilizes community strengths to support families of varying make-up in their own homes and communities. The Isibindi program is one that offers promise for application in a multitude of contexts. The UN has explored it for use in refugee situations, and perhaps it is a model that remote and Northern communities in Canada could use.

PROFESSIONALISM/PROFESSIONALIZATION

The complexity of working with families has been clearly outlined. The possibility of more adequately supporting children and families using a CYC approach to family intervention has been identified. Specific recommendations have been made for the development of a national service delivery model that allows family to be at the centre of intervention much differently than it is currently. Yet there are still barriers. Often, these are explicitly about licensing and registration. Organizational liability is lessened if individuals belong to a professional body that is legislated and regulated externally. In Canada, however, CYC practitioners are neither legislated nor regulated, although Alberta and Ontario are engaged with their governments towards this end. No province requires specific education to be a CYC practitioner, and any general educational requirement is practice-sector specific. There are exceptions, and examples of this would include that a diploma in CYC or a degree in a related discipline is required to work in school-based or secure treatment settings.

Nine provinces have established CYC professional associations, and each association has a unique mandate. A national unifying body—the Council of

Canadian Child and Youth Care Associations (CCCYCA)—supports advocacy of quality care for children, youth, and families as well as the direction of each provincial association towards professionalizing in the way that is most meaningful and specific to each province.

Competency-based CYC certification is available in a number of provinces utilizing two similar models: the Alberta Certification process (http://www.cycaa.com/certification/purpose/) or the Child and Youth Care Certification Board process (https://cyccb.org). Even though provincial professional CYC associations endorse, support, facilitate, and advocate for CYC certification and the benefits for parents, youth, and families, certification is not a hiring requirement in any province, but it is sometimes seen as an asset. Currently, CYC certification is voluntary; thus individuals who choose to pursue certification are intrinsically motivated to do so, and those that do are often recognized as high performers by their supervisors (Curry, Eckles, Stuart, Schneider-Munoz, & Qaqish, 2013).

Continued exploration of the professionalizing of child and youth care practitioners might support increased practice areas if this includes legislation and regulation congruent with other professional bodies nationally (e.g., psychologists, social workers, counsellors). This is a complicated venture as previously identified in this chapter, yet one which has merit.

BUT … MAYBE …

Uri Bronfenbrenner suggested that North American society and government needed to examine how they value family, individuals who are struggling, and children (Bronfenbrenner, 2012). Perhaps it is our socio-cultural and socio-political system that perpetuates the challenges that our social welfare system encounters as it positions within legislation and policy to support family (Freistadt, 2010). Perhaps, as Hans Skott-Myhre (2013) suggests, family—as we imagine it should be, defined by legislation and policy—is not the foundation of society. This is another layer of the intricacy of our practice when we work with family.

CONCLUSION

It is weighty, yet imperative, that we balance *these* tensions: our practice environments that are primarily influenced by the social policies of our country; our responsibility to negotiate the mandate of our employers; and our professional, ethical responsibility as relational practitioners to be reflective, constantly engaged in our own change process. It is important that we recognize our responsibilities as advocates and ensure that we challenge legislation, policy, and program mandates in the best interest of children, youth, and family. This responsibility extends to education, training, supervision, and support of CYC practitioners.

Jones (2007) indicated that most CYC practitioners do not graduate from their pre-service program prepared for the complexity of working with family, and they would therefore benefit from experience in residential CYC practice where there is a mix of beginning and seasoned practitioners. The mentorship and supervision offered in a residential environment are important in supporting practitioner development. Child and youth care practitioners who spend time working in residential/group care programs before they begin doing family work use that experience to support their navigation of the intricacies of relationship and the complexity of experience. Without this valuable experience, they would be unable to effectively engage with family.

As a collective, we need to continue to build on our body of literature strengthening what is known about the value of including family when working with children (whether those families are living intact or parents and children are living apart from each other). We need to remember that because of the contextual nature of CYC practice, we are always working with family.

Continued exploration of what is meant when we refer to CYC practice with families would be valuable. This would support clarity and increase opportunity for supervisory and training support that is specific to this unique practice area. No matter the practice arena, it is important that CYC practitioners have supervision that is meaningful. Working with family requires supervision that is responsive to the unique challenges of this practice: the isolation, the complicated relationships, the feelings of responsibility and anxiety.

The Association for Children's Residential Centres (ACRC) provides multiple training and education opportunities for practitioners whose primary focus is residential practice. They support advocacy, a research base, and a network for organizations and individuals. CYC practitioners who work external to a residential centre could benefit from a network, perhaps based within the provincial professional associations, similar to the ACRC yet focused on the unique practice intricacies encountered when working solo in the community or with family in their own homes.

REFERENCES

Anglin, J. (2002). *Pain, normality and the struggle for congruence: Reinterpreting residential care for children and youth*. New York: Haworth Press.

Bellefeuille, G., & Ricks, F. (Eds.). (2008). *Standing on the precipice: Inquiry into the creative potential of child and youth care practice*. Edmonton: MacEwan Press.

Brendtro, L. K., & Mitchell, M. L. (2011). Families as life span experts. *Reclaiming Children and Youth, 20*(3), 8–14.

Bronfenbrenner, U. (2012, April). Children and communities. *CYC-Online*. Retrieved from http://www.cyc-net.org/cyc-online/april2012.pdf#page=12

Charles, G., & Gabor, P. (2006). An historical perspective on residential services for troubled and troubling youth in Canada. *Relational Child and Youth Care Practice, 19*(4), 17–24.

Charles, G., & Garfat, T. (2009). Child and youth care practice in North America: Historical roots and current challenges. *Relational Child and Youth Care Practice, 22*(2), 17–28.

Charles, G., & Garfat, T. (2010). Beyond residential and community based services: A conceptual model for an integrated youth and family service delivery system in Canada. *Relational Child and Youth Care Practice, 23*(4), 46–52.

Curry, D., Eckles, F., Stuart, C., Schneider-Munoz, A., & Qaqish, B. (2013). National certification for child and youth workers: Does it make a difference? *Children and Youth Services Review, 35*, 1795–1800.

Denholm, C., Ferguson, R., & Pence, A. (Eds.). (1987). *Professional child and youth care: The Canadian perspective*. Vancouver: University of British Columbia Press.

Fewster, G. (1991). The paradoxical journey: Some thoughts on relating to children. *Journal of Child and Youth Care, 6*(4), 85–91.

Fewster, G. (2001). *Going there from being here*. Retrieved from http://www.cyc-net.org/cyc-online/cycol-0201-fewster.html

Fewster, G., & Garfat, T. (1993). Residential child and youth care. In C. Denholm, R. Ferguson, & A. Pence (Eds.), *Professional child and youth care* (2nd. ed., pp. 15–43). Vancouver: University of British Columbia Press.

Freistadt, J. (2010). Navigating potentially conflicting political rationalities: Discursive strategies about "family" in Alberta's child welfare law. *Canadian Journal of Family Law, 26*(1), 219–267.

Fulcher, L., & Garfat, T. (Eds.). (2015). *Child and youth care practice with families*. Cape Town, South Africa: CYC-Net Press.

Garfat, T. (2000). Editorial: On the development of family work in residential programs. *Journal of Child and Youth Care, 14*(2), iii–iv.

Garfat, T. (Ed.). (2003). *A child and youth care approach to working with families*. New York: Haworth Press.

Garfat, T. (2007). *Who are we working with? A short history of child and youth care involvement with families*. Retrieved from http://www.cyc-net.org/cyc-online/cycol-0708-garfat.html

Garfat, T. (2008). The inter-personal in-between: An exploration of relational child and youth care practice. In G. Bellefeuille & F. Ricks (Eds.), *Standing on the precipice: Inquiry into the creative potential of child and youth care practice* (pp. 7–34). Edmonton: MacEwan Press.

Garfat, T., & Charles, G. (2007). How am I who I am? Self in child and youth care practice. *Relational Child and Youth Care Practice, 20*(3), 6–16.

Garfat, T., & Fulcher, L. C. (2012). Characteristics of a child and youth care approach. In T. Garfat, L. C. Fulcher, & J. Digney (Eds.), *Readings for the therapeutic use of daily life events* (pp. 12–34). Cape Town, South Africa: Pretext Publishing.

Geurts, E., Knorth, E., & Noom, M. (2007). Contextual, family-focused residential child and youth care: Preliminary findings from a program evaluation study. *Relational Child and Youth Care Practice, 20*(4), 46–58.

Hill, M., & Garfat, T. (2003). Moving to youth care family work in residential programs: A supervisor's perspective on making the transition. In T. Garfat (Ed.), *A child and youth care approach to working with families* (pp. 211–223). New York: Haworth Press.

Jones, L. (2007). Articulating a child and youth care approach to family work. *CYC-Online*. Retrieved from http://www.cyc-net.org/cyc-online/cycol-0709-jones.html

Jones, L., & Kruk, E. (2005). Life in government care: The connection of youth to family. *Child & Youth Care Forum, 34*(6), 405–421.

Kelly, M. (2004). *Some key characteristics of child and youth care workers*. Retrieved August 12, 2009, from http://www.cyc-net.org/cyc-online/cycol-1004-maxinekelly.html

Krueger, M. (1999). Presence as dance in work with youth. *Journal of Child and Youth Care, 13*(2), 59–72.

Lundy, T. (2008). Presence and participation: Being at the heart of change. In G. Bellefeuille & F. Ricks (Eds.), *Standing on the precipice: Inquiry into the creative potential of child and youth care practice* (pp. 207–230). Edmonton: MacEwan Press.

Maier, H. (1987). *Developmental group care of children and youth: Concepts and practice*. New York: Haworth Press.

McElwee, N., & Garfat, T. (2003). What's in a name? Exploring title designations in child and youth care in Ireland. *Irish Journal of Applied Social Studies, 4*(1), 5–19.

Metselaar, J., Knorth, E., & Van den Berg, P. (2007). Needs-led and family centered Child and Youth Care: Theoretical considerations and evaluation in practice. *Relational Child and Youth Care Practice, 20*(2), 38–46.

Minuchin, P. (1985). Families and individual development: Provocations from the field of family therapy. *Child Development, 56*(2), 289.

Modlin, H. (2015). Initiating family involvement in residential care: Reflections on the journey. In L. Fulcher & T. Garfat (Eds.), *Child and youth care practice with families* (pp. 104–120). Cape Town, South Africa: CYC-Net Press.

Nickerson, A., Colby, B., Brooks, S., Rickert, A., & Salamone, J. (2007). Transitioning youth from residential treatment to the community: A preliminary investigation. *Child and Youth Care Forum, 36*(2), 73–86.

Phelan, J. (2004). An explanation of family support work. Retrieved from http://www. cyc-net.org/cyc-online/cycol-1204-familysupport.html

Redl, F., & Wineman, D. (1952). *Controls from within: Techniques for the treatment of the aggressive child*. New York: The Free Press.

Ricks, F. (2001). Without self there is no other. *CYC-Online*. Retrieved from http://www. cyc-net.org/cyc-online/cycol-0401-ricks.html

Shaw, K. (2009). *Barefoot in their home: A phenomenological inquiry into child and youth care workers experience of self in family homes*. Unpublished master's thesis, Mount Saint Vincent University, Halifax, Nova Scotia.

Shaw, K., (2015). From front line to family home: A child and youth care approach to working with families. In L. Fulcher & T. Garfat (Eds.), *Child and youth care practice with families* (pp. 85–103). Cape Town, South Africa: CYC-Net Press.

Shaw, K., & Garfat, T. (2003). From front line to family home: A child and youth care approach to working with families. In T. Garfat (Ed.), *A child and youth care approach to working with families* (pp. 39–54). New York: Haworth Press.

Skott-Myhre, H. (2013, May). Down with the family. *CYC-Online*. Retrieved from http://www.cyc-net.org/cyc-online/may2013.pdf#page=20

Thumbadoo, Z. (2011). Isibindi: Love in caring with a child and youth care approach. *Relational Child & Youth Care Practice, 24*(1/2), 193–198.

CHAPTER 4

Community Settings, Outreach, and Youth Engagement

Janet Newbury and Wolfgang Vachon[1]

We are writing this chapter as an experiment in the generative potential of thinking together across differences. While we share several perspectives on, experiences with, and commitments to child and youth care (CYC) practice, the ways we have come to what we know and the ways we engage based on what we know differ greatly. We represent different genders, have different professional and academic backgrounds, live in different geographic and demographic contexts, and we have no prior relationship with each other. Do these differences preclude us from working collaboratively? If we believed that to be the case, then we would certainly see no possibilities for intergenerational and intercultural work in communities. Instead, we strongly believe in the creative, therapeutic, and community-building potential of connecting across differences.

In the pages that follow, we will explore collaborating across differences particularly in relation to *community, outreach,* and *youth engagement.* To begin, we look at how each of these three terms is commonly understood within the field of CYC and beyond. Next, we unpack these ideas further, in order to widen the scope of possibilities for practice. We advocate for an approach put forward by thinkers/practitioners before us (Aldarondo, 2007) who recognize the potential of emphasizing collaborative engagement over service delivery and the political imperative for such practices. At the same time, we recognize some of the practical and ethical challenges inherent within this approach including the negotiation of power dynamics (Madsen & Gillespie, 2014). We conclude with an invitation to extend the conversation by reflecting on some lingering questions and a practice scenario.

CLARIFYING OUR TERMS

In order to increase our chances of beginning from a place of common understanding, we will briefly discuss the three terms that comprise the core of this chapter: community, outreach, and youth engagement.

Community

Community is most often thought of as a group of people in some sort of shared relationship; it is also frequently thought of in terms of sameness. For instance, communities are sometimes described on the basis of shared values or concerns (i.e., faith-based), shared experiences (i.e., sports teams), shared identity (i.e., the Queer community), and of course shared place (i.e., a particular neighbourhood, town, or country). Communities of sameness can be important in that they offer a sense of belonging and solidarity (Cameron & Gibson, 2001). Particularly when mobilizing for social change in the direction of justice, such communities can be powerful forces (Etmanski, Hall, & Dawson, 2014).

However, it is easy to see some practical and ethical difficulties when it comes to defining communities in terms of sameness alone. What does it mean when it comes to welcoming or excluding newcomers (see James, this volume)? How well does the community change or adapt to new circumstances? How is diversity *within* communities negated when defined by sameness? Cameron and Gibson (2001) suggest that sameness is not the only way to define community, and in fact is generally not the primary way we experience community. As a response to these considerations, they advocate the possibilities that emerge when we instead think about *communities of difference.* An intentional commitment to the openness required by communities of difference means we (individually and collectively) are not bound to behave in certain ways or believe in certain things in order to belong.

Instead, we can see community as a relational process in which we are always engaged. Community invites us to redefine ourselves anew in the context of one another (and different others over time) and, in doing so, support others to do the same. Communities of difference are porous and strengthen through curiosity about one another, as well as ourselves (Newbury, 2012). Importantly, this notion of community takes into consideration our relations with not only other people, but also animals, the material world, spiritual realities, and other important elements of community life (Taylor & Pacini-Ketchebaw, 2015). Considering CYC practice from this perspective invites us to recognize that we all simultaneously identify with multiple communities, in many different ways, and that communities are not necessarily rigidly defined collections of individuals specific to certain places (Newbury, 2014; Richardson & Reynolds, 2012). With this in mind, we suggest community practice takes place every time CYC practitioners and young people come together, including all the locations and practices within this book.

Outreach

Outreach targeting young people is usually understood as a practice that identifies and locates people in their milieu. Workers form relationships with individuals, help them become aware of services, and offer these services in diverse formats (Connolly & Joly, 2012). Historically, outreach programs focusing on children and youth frequently had interventionist, moralistic, and coercive agendas (Crimmins et al., 2004), some tenets of which remain to this day, as will be discussed below. Outreach programs can be "fixed" or "mobile" (Saldanha & Parenteau, 2013), although one does not necessarily preclude the other. Fixed outreach involves placing services in specific communities that people access, whereas mobile outreach is bringing services directly to people (see Martin & Stuart, this volume). Drop-ins, shelters (Slesnick, Dashora, Letcher, Erdem, & Serovich, 2009), or supervised injection sites would be examples of fixed outreach. Going to locations where young people spend time, such as malls, bars, parks, and schools (Connolly & Joly, 2012), would be considered mobile. There is also outreach for specific populations such as sex workers (Saldanha & Parenteau, 2013), homeless youth (Connolly & Joly, 2012), or gangs (Klein, 2011). In a review of published literature on outreach with street-involved youth, Connolly and Joly (2012) identify three key philosophies that guide outreach: client-centred, developmentally sensitive, and strength-based.

CYC is a practice of entering and leaving. Young people come into our care, programs, and lives. Similarly (and yet completely differently), we enter and leave their lives. We recognize that when people approach, we also need to *reach out* to welcome them, and if they don't come to us, we may need to *reach in*, assess why, and then ask if we should outreach to them. In this chapter, we would like to extend our understanding of what is meant by outreach to include these important informal and reflexive processes.

Youth Engagement

There is a growing body of literature regarding engagement and young people, coming from multiple disciplines such as education (Hattie, 2009), social work (Naccarato, Brophy, & LaClair, 2013), and sociology (Nenga & Taft, 2015), among others. It is also something we speak of often in CYC practice, although there has been little CYC-specific research on engagement. Perhaps because of this we have to be careful about what we mean when we—sometimes too casually—use this term.

In an undergraduate CYC course taught by one of the authors, which included a component on youth engagement, many of the students were looking for "techniques to engage youth," that is, ways to convince youth to take part in the great programs on offer. They understood engagement as compliance; this is not uncommon. We often look for evidence of "buy-in" to our programs or activities (Naccarato, Brophy, & LaClair, 2013; Yachmenoff, 2005; see also Gharabaghi & Charles, this volume). In these instances, we seek engagement that "consists of a cognitive component, an affective component, and a behavioral component—Head, Heart, Feet" (Centres of Excellence for Children's Well-Being, 2012). As CYC practitioners (CYCs), we may practise this form of engagement through applying methods of coercion, and measure success as the young person's (or family's) mental, emotional, and behavioural obedience to our agenda. We may unwittingly expect those we work with to not only behave as we would like them to, but to also think and be emotionally committed to *our* vision (Gharabaghi, 2008). In addition to being potentially oppressive, this approach can be frustrating for all parties, leading to resentment and a dismissal of engagement as a useless or even detrimental process. Thus it can limit opportunities for other types of engagement.

When discussing engagement in this chapter we are referring to a more collaborative process than the one described above. According to Lenihan (2012), engagement is a methodology for collaboration in which "empowerment and responsibility are two sides of the same coin" (p. 72). As CYCs working from an engagement orientation, we seek to have young people meaningfully participating in decision-making, based upon *their* individual capacities and visions, from our earliest interactions. Engagement cannot be meaningful—and will not be successful—if it is only the last step (Lenihan, 2012). True youth engagement is thus participatory—not just in activities or outcomes, but in decision-making, goal-setting, and other processes that contribute to their development. Here we draw upon a definition provided by Checkoway (2011): "Youth participation is a process of involving young people in the institutions and decisions that affect their lives" (p. 341). We argue that this approach to child and youth care can be applied in multiple contexts and is ultimately beneficial for those we work with, the organizations we work for, and to ourselves as practitioners.

A CLOSER LOOK AT COMMUNITY, OUTREACH, AND YOUTH ENGAGEMENT

From our standpoint, *community* can be understood as the various ways we come together in different times and places; *outreach* can be understood as those practices that strive to include even the most marginalized among us in these community processes; and *engagement* can be understood as participatory and collaborative ways of facilitating these practices.

Understanding these terms in these ways, we deliberately resist the temptation to consider community, outreach, and youth engagement as comprising a particular "sector" within the diverse field of Child and Youth Care. Rather, we understand them to be *ways of engaging* that can show up in many ways—and in many "sectors." In order to begin unpacking them a bit further, let us now consider these ideas by way of a scenario.

An experienced CYC practitioner and educator was invited to provide training for staff at a residential treatment program for adolescent females. Shortly into the day, it became clear that the manager and staff were troubled by the lack of compliance among residents. The residents stayed out well past curfew, swore, smoked behind the house, and skipped chores. Staff were looking for new ways to address these issues.

The trainer asked them to shed light on the rules, rationales, and sanctions that were upheld at the institution. He then followed up with some questions about their development:

"Were the young women who live here involved in creating the rules?"

"No."

"Were there any opportunities for them to have an input into the rules?"

"No."

"Can I ask why not?"

(With a smile) "Come on, these girls don't have the skills or ability to do so responsibly, that's part of the reason they're here. If we gave them a say, they would choose to have very lax or no rules at all, and they'd not make effective consequences."

"Okay … and are the current rules and consequences effective?"

"No."

"Would you consider collaborating with them to find out what they think would be fair and if there is a way to establish rules and consequences together this way?"

The trainer was diplomatically told he did not understand the context, and his ideas were naïve.

Take a moment to reflect on this scenario, and consider (a) why the manager might have been resistant to a more collaborative approach, (b) your own experience with collaborative practices and the challenges that arise (particularly in involuntary practice contexts), and (c) what you think some possible outcomes of the proposed approach might be.

We will now return to our discussion, suggesting that you keep this scenario in mind.

PARTICIPATORY DECISION-MAKING

There are ways of conceptualizing and implementing engagement in CYC practice that are anti-oppressive, rights-based, *and* therapeutic. One such example comes from youth-adult partnerships (Y-AP). Multiple models of Y-AP, such as Hart (2008), Shier (2001), and Wong, Zimmerman, and Parker (2010), demonstrate how effective Y-AP focuses less on changing young people and more on what (and how) young people and adults can effectively work together on issues affecting youth. This is not to say, though, that Y-AP are not also therapeutic. Zeldin, Christens, and Powers (2013) define Y-AP as follows:

Youth-adult partnership is the practice of: (a) multiple youth and multiple adults deliberating and acting together, (b) in a collective [democratic] fashion, (c) over a sustained period of time, (d) through shared work, (e) intended to promote social justice, strengthen an organization, and/or affirmatively address a community issue. (p. 388)

There are well-documented benefits to young people who are engaged in inter-generational partnership activities (Ramey, Lawford, & Vachon, 2017). These include skills in teamwork, communication, and presentation abilities; new friendships; increased knowledge; and feeling valued and empowered (Howe, Batchelor, & Bochynska, 2011). Morciano, Scardigno, Manuti, and Pastore (2014) found that participation in decision-making by young people seemed to contribute to an increased sense of empowerment and self-efficacy. Larson and Angus (2011) identified agency and strategic thinking in young people who par-ticipated through collaborative arts-based processes. A crucial aspect of their study was that the adult advisors gave young people control of the programs. Larson (2011) found greater self-regulation in young people who were engaged in arts, technology, and leadership programs.

Clearly, there are many ways that engagement positively impacts young people. As one goes deeper into the literature, it becomes clear that when young people are involved in decision-making, there are also benefits to organizations and workers. For example, Ramey (2013) found that youth involvement in organizational decision-making was perceived as leading to improved services, more service utilization, youth delivery of services, im-proved youth-adult interactions, and more participatory practices (p. 498). The perceived outcomes for staff included changes to attitudes, knowledge, and skills in their work with youth, and increased motivation, self-efficacy, engagement, and confidence (p. 499). Importantly, Ramey (2013) also identi-fies some challenges for adults working in organizations that implemented youth engagement models. She found that youth engagement led to greater stress and responsibility for staff, and the need for additional resources (such as more staff) from the organization. This suggests that developing engage-ment skills could be a useful aspect of CYC training.

AN ASSET-BASED APPROACH

The approach embraced by the trainer in the earlier scenario—and in this chapter as a whole—is informed by asset-based thinking, which recognizes that *all* com-munity members have something to contribute, and that their inclusion strength-ens communities (Kretzmann, McKnight, Dobrowolski, & Puntenney, 2005).

From this perspective, our primary role as CYCs is to support the identification and mobilization of existing assets so that together we can create stronger communities (see also Lord & Hutchinson, 2007). This does not ignore that needs exist, but recognizes that a problem-oriented approach rarely leads to the elimination of problems and can sometimes lead to stigmatization (McKnight, 1995). An asset- or strength-based perspective, on the other hand, builds resilience in a way that preserves and even enhances human dignity (Madsen & Gillespie, 2014; Richardson & Reynolds, 2012). Because of the systemic marginalization many of those we work with experience in aspects of their lives (de Finney, Dean, Loiselle, & Saraceno, 2011), the political imperative for such practices becomes even more apparent.

Decades of evidence supports an asset-based approach in addressing such challenging community issues as suicide (Kral et al., 2009), HIV prevention (Thoms, 2007), child protection (Madsen & Gillespie, 2014), child poverty (Albanese, 2010), inclusion of people with disabilities (Lord & Hutchison, 2007), and community-based economic development (Gibson-Graham & Roelvink, 2011). And current studies show that communities in which more people are supported to meaningfully contribute and belong are communities that thrive both socially and economically, even despite material, political, and economic challenges (Knight Foundation, 2010).

PRACTICAL AND ETHICAL CHALLENGES

Involving young people in decision-making can evidently benefit them, practitioners, and communities. This is not to say it is easy or that there are no challenges that need to be navigated. However, as Larson (2011) points out, challenges are where young people develop (and *all* of us do). In this section we consider some significant challenges that present themselves when striving to do effective outreach and youth engagement in community settings.

Access and Effectiveness

There are numerous barriers to establishing the kinds of meaningful partnerships described above. How can we connect across sometimes seemingly insurmountable divides? Connolly and Joly (2012) identify outreach workers' and young people's views of outreach program effectiveness. Workers in several programs identify *peer* outreach workers as important to program effectiveness, while participants identified youth ("in age or at least attitude" [p. 531]) as beneficial but did not indicate peer identity as important. In fact, some participants were irritated by peer workers who "lecture them about practices the workers still engage in," such as drug use (p. 531). Saldanha and Parenteau (2013) write about an outreach program targeting sex workers in Toronto in which peer outreach was perceived as a significant asset. However, in a policy essay, Klein (2011) discusses the lack of empirical support for peer interventions in gangs and even identifies several associated risks. The Ella Baker Centre (n.d.) in Oakland, California, did a Youth Participatory Action project called Heal the Streets. This study found that young people thought adults from the community were better positioned to intervene with young people than adult professionals. Such results raise important questions about discerning when expert knowledge is or isn't potentially beneficial and/or therapeutic (Hoskins, 2011). Clearly, there are no definitive answers to this question of access and effectiveness, but it is something to which we should be attuned as practitioners working with(in) diverse communities.

Power Dynamics

Who determines the content of our programs or services? If those we are trying to serve reject our services, should we abandon what we believe to be helpful, find ways to entice participants, or involve them in the creation of services? Do we relinquish our commitments to certain outcomes for young people if they don't share our views, or do we relinquish our commitments to those particular young people? In other words, how do we negotiate the power dynamics at play as CYCs?

At first, the answers to the questions above seem obvious. Our programs and services are meant to support young people, and if they don't connect, there is little value. This perspective would be exemplified by detached youth work (Crimmins et al., 2004), which is based upon the relationship between the two parties. The workers respond to the identified needs of the young person; they do not enforce, sanction, or otherwise try to coerce the young person. In other words, they do not have specific interventionist aims and intended outcomes.

In more interventionist approaches, it may seem that the agenda of the worker or agency takes precedent. Saldanha and Parenteau (2013) were both outreach workers with a program called Street Trade Alternatives and New Directions (STAND). They are clear regarding their own agenda (for people to leave the sex trade); however, they also grew to accept that trying to force people to leave is unlikely to be successful. This awareness is exemplified in how they came to understand outreach as:

> *an active form of waiting* ... Waiting communicates respect towards the individual. It acknowledges that street youth are on their own stage of the journey and will not be ready or able to make changes in their life just because we want them to or because we happen to have room in our program for them at that time. Waiting shows people that outreach workers care about them, not just about helping them; while we wait we spend time with people just as they are. (p. 1278; italics in original)

Interventionist, moralistic, and coercive agendas were a topic of discussion at a panel presentation by sex workers, all of whom started working while they were legally minors.[2] All said they did it through choice, did not have "pimps," and found interventions trying to stop them to be oppressive. They saw professional interventions as hypocritical, as an example of people trying to *control* their bodies, while saying it was to protect their bodies. This sentiment is captured by Canadian sex worker Evans (2016), who writes, "swinging in on a vine to save someone who does not want to be saved is not an act of liberation; it is a perpetuation of the kinds of power imbalances that feminism is supposed to fight" (para. 18). Several members of the panel used the term "rescue industry," referring to practices such as those implemented by initiatives like STAND. The rescue industry is the system designed to prevent (rescue) young people from doing what they are doing (see also McKnight, 1995). The panellists identified it as *more* oppressive, more abusive, and ultimately more dangerous than the people who were their customers. For them, outreach workers were, usually, people best avoided.

 As we reflect on this example, we ask ourselves what other CYC practices might be characterized as part of the rescue industry? What does this mean for us as a profession? How can we ensure our practices are not perpetuating or otherwise replicating the inequitable power dynamics we aim to overcome?

Legacies of Oppression

This becomes very uncomfortable for us as authors. On a personal and political level, we see sex work by young people as indicative of many issues within our culture that should be addressed (Reynolds, 2014). We understand those who argue against even using the term *sex work* to describe people who are under the legal age of consent. *And* we ally with young people who are involved. We entered this field because of our love for and commitment to supporting young people (Skott-Myhre & Skott-Myhre, 2007). Sometimes in CYC our values can become uncomfortable for us when understood in context.

Effective outreach requires us to look inward in these ways. To challenge our taken-for-granted assumptions, to be willing to be challenged by others, and to have the humility to acknowledge that we do not always know what "best practice" actually is, are also part of our jobs (Thoms, 2007). It is important that we recognize the damage that has been done historically by professionals who think they know best (Charles & Gabor, 2006). Canada's legacies of residential schools (Truth and Reconciliation Commission of Canada, 2015) and institutionalization of people with disabilities (Pfeiffer, 1993) are two examples that continue to play out in our policies and practices. Uninvited or coercive practices—regardless of the intentions behind them—can have devastating implications (Fadiman, 1998).

Rather than thinking of best practices for community work, outreach, and youth engagement, we can more tentatively consider the notion of "wise practices." According to Wesley-Esquimaux and Snowball (2010), wise practices are "a way to foster culturally appropriate support and health care" (p. 121). They developed the concept in response to the imposition of universalized interventions in Indigenous communities despite diverse histories, capacities, and challenges. We see value in the approach for all relational practice in that it uses dialogue to help us respond to diverse needs and strengths in a more contextualized way. Considering the above discussions of access and effectiveness, power dynamics, and legacies of oppression, perhaps wise practices can help us navigate the complex realities in which we are enmeshed.

PIECING IT TOGETHER

We have explored three related concepts in an effort to widen the scope of, and critically engage with, what we understand CYC practice to be. What does this mean for CYCs working with young people and families (see also Shaw, this volume)? What are the foundational skills that will equip us to partner within communities, identifying and mobilizing assets? Is there a place for expert-knowledge, and if so, what is the crucial knowledge CYCs should be proficient in (Hoskins, 2011)?

With these and other lingering questions in mind, we now turn to a practice scenario to illustrate the potential of this approach to CYC practice.

....

Coco was enjoying an afternoon at the young parents' program at the youth resource centre where she worked. This was a voluntary program, and the young parents and their children enjoyed it largely for the sense of belonging it fostered. This particular afternoon, Coco was playing with a few children while their moms enjoyed conversation and a coffee. The conversation casually turned to an upcoming event: August 6th was the anniversary of the day Hiroshima was bombed, and there would be a peace rally at the park that night.

"Are you going?" one parent asked.

"Oh yeah, we'll be there."

"Us too."

"Not me. They deserved to die."

The room stood still. Coco could practically hear hearts sinking. The children continued to play, but it was clear they were keenly aware something had just happened. Coco knew her role was to ensure this space was as safe as possible—emotionally and otherwise—for everyone who attended. What to do in this particular situation? She made the decision that this would require careful follow up, rather than immediate intervention.

That evening, Sachie, a Japanese mother who was present, called Coco in tears. Feeling she would never again be able to comfortably go to the youth resource centre—which up until then had been a refuge for her in that city—she was at a loss. The comment hurt her and also left her dumbfounded as to where it came from. Coco listened.

The next time Guo, the mother who made the comment, attended the centre, she and Coco went outside to chat. Guo, who was Chinese, was feeling a lot of turmoil. On the one hand, she could see the damage her comment had caused, and she regretted that. On the other hand, she was painfully aware that her relatives had experienced more than a single bombing at the hands of the Japanese—they'd been targeted for years. Why does the world not have a day of remembrance—like August 6th—to acknowledge that pain? She felt a deep loyalty to her ancestors and anger at the world's silence.

Coco and the other staff debriefed over the coming days, and the complexity of the intergenerational traumas both young women were processing became evident when a Métis staff member acknowledged how she could relate. It doesn't feel good to bear a grudge against an entire people; but it also doesn't feel good not to honour one's family history, lest the atrocities happen again. Letting go can feel like acquiescing. At this point, Coco recalled another community member, someone Sachie also knew and trusted, who had recounted a similar experience to her. Being Jewish, Mary had to actively overcome her involuntary dislike of Germans. She hated the feeling, but it was something she had to deliberately unlearn because of her own family history. Since Sachie had expressed a desire to understand and come to a place of peace with Guo (whom she regularly encountered), Coco suggested she babysit her daughter so Mary and Sachie could go for a walk and discuss some of these matters—from their two very different perspectives. Coco called Mary and presented the situation, being sure to protect the anonymity of others involved. Mary hoped her perspective could help and was intrigued by the possibility.

The conversation changed things for Sachie. And Guo also came to a place of deeper compassion through the conversations and opportunities to come together. Weeks and months passed, and while it was sometimes awkward, all community members offered their various assets. The healing that took place was immense.

· ·

This kind of practice scenario is not one that could be described in such prescriptive terms as "best practices." It is also not one that clearly fits within a particular program or setting. Rather, it is about remaining curious, sharing leadership, honouring communities of difference, and creating space for our strengths so that by drawing on them our communities can flourish. As Doherty and Carroll (2007) observe:

> Missing from our discourse is a way to think of ourselves as citizens, not just providers, as people engaged in partnerships with other citizens to tackle public problems. Also missing is the idea of our clients as citizens with something to contribute to their communities ... The provider/consumer dichotomy leaves out a third alternative—citizen partnerships where we are neither providers nor consumers—which our world sorely needs in an era of widespread disengagement from civic life. (p. 225)

Coco's role here was less about unilaterally providing "services" to clients than it was about fostering meaningful community outreach and intergenerational engagement on a number of levels, by drawing out the capacities of those who were involved (Aldarondo, 2007), casting the net wider to include more community members, and increasing the circle of support (Denborough, 2008). By doing so, she not only supported individuals with challenges but—and this is central to an asset-based approach—she also supported them to help cultivate a context that supports the well-being of others.

CYCs are *always* working in community. The ideas outlined here are not restricted to street outreach, working in resource centres, or developing drop-in programming, although these are all potentially receptive starting points for CYCs who want to work from an explicitly anti-oppressive, Y-AP, community-focused approach.

The core aspects of what we have explored here are useful in all settings and contexts. Specifically, the value of (1) seeing one's professional self as part of an intergenerational *community*, (2) *reaching out* to those one is in relationship with (which also includes an imperative to reach *in*), and (3) seeing ongoing *engagement* as a route towards wise practice and social justice. This requires commitment to making such connections and consideration of the complexities identified above; it also requires a deep respect for the expertise others bring to any situation (see Shaw, this volume). Being able to identify and bolster the assets of others in a way that contributes to the emergence of something new (Wheatley, 2012) is at the heart of the kind of CYC practice we are advocating, one that goes across all sectors.

NOTES

1. Authors are listed alphabetically, although this chapter was written collaboratively.
2. Those who were no longer minors spoke for themselves on the panel, while the submissions of those who were still minors were read by other panelists.

REFERENCES

Albanese, P. (2010). *Child poverty in Canada*. Don Mills, ON: Oxford University Press.
Aldarondo, E. (Ed.). (2007). *Advancing social justice through clinical practice*. Mahwah, NJ: Lawrence Erlbaum Associates.

Cameron, J., & Gibson, K. (2001). *Alternative pathways for communities and economies: A resource kit.* Melbourne, VIC: University of Newcastle and University of Western Sydney.

Centres of Excellence for Children's Well-Being. (2012). *Vision: Youth engagement.* Retrieved from http://www.engagementcentre.ca/vision.php

Charles, G., & Gabor, P. (2006). An historical perspective on residential services for troubled and troubling youth in Canada revisited. *Relational Child and Youth Care Practice, 19*(4), 17–26.

Checkoway, B. (2011). What is youth participation? *Children and Youth Services Review, 33,* 340–345.

Connolly, J. A., & Joly, L. E. (2012). Outreach with street-involved youth: A quantitative and qualitative review of the literature. *Clinical Psychology Review, 32,* 524–534.

Crimmins, D., Factor, F., Jeffs, T., Pitts, J., Pugh, C., Spence, J., & Turner, P. (2004). *Reaching socially excluded young people: A national study of streetbased youth work.* Leicester, UK: Joseph Rowntree Foundation.

de Finney, S., Dean, M., Loiselle, E., & Saraceno, J. (2011). All children are equal, but some are more equal than others: Minoritization, structural inequities, and social justice praxis in residential care. *International Journal of Child, Youth, and Family Studies, 2*(3/4).

Denborough, D. (2008). *Collective narrative practice: Responding to individuals, groups, and communities who have experienced trauma.* Adelaide, SA: Dulwich Centre Publications.

Doherty, W., & Carroll, J. (2007). Families and therapists as citizens: The families and democracy project. In E. Aldarondo (Ed.), *Advancing social justice through clinical practice.* Mahwah, NJ: Lawrence Erlbaum Associates.

Ella Baker Centre. (n.d.). *Heal the Streets.* Retrieved from http://ellabakercenter.org/our-work/heal-the-streets

Etmanski, C., Hall, B. L., & Dawson, T. (Eds.). (2014). *Learning and teaching community based research: Linking pedagogy to practice.* Toronto: University of Toronto Press.

Evans, M. (2016, January 4). *7 logical fallacies you will encounter as a sex worker* [Blog post]. http://shamelessmag.com/blog/entry/7-logical-fallacies-you-will-encounter-as-a-sex-worker

Fadiman, A. (1998). *The spirit catches you and you fall down: A Hmong child, her American doctors, and the collision of two cultures.* New York: Farrar, Straus and Giroux.

Gharabaghi, K. (2008). Contextual dialectics in relational work with youth. *Relational Child and Youth Care Practice, 21*(2), 5–9.

Gibson-Graham, J. K., & Roelvink, G. (2011). The nitty gritty of creating alternative economies. *Social Alternatives, 30*(1), 29–33.

Hart, R. (2008). Stepping back from "the ladder": Reflections on a model of participatory work with children. In A. Reid, B. B. Jensen, J. Nikel, & V. Simovska (Eds.), *Participation and learning: Perspectives on education and the environment, health and sustainability* (pp. 19–31). Dordrecht, Netherlands: Springer.

Hattie, J. (2009). *Visible learning: A synthesis of over 800 meta-analyses relating to achievement.* New York: Routledge.

Hoskins, M. (2011). Not-knowing or knowing naught: Revisiting the concept of collaboration and expertise in child and youth care practice. *Child & Youth Services, 32*(2), 124–134.

Howe, D., Batchelor, S., & Bochynska, K. (2011). Finding our way: Youth participation in the development and promotion of youth mental health services on the NSW Central Coast. *Advanced in Mental Health, 10*, 20–28.

Klein, M. W. (2011). Comprehensive gang and violence reduction programs: Reinventing the square wheel. *Criminology & Public Policy, 10*(4), 1037–1044.

Knight Foundation. (2010). *Knight soul of the community 2010: Why people love where they live and why it matters: A national perspective.* Miami, FL: John S. and James L. Knight Foundation in partnership with Gallup.

Kral, M. J., Wiebe, P. K., Nisbet, K., Dallas, C., Okalik, L., Enuaraq, N., & Cinotta, J. (2009). Canadian Inuit community engagement in suicide prevention. *International Journal of Circumpolar Health, 68*(3), 292–308.

Kretzmann, J., McKnight, J., Dobrowolski, S., & Puntenney, D. (2005). *Discovering community power: A guide to mobilizing local assets and your organization's capacity.* Evanston, IL: Asset-Based Community Development Institute.

Larson, R. W. (2011). Adolescents' conscious processes of developing regulation: Learning to appraise challenges. *New Directions for Child and Adolescent Development, 133*, 87.

Larson, R. W., & Angus, R. M. (2011). Adolescents' development of skills for agency in youth programs: Learning to think strategically. *Child Development, 82*, 277–294.

Lenihan, D. (2012). *Rescuing policy: The case for public engagement.* Ottawa: Public Policy Forum.

Lord, J., & Hutchison, P. (2007). *Pathways to inclusion: Building a new story with people and communities.* Concord, ON: Captus Press.

Madsen, W., & Gillespie, K. (2014). *Collaborative helping: A strengths framework for home-based services.* Hoboken, NJ: John Wiley and Sons.

McKnight, J. (1995). *The careless society: Community and its counterfeits.* New York: Basic Books.

Morciano, D., Scardigno, A. F., Manuti, A., & Pastore, S. (2014). An evaluation study of youth participation in youth work: A case study in Southern Italy. *Educational Research for Policy and Practice, 13*, 81–100.

Naccarato, T., Brophy, M., & LaClair, K. (2013). Summer engagement for at-risk youth: Preliminary outcomes from the New York state workforce development study. *Child and Adolescent Social Work Journal, 30*(6), 519–533.

Nenga, S. K., & Taft, J. K. (2015). Introduction: Conceptualizing youth engagement. In L. E. Bass (Ed.), *Youth engagement: The civic-political lives of children and youth* (pp. xvii–xxiii). Yorkshire, UK: Emerald Insight.

Newbury, J. (2012). Creating community: Reconsidering relational practice. *Relational Child and Youth Care Practice, 23*(5), 6–20.

Newbury, J. (2014). Inquiring into life as we live it. *Child and Youth Studies, 35*(3), 196–215.

Pfeiffer, D. (1993). Overview of the disability movement: History, legislative record, and political implications. *Policy Studies Journal, 21*(4), 724–734.

Ramey, H. L. (2013). Organizational outcomes of youth involvement in organizational decision-making: A synthesis of qualitative research. *Journal of Community Psychology, 41*, 488–504.

Ramey, H. L., Lawford, H. L., & Vachon, W. (2017). Youth-adult partnerships in work with youth: An overview. *Journal of Youth Development, 12*(4), 38–60.

Reynolds, V. (2014). Resisting and transforming rape culture: An activist stance for therapeutic work with men who have used violence. *The No to Violence Journal,* Spring, 29–49.

Richardson, C., & Reynolds, V. (2012). "Here we are amazingly alive": Holding ourselves together with an ethic of social justice in community work. *International Journal of Child, Youth and Family Studies, 1*, 1–19.

Saldanha, K., & Parenteau, D. (2013). "Well, if you can't smile you should go home!" Experiences and reflective insights on providing outreach to young sex trade workers. *Children and Youth Services Review, 35*, 1276–1283.

Shier, H. (2001). Pathways to participation: Openings, opportunities and obligations. A new model for enhancing children's participation in decision-making, in line with Article 13.1 of the UNCRC. *Children & Society, 15*, 107–117.

Skott-Myhre, H., & Skott-Myhre, K. (2007). Radical youth work: Love and community. *Relational Child and Youth Care Practice, 20*(3), 48–57.

Slesnick, N., Dashora, P., Letcher, A., Erdem, G., & Serovich, J. (2009). A review of services and interventions for runaway and homeless youth: Moving forward. *Children and Youth Services Review, 31*, 732–742.

Taylor, A., & Pacini-Ketchabaw, V. (2015). Learning with children, ants, and worms in the Anthropocene: Towards a common world pedagogy of multispecies vulnerability. *Pedagogy, Culture, and Society, 23*(4), 507–529.

Thoms, J. M. (2007). *Leading an extraordinary life: Wise practices for an HIV prevention campaign with two-spirit men*. Toronto: 2-Spirited People of the 1st Nations.

Truth and Reconciliation Commission of Canada. (2015). *Honouring the truth, reconciling for the future: Summary of the final report of the Truth and Reconciliation Commission of Canada*. Ottawa: Government of Canada.

Wesley-Esquimaux, C. C., & Snowball, A. (2010). Viewing violence, mental illness and addiction through a wise practices lens. *International Journal of Mental Health and Addiction, 8*, 390–407.

Wheatley, M. (2012). *So far from home: Lost and found in our brave new world*. San Francisco, CA: Berrett-Koehler Publishers.

Wong, N. T., Zimmerman, M. A., & Parker, E. A. (2010). A typology of youth participation and empowerment for child and adolescent health promotion. *American Journal of Community Psychology, 46*, 100–114.

Yachmenoff, D. K. (2005). Measuring client engagement from the client's perspective in nonvoluntary child protective services. *Research on Social Work Practice, 15*(2), 84–96.

Zeldin, S., Christens, B. D., & Powers, J. L. (2013). The psychology and practice of bridging generations for youth development and community change. *American Journal of Community Psychology, 51*, 385–397.

CHAPTER 5

Outdoor Adventure and Child and Youth
Care Practice: Intersections and Opportunities

Emily Carty, Nevin Harper, and Doug Magnuson

Outdoor recreation programming as a "service" for young people began in the mid-1800s, and over the next 100 years, summer camps especially became a mainstream activity in Canada. In 1878, the YWCA began its first summer camp for women, and in 1894 Camp Keewaydin became the first Canadian summer camp (acacamp.org). By the 1950s, summer camps were an essential service of most voluntary youth organizations, churches, and synagogues, and were emulations of Indigenous and early explorer activities and living conditions with teepees, cabins, canoes, and the fire-pit as a gathering place (Henderson & Potter, 2001; Potter & Henderson, 2004).

Like other youth movements of the late 19th and early 20th centuries, the growth in camping and outdoor pursuits was in response to urbanization and industrialization, the sense of loss of community, and an ethos associated with village and agricultural life. Cities were crowded and dirty and believed to be morally tainted. Work for many, especially the working class, was often danger-ous and repetitive. The ideals of community, harmony with nature, and mean-ingful work became romantic longings, and summer camping became the place for a respite from city life and for the instillation of moral values believed to be associated with hardy outdoor life (see, for example, Paris, 2008; Wall, 2008; Van Slyck, 2006).

During the first half of the 20th century, progressive educators and outdoor educators discovered each other. John Dewey (1916) was writing about educational pedagogy, and his theory was attractive to outdoor educators because of its emphasis on meaningfulness, experience, group life, democracy, and the development of the whole person (Quay & Seaman, 2013). These ideas received some support from other influential educators such as William Kilpatrick, who endorsed summer camping as a model of progressive education (Kilpatrick, 1931), and Charles Eliot, the president of Harvard who was widely quoted for saying in 1922, "I have the conviction that a few weeks in a well-organized summer camp may be of more value educationally than a whole year of formal school work" (cited in Keller, 2012). These ideas were also taken up by influential Progressive Era reformers, including Jane Addams, who was associated with the origins of youth work and had both practice and academic credibility (Addams, 1909).

This was a unique moment, because the same theories of how young people learn anchored initiatives in both formal and informal education. For example, Hedley Dimock took up Dewey's interest in democracy and citizenship in *Camping and Character* (Dimock & Hendry, 1929). Dimock and Hendry wrote about the democratic organization of a summer camp (Dimock, 1931), and he also chaired a series of Camp Institutes at George Williams College in Chicago between 1930 and 1947, which produced 10 monographs on how to organize group-centered, democratic camp work (see, for example, Dimock, 1931).

The idea that outdoor experience needed theorizing also influenced those offering more intensive outdoor adventure programs. In the UK, Kurt Hahn began an outdoor program, later known as Outward Bound (OB), with physical and interpersonal challenges out of doors that aimed to inculcate the spirit and practice of leadership and service to others (Flavin, 1996). The OB approach to youth development grew quickly with OB schools being established around the world; there are now more than 30 schools serving over 7 million worldwide. In Canada, prior to established OB programs, youth-serving organizations implemented similar outdoor intervention programs for youth involved in the justice system and those with behavioural issues (Church Council of Justice and Corrections, 1996).

Other significant factors influencing the development of outdoor adventure programs for youth in Canada include a history of extended wilderness expeditions, government funding (e.g., youth justice camps), psychoeducational and positive youth development strategies, and practices over clinical approaches (Harper et al., 2006). Of note nationally are Wendigo Lake Expeditions in Ontario (est. 1971), Enviros Wilderness School Association in Alberta (est. 1976), and Coastline Challenge Camp in BC (est. 1980, closed 2016). Concurrent with the growth in camping and scouting movements, wilderness and adventure-based adolescent social service and youth corrections camps and programs flourished until the early 2000s and were primarily funded through contracted services from provincial or federal sources (Harper & Scott, 2006).

Although only a small minority of children and youth now attend sleep-away summer camp, the idea that nature is good for you is widely accepted in the general population. There is also now research evidence that supports the benefits of learning outdoors compared with indoors: Learning is accelerated via reduced stress, increased directed attention, improved energy levels, and reduced negative emotion (see Maller, Townsend, Pryor, Brown, & St. Leger, 2005). It is easy to convince stakeholders and communities that outdoor experience is good for a wide variety of children and youth to enhance their development and for therapeutic purposes, although it is far more difficult to convince parents to send their children away for days and weeks at a time due to cost, concerns for safety, and the logistics of today's hurried lifestyles. In recent decades, programs have become more specialized and of shorter duration, while the expectations for outcomes are much higher. Adventure, solitude, or communing with nature are not usually justification enough for a program. Outdoor programs are expected to treat socio-emotional problems, cure addictions and PTSD, reduce recidivism, and diminish risk in the "youth-at-risk" formula.

In this chapter, we address some of these contemporary challenges and opportunities of the outdoor adventure field with a particular focus on the contribution that outdoor adventure might make to child and youth care, as well as the contribution that child and youth care might have for the outdoor adventure field.

OUTDOOR ADVENTURE

We use the phrase *outdoor adventure programming* to capture a diverse scope of practice, primarily outdoor, risk-based activities that are designed systematically for desired educational or therapeutic goals. Setting outdoor adventure apart from related and often interchangeable practices such as leisure, outdoor recreation, experiential education, and environmental education is the inherent and intentional use of risk and the underlying intentions of the activities and processes used.

Outdoor adventure programming often involves multi-day expeditions incorporating activities like canoeing or backpacking where participants learn travel skills and outdoor living skills. Alternatives to multi-day programs may include high or low ropes courses, team initiatives, or climbing elements where levels of physical, social, and emotional risk are utilized. The aims of these programs may include team building and leadership, individual growth and self-reliance, or working on an aspect of an individual's mental well-being.

Many outdoor adventure programs claim expertise about experiential learning in which people learn by "doing," physically and emotionally, followed by reflecting (Gass, 1993, p. 4). "Experiential education is a process through which a learner constructs knowledge, skills, and value from direct experiences" (Luckmann, 1996, p. 7). In the past 25 years, this generalist understanding of experiential learning has been losing ground to more specialized foci including wilderness therapy, adventure therapy, nature therapy, adventure-based counselling, ecotherapy, and, in Australia, bush adventure therapy (Richards, Carpenter, & Harper, 2011). Wilderness therapy was in part adapted from Kurt Hahn's Outward Bound model of outdoor education and experiential education with the overarching goals of service, leadership, and citizenship (Gass, 1993), as well as in recognition of the inherent health benefits of "contact with nature" through outdoor living and travel (Maller et al., 2005).

Adventure therapy intentionally addresses underlying issues and presenting behaviours by engaging and challenging clients through experiential activities, such as high ropes courses or initiative activities. Adventure therapy has been defined as "any intentional, facilitated use of adventure tools and techniques to guide personal change toward desired therapeutic goals" (Alvarez & Stouffer, 2001, p. 87). A second definition is "the prescriptive use of adventure experiences provided by mental health professionals, often conducted in natural settings that kinesthetically engage clients on cognitive, affective, and behavioral levels" (Gass, Gillis, & Russell, 2012, p. 1). International adventure therapy theorists and practitioners have recently criticized the increased exclusive nature of the second definition—specifically the terms "prescriptive" and "mental health professionals"—as limiting the recognition of the wide array of practice and practitioners utilizing adventure activities and processes in their work (Harper, Peeters, & Carpenter, 2015). The contrast between adventure experience for the development of service, leadership, and citizenship, as described by Hahn and Dimock, with adventure for therapeutic purposes is a contrast between self-transcendence and self-focus.

Risk

Physical and emotional risk are key elements of outdoor adventure programming, particularly "perceived" risk (Davis-Berman & Berman, 2002). Perceived risk is a consequence of previous experience and abilities. For example, a multi-day canoe expedition set in a remote location or a high ropes course in a natural setting can be perceived as extremely risky by participants who do not have experience in these activities or who have a fear of water or heights.

Due to its experiential approach, participants are highly engaged in outdoor adventure programs and will comprehend and learn the most when challenged to explore the territory up to and beyond their comfort zones. Instructors assess and apply an appropriate amount of risk for each individual participant relative to their capacities; the balance of challenge and support is key to developmental gains (Kegan, 1994). A participant's comfort or anxiety and capacity for learning depend on the individual's experience and state of mind. Vygotsky (1978) reminds us of the interaction between instruction and learning and of being under- or over-challenged relative to one's competencies and capacities. If a participant is challenged beyond the zone of optimal learning, fear and anxiety take over; by contrast, too little challenge leads to boredom and distraction (Vygotsky, 1978). The optimal zone, often called the learning or growth zone, is where participants best develop and grow (Rogoff, 1984).

Outdoor adventure programs usually involve the group as a mechanism of change, which creates a sense of community wherein youth work together to achieve common goals. Throughout a participant's experience, a variety of emotions can arise, including anxiety, trust, and empowerment. Participation provides opportunity for youth to experience these feelings while working on individual therapy goals. Participants learn to manage various emotions that arise throughout the wilderness experience. The experiential learning component of reflection is an important element of wilderness and adventure therapy, integrating typical personal development goals with therapeutic goals (Bruyere, 2002).

The emotional risk participants experience may outweigh the physical risk in the activities. The emotional risk can be associated with the physical tasks and also with participants' social roles as members of a group. For the purposes of development and therapeutic growth, emotional risk and vulnerability are usually the most important factors. Like physical risk, it is the perception of emotional risk that matters, but perceived emotional risk is a more delicate, complicated dynamic that takes experience and training for instructors to manage.

Management of these perceived risks is a challenge for leaders under the best of conditions, because individual group members have different levels of perceived risk and vulnerability, and experiences have to be managed for both the group and individuals. Under the best of conditions, the varying strengths and weaknesses of group members create interdependence and mutuality, where conflict is productive and contributes to learning.

Challenges

Risk inherent in outdoor adventure programs has been criticized as being used haphazardly and without adjustment for individual preparation and capacity for accepting and growing within the above "developmental recipe" (Davis-Berman & Berman, 2002). Since most programs operate with a group as the central feature, the experience of the individual deserves further research and attention in program facilitation.

Other challenges include the leader's own perceived risk related to the emotional and physical challenges, the limited information that most leaders have about participants, and environmental factors outside of the leader's control such as the weather. Leaders usually have extensive outdoor adventure experience and are physically fit. Those whose experience is primarily on the activity side of outdoor adventure do not often receive much training, coaching, or counselling to help them understand and cope with the differences between their own abilities and those of their charges, differences that can be frustrating. Further, these leaders do not always have experience in learning about how their own emotional experience may be implicated in their leadership.

Children and youth are often unknown by the outdoor adventure instructors, with pertinent information available to them too often limited to physical safety concerns such as allergies or epilepsy and not usually including mental health factors. Outdoor adventure instructors have limited time with participants prior to courses, and with the increasing specialization and decreasing length of courses, there is often limited time available for contemplation and adequate reflection on the activities.

Instructor Role

Instructors and leaders are crucial to the success of the experience. Participant behavioural, psychological, and social goals along with emotional and physical risks are important elements for leaders to recognize and to which they want to be responsive. Instructors need to learn how to navigate participant anxiety, trust, empowerment, and other feelings that naturally arise throughout outdoor adventure programming. When instructors are able to understand and incorporate participant goals, behaviours, and needs, then overall risk may be lessened.

Outdoor adventure instructors are expected to acquire a wide range of competencies and certifications in the activities they will lead; these may include water-based activities, mountaineering and climbing, backpacking, sailing, and first aid response and rescue, as well as an acceptable level of fitness. Although the means for acquiring technical competence are varied and scattered, as well as expensive to acquire, there are well-organized professional training programs. The foundation exists for instructors to help participants learn the technical and physical skills in a wide range of activities; this learning can lead to new-found confidence in one's own competence and ability to learn. The training in technical skills in the outdoor adventure field by activity-specific professional associations and guide- and instructor-training institutions has focused on the physical and technical realities of leadership at the expense of the human and social-emotional elements of group leadership.

There is less of a foundation and fewer resources for learning the leadership and soft skills; as Gass (1993) has said, successful adventure therapy programs have leaders who also see themselves as counsellors or therapists. Such an outlook "reminds professionals that the therapeutic means (e.g., the wilderness) are secondary to the therapeutic ends (i.e., therapy/evaluation)" (p. 155). Therefore, programs designed as "adventure therapy" should have leaders educated and trained in the therapeutic skills. One place these skills might be acquired is in child and youth care.

TRANSFERABLE CYC SKILLS

Child and youth care practitioners learn and develop many of the skills that outdoor adventure leaders practise such as group programming, facilitating day-to-day living, and building relationships. CYC professionals often work on the front line in a "life-space intervention" capacity (Gharabaghi & Stuart, 2014). Empathetic, trusting, and caring relationships are built through the day-to-day interactions that take place between child and youth care practitioners and the youth. Working within the realm of life-space intervention appears similar to the wilderness therapy field, particularly in situations where youth and staff are living and working together to achieve a common goal, such as setting up camp or cooking dinner. The intensity of relationships between outdoor adventure instructors and youth coincides with what child and youth care students learn and practice. CYC professionals explicitly learn and practise skills such as validating, mirroring, and observing body language, for example, which help build relationships and create space for growth and change.

Safe Spaces and Power Differentials

Child and youth care practitioners learn the importance of creating a safe space to allow for participant growth. The conception of personal change often stems from the processing of events and transference of learning, which occurs when participants are able to be open and vulnerable. In creating a safe space, instructors must have the skills to set the tone of the group. CYC students learn about the "therapeutic milieu," which takes into account cultural, emotional, ideological, social, and physical safety (Burns, 2006). The physical spaces offered up in nature provide a wide array of opportunities for reflection, comfort, and challenge. The group size and diverse roles and responsibilities of an outdoor adventure instructor, however, increase the need for sensitivity to participant social and psychological safety.

Participant and instructor relationships are important when creating a safe space. Youth participants in outdoor adventure programs may perceive their relationship with the instructor as "egalitarian and based on mutual trust" (Ungar, Dumond, & McDonald, 2005, p. 328). During wilderness expeditions, participants witness leaders hiking the same trail and enduring the same weather, which can humanize instructors. CYC practitioners learn that although supporting in the life-space of a child or youth, the perception of an egalitarian relationship is superficial due to the realities of accountability for risk management and curricular and logistical decisions. As well, children and youth have become more disconnected to the natural world, and in turn can be extremely reliant on instructors (McBride & Korell, 2005). The ideal is that participants benefit from respect in the participants' relationships with the staff team and their ongoing support.

CYC practitioners utilize various approaches to deconstruct power differentials, including person-centred approaches, which allow the children and youth to be involved as much as possible in decision-making while on programs. Once instructors become familiar and comfortable with a person-centred approach, the sense of an egalitarian relationship increases as the perceived power difference decreases (Estes, 2004).

Countertransference

CYC practitioners learn the importance of revisiting one's theoretical orientation knowing that, similar to participants, an instructor's knowing and doing will develop and change over time due to personal experience (White, 2007). While on a multi-day expedition, instructors have the responsibility to recognize and address their own individual needs and feelings and to be able to model how to manage their emotions, especially when instructors feel they need to be emotionally available for participants (McBride & Korell, 2005). If an instructor is experiencing any emotional detachment, irritation, or other conflicted feelings, other instructors need the skills to debrief and process with each other since supervisor support is often unattainable due to isolated locations or lack of direct means of communication.

Multi-day expeditions do not allow time for supervision, which is when conversations about safety, quality of care, and overall learning occurs (Halpern & McKimm, 2009). Supervision increases employee morale and overall job satisfaction. Without the ability to connect and obtain supervision, practitioners must be able to draw on various interpersonal skills to manage situations as they arise. Therefore, the hiring of an outdoor adventure practitioner can be a dilemma; the instructor must be able to work alone or with one or two other instructors without support from a supervisor. Instructor role modelling is important throughout the program for participants to witness and be a part of positive social interactions (Russell, 2006); the instructors are integral parts of a social ecology and can share their personal, parallel process with participants as part of their modelling.

Instructors' Interpersonal Skills

Interpersonal skills are frequently discussed in the outdoor adventure literature (Miles & Priest, 1990; Shooter, Sibthorp, & Paisley, 2009; Smith, Roland, Havens, & Hoyt, 1992; Ungar et al., 2005). However, as Attarian (2001) states, interpersonal skills are hard to evaluate and more difficult to train. Kalisch (1979) wrote a book focused more narrowly on the leader's role in Outward Bound-style programs: "A most significant element of both program and process is the *instructor*" (p. 3; italics in original). Kalisch's idea of "role" includes metaphorical and analogical allusions, including "an effective skill trainer, program designer, translator, group facilitator and 1:1 counselor" (pp. 24–25).

Throughout the outdoor adventure literature, various interpersonal skills are mentioned directly such as empathy, listening, and validating. However, there are a number of skills that are implicit, such as the ability to empower participants or co-create an experience through "doing with" (Garfat & Fulcher, 2012; Ungar et al., 2005). These implicit interpersonal skills would include the ability to listen, understand, and show respect to the participant and the group as a whole. All of these skills are important when working with children and youth.

CYC practitioners develop and hone the interpersonal skills that the outdoor adventure literature recognizes as imperative when working with children and youth. CYC practitioners are extensively trained in communication skills, such as when to use tentative language. They also learn how to recognize and point out one's own—and participants'—nonverbal communication and why it is important, including cautions around assuming meanings (Corey, Corey, Callanan, & Russell, 2004). CYC students learn about being genuine, attentive, and skilled observers. These skills are important for creating a safe space for children to learn and grow, particularly in a group context.

The interpersonal skills CYC practitioners acquire allow space for relationship building and risk assessment. CYC practitioners learn how to adapt techniques based on group needs, as well as how to speak to reactions in a group situation, such as resistance, and can provide understanding of participants' current experiences. Corey and colleagues (2004) explore the "thinking, feeling, and behaving dimensions of human experience" (p. 7) as a conceptual framework when working with a group. Leaders are encouraged to "assist" and "help" participants explore past and current thoughts and feelings and how they have behaved based on their thinking and feeling. CYC practitioners are encouraged to respectfully describe what they are witnessing within the group, to encourage reflection among participants, as well as to process what is going on for participants in the moment. Using the group as a resource is encouraged; practitioners do not need to always have the "right" answer or technique. CYC practitioners are encouraged to be genuine and present, allowing for a safe space for children and youth to be genuine and take risks.

Outdoor adventure instructors are therefore encouraged to have an understanding of psychological concepts and social interactions in order to facilitate programs, including knowing the appropriate amount of risk and challenge for each group (Ringer & Gillis, 1995; Ungar et al., 2005). Group challenges can trigger participants for various reasons, including not being successful in the activity or not being listened to by other group members. Behavioural or risk-seeking tendencies could also arise during the activities, and instructors must be able to facilitate and intervene when necessary. Instructors can use moments of escalation or frustration from participants as "teachable moments" by intervening and posing questions about what is happening and how participants are feeling. Instructors can also alter the participants' experiences throughout the activity by decreasing or increasing the challenge based on the response of participants. While the duration of many outdoor adventure programs usually affords instructors ample opportunities for interventions, it should be tempered with the realities of how physically and emotionally tiring this type of work can be. Managing group dynamics/behaviour, delivering curriculum, leading technical activities, and maintaining open communications between staff and participants while also ensuring self-care is a calling of high order.

The instructor is required to develop and facilitate the program, intervene if concerns arise, and facilitate meaning-making that uncovers hidden strengths and can elicit a "transference of learning" to relate participants' experiences to their day-to-day lives (Gass, 1985). This transference of learning may be accelerated during or after participants' experiences in outdoor adventure programming through meaningful questions and dialogue with the instructor and other participants. The transfer of learning is important to consider as participants are encouraged to reflect on their thoughts and feelings about their experiences and lives. Significant learning for the group can occur when instructors facilitate the experience with intention, when instructors ask questions that allow meaning to emerge and participants to make connections to their day-to-day lives. Critics have identified outdoor adventure programs as not representing the life-space of children and youth served, and have suggested that the transfer of learning pales compared with in-program learning experiences. The outdoor adventure field has long relied on its earlier literature and strength of beliefs that outcomes stick long-term, but this has not been well supported empirically.

At the same time, outdoor adventure programming literature has probably over-emphasized the cognitive and verbal skills of debriefing and reflection (Brown, 2002) and under-emphasized bodily experience and non-cognitive learning. Too much emphasis on debriefing and the pressure to produce results may lead facilitators to manipulate or direct the conversation towards leader-defined goals rather than participant goals and interests, in effect undermining the experiential learning process. If truly experiential, then meaning should emerge and not be pre-determined—as many programs are, due to the need for outcomes. Again, the field has been criticized for falling into a factory-style delivery of programs, consistently meeting the desired outcomes at the expense of emergent outcomes, meaning, and experience (Loynes, 1998).

CREATING OUTDOOR ADVENTURE CHILD AND YOUTH CARE

Natural World

Relationships are the foundation of child and youth care, which can include human relationships to the natural world. Often in wilderness programs, participants are implicitly reconnecting with the natural world. Rutko and Gillespie (2013) conclude that there still exists a theoretical uncertainty as to why the adventure activities take place in the wilderness and what the impact of the wilderness has on these activities. Meanwhile, Gass and colleagues (2012) find that "nature is restorative and promotes healthy physical, psychological, and emotional development, especially for youth" (p. 107). Perhaps CYC practitioners can include alongside the "risky" and technical skill-based adventure therapy a more ecologically based approach, where instructors can facilitate purposeful and powerful reconnections with nature for participants.

There is again some movement in adventure-based education and therapy towards land-based, Indigenous, and spiritual aspects of connecting with the more-than-human world (Harper, Carpenter, & Segal, 2012; Jordan, 2015). Nature provides a projection screen for individuals; it is neutral and both easily produces metaphor for experience and acts as a receptacle for projections. One's sense of self and understanding and owning of personal traits and behaviours become more obvious when outdoor living and travelling (e.g., when it is raining and the trail is slippery, one has a choice to project negativity onto the environment, or own the decision to accept the weather as is by putting on appropriate clothing and choosing one's steps more wisely).

Human contact with nature has been found to decrease stress and aggression, increase life satisfaction and productivity, and shorten recovery time from illness (Hartig et al., 2011; Maller et al., 2005). Naturalized or "green" schoolyards show an increase in cooperation, engagement, and student-teacher relationships, and decreases in bullying, hostility, and injuries (Chawla, Keena, Pevec, & Stanley, 2014; Harper, 2008). Further, Tremblay and colleagues' 2015

"Position Statement on Active Outdoor Play," backed with two current systematic reviews, argues for unstructured play in natural environments as a developmental need. Children who play outside, specifically unsupervised, are more active than children who spend time inside, and increased activity is paralleled to increased health benefits, including physical and mental health (Duncan et al., 2014). Play in natural environments increases children's curiosity, creativity, and sensory experiences. Children engaged in natural outdoor play have been found to have increased "resilience, self-regulation and develop skills for dealing with stress later in life" (Tremblay et al., 2015, p. 6486). Less structured and adult-directed outdoor play allows children to interact and connect with peers, increasing interpersonal skills (Chawla et al., 2014).

Child and youth care practitioners work with youth to develop the skills that unstructured outside play in nature also builds. Engaging children and youth with the natural world does not require technical skills nor travelling to the wilderness. Time simply spent in "nearby nature" such as local and accessible green spaces, has been shown to assist in buffering life stress and increase attention in children and youth (Wells & Evans, 2003; Faber Taylor, Kuo, & Sullivan, 2001). CYC practitioners can organize unstructured time outdoors by going on a nature walk in the woods, or allowing space to run and explore. Practitioners often choose program activities such as "sit spots" or a more active game of "camouflage" where children or youth run and hide in the woods and, in that time hiding alone in the silence of the forest, the youth may make a connection to the natural world through sensory contact or discovery of a unique plant or animal. In the natural world, children's innate sense of curiosity emerges (Cornell, 2009). CYC practitioners can use their interpersonal skills to deepen that curiosity, and in turn their connection to the natural world. When a child or youth asks what kind of tree they are looking at, a CYC practitioner can ask further questions, such as what do the leaves and bark look and feel like, encouraging deeper exploration beyond labelling species.

The types of knowledge invoked by "place" can be powerful antidotes to children or youth who feel disconnected. Place names and histories, the feelings one gets from a particular place, and the experiences one has in that place result in an increased "sense of place" and contribute to our personal memories and autobiographical selves, arguably mediating one's sense of self (Harper et al., 2012; Knez, 2014). CYC practitioners can facilitate these experiences of connecting to place through storytelling about a place and creating lived experiences (Baker, 2005). This type of experience is readily available to child and youth workers via parks, gardens, ravines, and other natural spaces, creating an affordable and accessible intervention with nature as milieu and co-facilitator (Berger & McLeod, 2006).

Integration of Outdoor Education

While CYC students learn excellent interpersonal skills, post-secondary child and youth care education in Canada struggles to maintain connections to experiential, space-, and place-based activities like outdoor experiences. It is easy to forget the efficacy and power of somatic experience and the confidence and joy from learning to be competent in a new setting, experiences central to outdoor activities. The outdoor adventure field can also help CYC maintain its focus on the curative powers of human development and play in contrast to medicalized treatment and diagnostic strategies.

Further, while the roots of CYC and youth work are in the use of "everyday life" experiences for learning and therapeutic purposes, CYC post-secondary educators struggle to maintain that emphasis. The more successful CYC becomes in gaining access to professional arenas and to higher education, the less likely it is that outdoor experience and experiential education are included in the curriculum and the less likely it is that practitioners are working in everyday life practices. Counselling, mental health, child welfare, education, and child life, among others, are practice fields increasingly open to CYC and whose institutional practices are stylized and organized self-referentially.

Outdoor adventure in its best form is a temporary community organized to accomplish concrete everyday life tasks and, like residential camping before it, is a fantastic training ground for CYC students to learn the practices of everyday life work. Outdoor adventure requires challenges to overcome and a ladder of increasing technical and interpersonal competence, with immediate and clear consequences linked to success or failure. There are few CYC programs left that require concrete demonstrations of technical and interpersonal competence, and outdoor adventure is one of the arenas that can guide us back to everyday life.

One aspect of everyday life learning—and outdoor adventure—that is important to the learning experience is uncertain outcomes, occasional failure, and learning as a consequence of trouble—emotional, interpersonal, and physical. Counselling practices have strongly influenced CYC educators to over-emphasize safety and non-confrontational communication, and the reduction of risk. Context is everything, of course, and these practices are appropriate when working with clients whose everyday life is chaotic and threatening. Yet there is room in CYC practices for a greater variety of challenges and methods of learning, and outdoor adventure as a model and metaphor ought to be included in the family.

Finally, as CYC became established in higher education, classic experiential education practices have become more difficult to retain, other than internship experiences and practice-based skills courses such as group work or individual counselling. Colleges have had more success, but where there has been increasing pressure on faculty to do research, publish, and "be academic," the curricular and pedagogical practices linked to experiential learning are sometimes perceived by administrators and by colleagues in other programs as only "fun and games." The efficacy of our educational practices will depend on immersing our students in experiential education in a wide variety of arenas, and outdoor adventure can help us with this. Reflective of educational preparation in CYC, no specific references are made in industry documents such as the *Competencies for Professional Child and Youth Work Practitioners* (ACYCP, 2010) to prepare child and youth work practitioners to work outdoors or experientially.

CONCLUSION

We have suggested that the outdoor adventure field has something to learn from CYC, particularly more sophisticated interpersonal skills and group work practices. CYC professional practitioners in turn have something to learn from the outdoor adventure and outdoor experience fields about operationalizing experiential learning and integrating the natural world into the daily life of children, youth, and families. We also suggest that the outdoor adventure world can help CYC educational programs recover the educational and developmental benefits of experiential learning, whether outdoors or not.

The timing is right. As children and youth are spending less time outdoors, the CYC practitioner would be an ideal support to allow for that space for children and youth to connect and explore the natural world. Time in the natural world increases connections with our selves, community, and environment. Time outdoors increases children's curiosity, creativity, social engagement, self-regulation, interpersonal skills, and resilience. Children who spend time outdoors are more active, which is beneficial for their physical and mental health. CYC practitioners have the ability to use natural space for free play or intentional programming, which enriches children's sense and connection to the world, themselves, and each other.

The timing is also right for CYC's contribution to the outdoor adventure literature and outdoor adventure practices. In addition to the importance of technical and physical safety skills (Priest & Gass, 1997), emotional safety is as important. Outdoor adventure literature suggests that outdoor adventure leaders require interpersonal skills—training in emotional risk and counselling skills, along with technical skills. Child and youth care professionals benefit from learning communication skills, relationship building skills, and knowledge about creating a safe space and in turn cutting down risk. CYC practitioners can further attain the specific technical qualifications and certifications to be outdoor adventure youth workers.

There is a debate in the outdoor adventure literature about the necessary qualifications to work with specialized populations. For example, Davis-Berman and Berman (1994) question the ethics of running programs for "high-risk" youth with leaders who may not be fully trained to deal with psychiatric situations and mental health emergencies in a wilderness setting. Still, the ideal of having front-line staff who are highly trained in outdoor adventure technical skills, outdoor adventure leadership, and child and youth care or youth work is not realistic (Davis-Berman & Berman, 1994; Kalisch, 1979). The ideal minimum requirements may need further study and articulation.

This debate is similar to long-standing conversations in the wider human services field where, for example, practitioners may be expected to provide care or some kind of service to a wide variety of people with a wide variety of clinical challenges. One argument is that practitioners are generalists whose ethical orientation, relationship skills, and disposition can be effective in a wide variety of circumstances. In the outdoor field, many youth experience at least temporary success and reduced behavioural issues "on trail" as compared to their everyday life.

This success exists on the assumption that the natural environment has a stress-reducing and attention-restoring ability allowing children and youth increased locus of control and executive functioning (Berman, Jonides, & Kaplan, 2008). With proper assessment, intentional program designs, and well-prepared instructors, outdoor adventure experiences can produce valuable social and psychological benefits for children, youth, and families (Harper et al., 2015). Community-based adventure therapy programs for youth and families have begun to show positive results (Tucker, Javorski, Tracy, & Beale, 2013). With careful attention to the choice of environments and activities, similar results are possible in natural settings in urban centres and across CYC contexts, and they do not require immersion in wilderness or even high-risk adventure activity. Here too the claim is that there are common experiences in encounters with the natural world that benefit participants with diverse backgrounds and character-istics. These claims need further development, field testing, and research.

REFERENCES

ACYCP. (2010). Competencies for professional child and youth work practitioners. Retrieved from https://cyccb.org/competencies/

Addams, J. (1909). *The spirit of youth and the city streets* (Vol. 80). Chicago: University of Illinois Press.

Alvarez, A. G., & Stouffer, G. A. (2001). Musings in adventure therapy. *Journal of Experiential Education, 24*(2), 85–91.

Attarian, A. (2001). Trends in outdoor adventure education. *Journal of Experiential Education, 24*(3), 141–149.

Baker, M. (2005). Landfullness in adventure-based programming: Promoting reconnec-tion to the land. *Journal of Experiential Education, 27*(3), 267–276.

Berger, R., & McLeod, J. (2006). Incorporating nature into therapy: A framework for practice. *Journal of Systemic Therapies, 25*(2), 80–94.

Berman, M. G., Jonides, J., & Kaplan, S. (2008). The cognitive benefits of nature. *Psychological Science, 19*(12), 1207–1212.

Brown, M. (2002). The facilitator as gatekeeper: A critical analysis of social order in facili-tation sessions. *The Journal of Adventure Education & Outdoor Learning, 2*(2), 101–112.

Bruyere, B. L. (2002). Appropriate benefits for outdoor programming targeting juvenile male offenders. *Journal of Experiential Education, 25*(1), 207–213.

Burns, M. (2006). *Healing spaces: The therapeutic milieu in child and youth work.* Kingston, ON: Child Care Press.

Chawla, L., Keena, K., Pevec, I., & Stanley, E. (2014). Green schoolyards as havens from stress and resources for resilience in childhood and adolescence. *Health & Place, 28*, 1–13.

Church Council of Justice and Corrections. (1996). *Satisfying justice: Safe community op-tions that attempt to repair harm from crime and reduce the use or length of imprisonment.* Ottawa: Correctional Services Canada.

Corey, G., Corey, M. S., Callanan, P., & Russell, J. M. (2004). *Group techniques* (3rd ed.). Belmont, CA: Brooks/Cole Cengage Learning.

Cornell, J. (2009). *Sharing nature with children.* Nevada City, CA: Dawn Publications.

Davis-Berman, J. L., & Berman, D. S. (1994). *Wilderness therapy: Foundations, theory &
research.* Dubuque, IA: Kendall Hunt Publishing Company.

Davis-Berman, J. L., & Berman, D. (2002). Risk and anxiety in adventure programming.
Journal of Experiential Education, 25(2), 305–310.

Dewey, J. (1916). *Democracy and education.* New York: Macmillan Press.

Dimock, H. S. (1931). Character education in the summer camp: Report of institute held
at Y.M.C.A. College, Chicago, April 4–7, 19–30.

Dimock, H. S., & Hendry, C. E. (1929). *Camping and character.* Camp Ahmek, ON:
Association Press.

Duncan, M. J., Clarke, N. D., Birch, S. L., Tallis, J., Hankey, J., Bryant, E., & Eyre,
E. L. (2014). The effect of green exercise on blood pressure, heart rate and mood state
in primary school children. *International Journal of Environmental Research and Public
Health, 11*(4), 3678–3688.

Estes, C. A. (2004). Promoting student-centred learning in experiential education. *Journal
of Experiential Education, 27*(2), 141–160.

Faber Taylor, A., Kuo, F. E., & Sullivan, W. C. (2001). Coping with ADD: The surprising
connection to green play settings. *Environment and Behavior, 33*(1), 54–77.

Flavin, M. (1996). *Kurt Hahn's schools & legacy.* Wilmington, DE: Middle Atlantic Press.

Garfat, T., & Fulcher, L. C. (2012). Characteristics of a relational child and youth care approach. In T. Garfat & L. C. Fulcher (Eds.), *Child and youth care in practice* (pp. 5–24).
Cape Town, South Africa: CYC-Net Press.

Gass, M. A. (1985). Programming the transfer of learning in adventure education. *Journal
of Experiential Education, 8*(3), 18–24.

Gass, M. A. (1993). *Adventure therapy: Therapeutic applications of adventure programming.*
Dubuque, IA: Kendall Hunt Publishing Company.

Gass, M. A., Gillis, L., & Russell, K. C. (2012). *Adventure therapy: Theory, research, and
practice.* New York: Routledge.

Gharabaghi, K., & Stuart, C. (2014). Life space intervention: Implications for caregiving.
Relational Child and Youth Care Practices, 27(3), 6.

Halpern, H., & McKimm, J. (2009). Supervision. *British Journal of Hospital Medicine,
70*(4), 226–229.

Harper, N. J. (2008). Therapeutic benefits of contact with nature: A primer for counsel-
ors and suggestions for schoolyard naturalization. *Insights: The Clinical Counsellors'
Magazine and News, 19*(4), 12–13.

Harper, N. J., Carpenter, C., & Segal, D. (2012). Self and place: Journeys in the land.
Ecopsychology, 4(4), 319–325.

Harper, N. J., Peeters, L., & Carpenter, C. (2015). Adventure therapy. In R. Black & K. S. Bricker (Eds.), *Adventure programming and travel in the 21st century* (pp. 221–236). State College, PA: Venture Publishing.

Harper, N., Potter, T. G., Bilodeau, M., Cormode, T., Dufresne, A., Dyck, B., ... & Turgeon, S. (2006). Wilderness expeditions, integrated service delivery models and democratic socialism: Canada and the state of adventure therapy. In D. Mitten & C. Itin (Eds.), *Connecting with the essence* (pp. 119–132). Boulder, CO: Association for Experiential Education.

Harper, N. J., & Scott, D. G. (2006). Therapeutic outfitting: Enhancing adolescent mental health service through innovative collaborations with a wilderness experience program. *Therapeutic Communities, 27*(4), 524–545.

Hartig, T., van den Berg, A. E., Hagerhall, C. M., Tomalak, M., Bauer, N., Hansmann, R., ... & Bell, S. (2011). Health benefits of nature experience: Psychological, social and cultural processes. In *Forests, trees and human health* (pp. 127–168). Amsterdam, the Netherlands: Springer.

Henderson, B., & Potter, T. G. (2001). Outdoor adventure education in Canada: Seeking the country way back in. *Canadian Journal of Environmental Education, 6*(1), 225–242.

Jordan, M. (2015). *Nature and therapy: Understanding counselling and psychotherapy in outdoor spaces.* New York: Routledge.

Kalisch, K. R. (1979). *The role of the instructor in the outward bound educational process.* Kearney, NE: Morris Publishing.

Kegan, R. (1994). *In over our heads.* Cambridge, MA: Harvard University Press.

Keller, J. (2012). In praise of summer camp. *The Atlantic.* Retrieved from www.theatlantic.com/national/archive/2012/06/in-praise-of-summer-camp/257336

Kilpatrick, W. (1931). Foreword. In H. S. Dimock & L. Hendry (Eds.), *Camping and character. A camp experiment in character education* (pp. vii–xi). New York: Association Press.

Knez, I. (2014). Place and the self: An autobiographical memory synthesis. *Philosophical Psychology, 27*(2), 164–192.

Loynes, C. (1998). Adventure in a bun. *Journal of Experiential Education, 21*(1), 35–39.

Luckmann, C. (1996). Defining experiential education. *Journal of Experiential Education, 19*(1), 1–2.

Maller, C., Townsend, M., Pryor, A., Brown, P., & St. Leger, L. (2005). Healthy nature healthy people: "Contact with nature" as an upstream health promotion for populations. *Health Promotion International, 21*(1), 45–54.

McBride, D. L., & Korell, G. (2005). Wilderness therapy for abused women. *Canadian Journal of Counselling, 39*(1), 3–14.

Miles, J. C., & Priest, S. (1990). *Adventure education*. State College, PA: Venture Publishing.

Paris, L. (2008). *Children's nature: The rise of the American summer camp*. New York: New York University Press.

Potter, T. G., & Henderson, B. (2004). Canadian outdoor adventure education: Hear the challenge—Learn the lessons. *Journal of Adventure Education & Outdoor Learning, 4*(1), 69–87.

Priest, S., & Gass, M. (1997). *Effective leadership in adventure programming*. Champaign, IL: Human Kinetics.

Quay, J., & Seaman, J. (2013). *John Dewey and education outdoors: Making sense of the "educational situation" through more than a century of progressive reform*s. Rotterdam, the Netherlands: Sense Publishers.

Richards, K., Carpenter, C., & Harper, N. (2011). Looking at the landscape of adventure therapy: Making links to theory and practice. *Journal of Adventure Education & Outdoor Learning, 11*(2), 83–90.

Ringer, M., & Gillis, Jr., H. L. (1995). Managing psychological depth in adventure programming. *Journal of Experiential Education, 18*(1), 41–51.

Rogoff, B. (1984). *Children's learning in the "zone of proximal development"* (No. 23). San Francisco, CA: Jossey-Bass.

Russell, K. C. (2006). Evaluating the effects of the Wendigo Lake expedition program on young offenders. *Youth Violence and Juvenile Justice, 4*(2), 185–203.

Rutko, E. A., & Gillespie, J. (2013). Where's the wilderness in wilderness therapy? *Journal of Experiential Education, 36*(3), 218–232.

Shooter, W., Sibthorp, J., & Paisley, K. (2009). Outdoor leadership skills: A program perspective. *Journal of Experiential Education, 32*(1), 1–13.

Smith, T. E., Roland, C. C., Havens, M. D., & Hoyt, J. A. (1992). *The theory and practice of challenge education*. Dubuque, IA: Kendall Hunt Publishing Company.

Tremblay, M. S., Gray, C., Babcock, S., Barnes, J., Costas-Bradstreet, C. C., Carr, D., ... & Brussoni, M. (2015). Position statement on active outdoor play. *International Journal of Environmental Research Public Health, 12*(6), 6475–6505.

Tucker, A. R., Javorski, S., Tracy, J., & Beale, B. (2013). The use of adventure therapy in community-based mental health: Decreases in problem severity among youth clients. *Child and Youth Care Forum, 42*(2), 155–179.

Ungar, M., Dumond, C., & McDonald, W. (2005). Risk, resilience and outdoor programmes for at-risk children. *Journal of Social Work, 5*(3), 319–338.

Van Slyck, A. A. (2006). *A manufactured wilderness: Summer camps and the shaping of American youth, 1890–1960*. Minneapolis: University of Minnesota Press.

Vygotsky, L. S. (1978). Interaction between learning and development. (M. Lopez-Morillas, Trans.). In M. Cole, V. John-Steiner, S. Scribner, & E. Souberman (Eds.), *Mind in society: The development of higher psychological processes* (pp. 79–91). Cambridge, MA: Harvard University Press.

Wall, S. Y. (2008). Making modern childhood, the natural way: Psychology, mental hygiene, and progressive education at Ontario summer camps, 1920–1955. *Historical Studies in Education, 20*, 73–111.

Wells, N. M., & Evans, G. W. (2003). Nearby nature: A buffer of life stress among rural children. *Environment and Behavior, 35*(3), 311–330.

White, J. H. (2007). Knowing, doing and being in context: A praxis-oriented approach to child and youth care. *Child and Youth Care Forum, 36*(5–6), 225–244.

CHAPTER 6

The Digital Life-Space as a Practice Setting

Jennifer Martin and Carol Stuart

The ascendancy of cyberspace as an extension of life-space has significant implications for child and youth care practice and education. Within the timespan of our professional careers, practice has evolved from handwritten reports (typed by the secretary if you were part of a big agency) to web-based "case files" accessed by multiple agencies; from "land-lines" and pagers to cell phones, telehealth, online gaming, apps, and Google. The transformation of the digital life-space has been exponential such that since we wrote together about the phenomena (Martin & Stuart, 2011), the changes have magnified tenfold.

The current wave of technological innovation is fast becoming part of the context in which child and youth care (CYC) practitioners train and practice. This evolution comes from the realization that the pace of technological change is accelerating and creating an increasingly complex and interconnected world. The rapid increase in the use of cyber technologies presents unique complexities that must be considered in CYC practice. In this chapter, we will discuss the influence of new digital technologies on traditional interventions with young people. We will focus on how technology is being integrated into traditional practice settings, while at the same time creating a new location for practice. We will explore challenges the Cybersystem is introducing to practice as well as some innovative approaches to practice in preparation for work with cyberspace in life-space work with children, youth, and their families. Ultimately, some practitioners will incorporate the Cybersystem into their current practice settings, while others are exploring how they can work more meaningfully within that space as a primary location or setting for practice.

THE EVOLUTION OF DIGITAL LIFE-SPACE WORK

Therapeutic life-space intervention is a central concept in working with children and youth in today's global context (see Gharabaghi & Charles, this volume). The core of child and youth care practice is to be with young people where their lives unfold (see Anderson-Nathe, this volume). The therapeutic relationship is integral to child and youth care practice (Gharabaghi & Stuart, 2013). There have been expressed reservations about whether mobile phones or other communication technologies can provide the necessary relational connection; can cyberspace be a place of connectedness? What are the required practitioner competencies for effectively establishing relationships for therapeutic intervention as mediated by technology? An increasing number of researchers have pointed out the potential advantages of using contemporary communication technologies to provide therapeutic interventions (see, for example, Martin & Stuart, 2011). Some evaluations have provided evidence for the success of technology-based programs that have operated in circumscribed ways to assist therapeutic engagement, address psychoeducation goals, or facilitate other interventions (Agyapong, Farren, & McLoughlin, 2011; Preziosa, Grassi, Gaggioli, & Riva, 2009). But research has also shown that there may be advantages to using these technologies to facilitate more complex therapeutic goals, including those that build on the therapeutic relationship (Martin & Stuart, 2011; Richards & Vigano, 2013).

We live in a digital society that has significantly changed the information landscape affecting every aspect of our lives. As we were writing this chapter, Facebook's Mark Zuckerberg announced the Connectivity Declaration campaign that intends to make the Internet available to everyone on the planet by the year 2020 (BBC News, 2015). Young people are growing up in a world in which access to communication technologies not available in previous generations is transforming and shaping their social interactions, networks, and relationships. As youth culture embraces rapid advances in technology, there are opportunities and challenges for CYC practitioners and others working with young people as they try to keep pace with their clients' priorities and expectations (see James, this volume). The ways in which interactive support services can be provided by mobile devices and applications, especially social media and text messaging, and how young people may experience these services, has evolved into a necessary component of practice. It seems reasonable to assume that young practitioners who are growing up with digital media will more naturally turn to digital technology as a component of their practice. It is also incumbent upon more mature practitioners to engage with technology as well as to understand and mediate its effects on the young people they work with in their practice.

The history and evolution of how practitioners incorporate digital technologies into their work is so short and varied that this section can only highlight briefly some of the practices and experiences that we are familiar with, before considering the significant challenges to practice that are raised. We can begin with what the cyber setting is *not*. Cyber counselling or E-counselling (services delivered via the Internet) has developed into a field of practice with certification that comes with a set of protocols, policies, and procedures (e.g., encryption); however, this is not what we are focusing on in this chapter. We are concerned with how CYC practitioners respond to and navigate the changing digital landscape in current practice—how do we work with cyberspace in life-space work with children, youth, and their families? In this context, there are no specific guidelines or procedures for CYC workers to follow, and our responses may be complicated by our own relationships with social media and by the existing policies and procedures of the organization that we work within. Existing organizational policies and procedures regarding offline ethical behaviour, client engagement, and privacy could be amended to include online activities, but this is not commonly done. As a result, a grey area exists in CYC practice approaches about whether and how practitioners engage with young people in cyberspace. Working with cyberspace is not addressed in CYC Codes of Ethics. Currently, there are no set guidelines around professional or ethical behaviour, although some agencies may specifically restrict the use of digital technologies to communicate with clients.

In previous work (Martin & Stuart, 2011; Martin, 2010) we described the concept of the Cybersystem as a digitally mediated virtual system that extends the environment beyond the restrictions of time, place, and three-dimensional space. Organizational restrictions on practitioners' use of digitally mediated communication are driven by risk management and the fear generated from incidents of cyber-bullying, sexting, online abuse, digital pornography, and more. Similarly, the popular social opinion that young people are too immersed in technology and are losing the ability to relate to each other is reflected in policies and procedures that limit the use of technology by young people who are service recipients. Current policies and procedures in various agencies and programs are meant to control the infusion of the Cybersystem and its effects on the lives of young people. But these policies and practices fail to acknowledge that the Cybersystem and its digital influence are here to stay and therefore require a more considered approach to helping young people manage, and benefit from, this aspect of their lives.

It is also worth keeping in mind that digital technologies are as pervasive as they are "invisible." Whether formally acknowledged or not, new information and communication technologies are transforming and challenging the way service users and care providers connect and the way service providers engage with clients (Midkiff & Wyatt, 2008; Rafferty & Steyaert, 2009). This is currently making it challenging for employers to monitor or update policies and practices or provide reasonable guidelines. The challenges of policies that simply seek to restrict CYC workers' use of digital technologies is illustrated by the following story.

After discussing the possibilities of digital technologies in CYC practice in a series of undergraduate classroom presentations, a student related to one of the authors how he routinely used text messages to communicate with young people in the group home where he worked. He reported using text messages to reprimand youth who were late for appointments or events, and to demand compliance with program rules in reaction to non-compliant behaviour. He said that before thinking about and reading about working with cyberspace in the lifespace and learning about cyber counselling as a therapeutic intervention, he had not considered using text messages at the program to engage relationships. He wondered out loud about sending a text to let the youth know he was thinking about them and asking if they wanted to play a game of pool at the group home at 10 o'clock (curfew) and ending with "see you then." He said that this represented a shift in his attitude—about how he thought about CYC work and what it meant to "care" for the youth. He also said that overall he was using technology against the organizational rules; the staff at the group home had been directed by management not to use email or text messages with youth. The participant said most of the staff used technology to communicate with the youth regardless of the rules, and that in his experience they often used it in a punitive way.

This story is counter to our own thinking about the potential for using the digital environment for relationship building and as a means of engaging young people's interests, but illustrates the unevenness of both practice and theory in this area. Our previous work and the foregoing story suggest the potential for practitioners and young people to engage with digitally mediated relationships, which can allow young people to choose when and where they will participate in relationships. Such mediated relationships also require careful thought about messages and images that can evoke emotional or historical connection. Anecdotally, some more progressive CYC practitioners are ignoring organizational protocols and thereby influencing the field towards more radical approaches.

Research on both the negative and positive effects of digital and social media reinforce the importance of practitioner capacity to intervene within cyberspace. For example, Kross and colleagues (2013) found that Facebook can reinforce feelings of loneliness even when it is experienced as a source for support and connection and even though a young person may have hundreds of Facebook "friends." Another study of adolescents (aged 12 to 20 years) demonstrated that online interactions provided social support while at the same time normalizing and encouraging self-injurious behaviours (Whitlock, Powers, & Eckenrode, 2006). On the positive side, a recent longitudinal study indicated that texting and online chatting provided young people with opportunities to practise social skills online and learn how to relate to a variety of people. This research suggested that social skills learned online are transferable to offline environments and can improve the capacity of young people to initiate offline friendships and interact with offline peers in emotionally meaningful ways (Koutamanis, Vossen, Peter, & Valkenburg, 2013). These studies demonstrate the potential for digital intervention by CYC practitioners through effective use of technology. However, common concerns about adopting technology as part of practice often centre on the privacy and safety of young clients and the blurring of professional boundaries because technology enables the potential for 24/7 access (Blanchard, Herrman, Frere, & Burns, 2012; Howard, Friend, Parker, & Streker, 2010). Another expressed concern is that cyber communication could allow clients to access practitioners regardless of whether the practitioner provides the client with their contact information (Mishna, Bogo, Root, Sawyer, & Khoury-Kassabri, 2012).

Research that has specifically examined the use of digital technology in human services has revealed several potential benefits of this practice. Email and text messaging can increase both the amount of time and frequency of contact between a youth and their worker (Mehta & Chalhoub, 2006). Young people may devote considerable time putting their thoughts into words in emails to their workers, and when they receive frequent brief feedback, they feel that their worker is present, listening, and thinking about them (Boydell et al., 2014). Texting can provide relatively immediate communication and relief through "real time" connections, creating a presence for the practitioners that extends beyond the physical. Text messaging, particularly as a crisis response, means the practitioner can respond immediately and explicitly validate the issue at hand. Online interactive games can present young people with engaging scenarios and serve as a catalyst for raising issues and discussing difficulties they may be experiencing (Burns, Webb, Durkin, & Hickie, 2010). The practical use of digital media, such as iPads for learning accommodations in schools, and the infusion of gaming and play that uses digital forums have become a point of connection for practitioners. While a game of basketball or checkers provides the opportunity to get to know each other with a non-threatening focus, so too does a video game for two or a discussion about the latest online version of a favourite game.

The exponential infusion and expansion of digital technology has left us without the theory, guidelines, and evidence required to consistently and thoughtfully manage the risk and potential of the Cybersystem for CYC practice. The challenges of working within the Cybersystem have different foci depending upon the age and stage of career that a practitioner has achieved. The challenges, as we can conceive of them today, are outlined in the next section.

THE CHALLENGES OF THE CYBERSYSTEM

Developing and maintaining effective use of technology is not simply about finding what works and sticking to it; rather, it is about anticipating and adapting to change. It is about transforming the research into day-to-day CYC practice as well as into programs that support today's young people. Digital technology has produced a wide range of challenges related to the application of CYC ethics and practice standards: informed consent; privacy and confidentiality; boundaries and dual relationships; and practitioner competence. There are also challenges regarding the misinterpretation of messages, the failure of the worker to recognize the urgency of a text-based message, and response timing. A not uncommon misstep in face-to-face practice is to "tiptoe" around, or even avoid, issues that may be uncomfortable for the practitioner or perceived by the practitioners as beyond their experience or training (Martin, 2014), so it seems reasonable to assume that this may occur in online practice. Developing and maintaining effective use of technology is not simply about finding what works and sticking to it; rather, it is about anticipating and adapting to change. It is about transforming the research into day-to-day CYC practice as well as into programs that support today's young people.

Blurring public and private boundaries in cyberspace may lead to unexpected or unintended consequences in the workplace. For example, the use of personal social media (Twitter or Facebook) by CYC workers whose accounts are publicly accessible can affect their ability to secure employment as prospective employers are increasingly examining applicants' web presence. There is also the potential for public trust and/or public opinion of the profession of child and youth care to be eroded. Finally, dual relationships may develop between practitioner and client since conversations are unmediated by non-verbal communications, and social media contacts range from professionals to family and friends. Recent studies on helping professionals in training indicated that 52 percent reported seeing unprofessional photographs of their colleagues on Facebook, including pictures of excessive drinking or various states of undress (Garner & O'Sullivan, 2010); 17 percent posted personal phone numbers; 22 percent revealed membership in potentially offensive group behaviour such as "perverts united" and included offensive language and rude humour (MacDonald, Sohn, & Ellis, 2010); 15–40 percent chose not to implement strict privacy settings, and 37 percent included personal information that they did not want their clients to see (Lehavot, Barnett, & Powers, 2010); and 32 percent reported reading client social networking sites, with 16 percent doing so without the consent of the client (Tunick, Mednick, & Conroy, 2011). CYC educators and organizational policies should provide guidelines and socialize practitioners to professional norms so they have the relevant knowledge for digital life-space work, including use of privacy settings and how the online presentation of self can have implications for their professional roles. The simple response of prohibiting communications and relationships through digital and social media is insufficient; yet the evolution of cyberspace is so rapid that staying current is almost a daily essential task.

It is crucial that practice standards and organizational policies address the negotiation and management of dual relationships in cyberspace. When Facebook provides no other options to the "accept a friend request," practitioners should pause to consider the implications of that message. It is a challenge to negotiate the meaning of a relationship and identify appropriate boundaries for both young person and practitioner within 280 characters in a tweet. Fortunately, digital media often provide an adjunct to the relationship that a practitioner has with a young person and family; some discussion about use of the various options, timing of messages, availability, and limits for the practitioner and for the young person are essential and must be handled with care and concern.

When we first wrote about working with cyberspace in the life-space of young people, there was much consideration given to CYC reactivity to unanticipated communication from their clients via digital technologies and to the lack of awareness that young practitioners had about their own online presence (Martin & Stuart, 2011). It is a sign of the times that CYC practitioners are now more concerned with becoming deliberate in how they connect with and respond to young people in cyberspace. However, CYC practitioners are not trained in the use of digital technologies for practice even though they are integral in the workforce today and will become even more important over time. Emergent research on the use of digital technology for counselling and crisis intervention needs to be reviewed, adapted, and evaluated in the CYC practice context. In the same way that the field has emerged from a multi-disciplinary background adapting techniques for the life-space intervention, we need to learn and adapt our techniques for intervention in cyberspace so that young practitioners are more conscious and purposeful in their use of technology.

Competence in working within cyberspace also requires addressing comfort with and knowledge of how young people's growth and development interacts with technology, as well as the abuse that can occur within that space. A vital aspect of digital practice in CYC is to provide young people with non-judgmental guidance and information regarding the legal and emotional consequences of online behaviour. CYC workers can inform and educate youth about, for example, cyberbullying laws for both the victim and the perpetrators, and child pornography and the legal ramifications of "sexy selfies" (e.g., no one under the age of 18 years can consent to recording of sexual images). Another important aspect of digital practice is knowledge about how, on the one hand, society fears that young people will be victimized online (Henson, Reyns, & Fisher, 2013); there are substantive online and offline programs to educate young people about how to stay safe in the cyber world. On the other hand, there is the belief that the Internet is responsible for increasing deviant or anti-social behaviour among young people (Guan & Subrahmanyam, 2009). For instance, current social and technological trends have made taking and sending imagery of oneself more mainstream than ever before. However, when teens share sexualized selfies, there is a tendency to consider such behaviour as the corruption of their morals and values. There is a societal tendency to blame and shame young people who are exploring their sexuality online, and they are threatened with criminal charges, yet exploration of the sexual self is a critical developmental task. At times, the "victim" is blamed when others copy and distribute the images without their permission (e.g., "if you hadn't snapped and shared the image, this wouldn't have happened"). This judgment comes from a culture that routinely sexualizes children in mainstream media. We have to recognize the need for young people to explore the world widely and build skills to engage in the cyber world. Restricting the mobility of young people, online and offline, curbs their ability to develop social skills writ large. This has nothing to do with technology but with the fears we have about "stranger danger" online—young people engaging or otherwise interacting with people outside of adult purview. Values will evolve alongside the evolution in ways of thinking and knowing. We will think differently, and a large part of that will be as a result of being capable of exploiting a cyberspace as a new communicative setting.

Whereas practitioners might previously have struggled with the following issue in a face-to-face dialogue with a young person, new practitioners identified this struggle with the labels and emotional inferences surrounding the concept of love in the context of a digital environment: What if a youth sent the CYC a text message saying they loved you—how would you respond? New practitioners might not know what to do with such a message. They might be very uncomfortable, and they might ignore it—not respond at all. Some might try to "unpack" the meaning of the word love with the young person. Others might rely on agency directives or redirect the young person by saying that they loved their parents or their brothers or sisters but that what they were feeling was not love for the CYC. What are the challenges of making these responses by text or email? The permanence that goes beyond that conversation is a vital consideration. Additional challenges include the possibility of a message being forwarded without the author's knowledge or consent; misinterpreting the context or the content of the message; or auto-complete making an error. There is little to guide practitioners with decision-making regarding mutual discussions about boundaries, or with what new competencies are required to engage in discussions through digital media.

Digital technologies go beyond those that mediate our communications to support activities of daily living as well as act as tools for identification. Both raise challenges to the work that we do. For instance, what privacy issues are involved in using GPS software to track the movements of youth in group homes or young criminal offenders? Facial recognition software currently used by law enforcement could just as easily be used to find young runaways as they travel the public transit system. Increasingly these technologies are built into devices, phones, and tablets that are readily available to CYC practitioners as well as the young people they work with, thereby mediating the privacy of their interactions and raising new questions about informed consent and confidentiality. Should text-based messages or Facebook posts sent to and received from youth be saved and/or printed and filed by the worker? Is consent implied when you respond to an email message? When working with young people and families, organizational policy often requires that they sign a consent form for release of information. How do these policies address the collection of information from digital communication? These are issues that must be addressed, and an important consideration is that the communication is already public, once posted on the Internet, and is often non-retractable. As illustrated in the following example, the public nature of Internet communication raises ethical dilemmas that practitioners must confront.

A CYC practitioner was working with a 16-year-old who had run away from the group home. The young person would not respond to the practitioner, and so the CYC took on the online identity of a friend of the 16-year-old and, using that identity, was able to connect with the young person online and arrange a meeting. At that meeting the young person was taken into custody. In this situation, the practitioner gave primacy to the safety of the young person over her own honesty and used the capacity of the Internet for disguise to connect with the young person. How is this different from the activities of adults who lure young people by creating an online presence of someone of the same age? One could argue that safety is the first consideration; the question of whether the young person, at 16, was actually unsafe is unclear. How can the practitioner assess this? When interacting with young people, practitioners represent not just themselves, but also the profession, and so the integrity of all practitioners could be called into question. Practitioners must have a forum for exploring these types of ethical dilemmas and the nuances of the digitally mediated approaches to practice that are possible as they work with young people, and organizations should expect such exploration on a regular basis.

THE FUTURE OF DIGITAL SETTINGS

Given the prevalence of online relationships, CYC practitioners should be aware of the potential therapeutic benefits (e.g., social support; see Martin & Stuart, 2011) and dangers (e.g., cyber-bullying; see Hinduja & Patchin, 2008a, 2008b) of cyberspace and must be engaged in discussion and practice regarding how relationships can be mediated by digital technologies. Currently, CYC training emphasizes in-person relationships, with little attention given to understanding the role of online relationships and digitally mediated relationships. Effective practice within the context of the Cybersystem requires that we discuss how current practice standards and principles translate to both the infusion of the Cybersystem into all practice settings as well as the creation of a new microsystem or setting for day-to-day practice. CYC practitioners who understand and are well-informed about both the risks and benefits of digital technologies are better equipped to help young people make informed decisions, identify choices, and understand potential consequences as they navigate and interact with the cyber world.

Working with cyberspace in the life-space of young people and their families means letting go of the fear of exclusion when innovating—that is, not worrying about institutional risk from a new or different way of relating to young people and instead actively seeking out ways of engaging with children and youth in cyberspace. Having the ability to explore the needs of young people in innovative ways online is essential (e.g., gaming and apps)—particularly for those young people who may already feel disenfranchised or marginalized. Professional associations and educational programs should identify and include these competencies as part of the practice standards and professional development of CYC practitioners. Competency goes beyond knowing how to use the technology, to a considered application based on particular client circumstances. The challenges noted above could be resolved if we permitted discussion about effective application within the principles of CYC practice.

Technology will enable young people to ignore political limitations, including geographic borders, and especially ignore time and distance as inhibitors to communications. The evolution of digital technology is also opening CYC practice internationally, creating the possibility of purely digitally based practice settings. The focus on activity-based relationships as a forum for transformation and the use of the events of daily living that have characterized many aspects of CYC practice could shift to helping young people negotiate cultural differences online and identify common issues for social change. Approaches that promote sharing of life-space characteristics while respecting personal information and private spaces through text and visual digital media become essential. While boundaries and limitations related to geographic borders, time, climate, and other characteristics of physical space may gradually disappear, we still need to be respectful and caring through an online presence that addresses interpersonal boundaries.

Information and representations of life-space that are posted on the Internet by young people on social media sites tend to often capture the highlights of life. True understanding comes from exploring the fullness of life, which includes the lowlights and the everyday. This balanced and full understanding is hard to achieve in the text, visual, or sound "bites" presented through digitally mediated opportunities. This will require a different way of working and new approaches that will emerge through the development of promising and best practices in negotiating cyberspace, which are grounded in CYC approaches such as life-space intervention, events of daily living, and relational practice.

Another challenge of technology is that it acts as an equalizer for those who have access and further marginalizes those who are left out. While, on the one hand, social media has been credited with facilitating social activism and empowering the disenfranchised, how do we address the "digital divide" where those without access to the Internet are increasingly marginalized? The embedded nature of CYC practice in multiple physical spaces such as schools, recreation and community centres, and residential settings enables practitioners to address these issues of marginalization in those settings. The *possibilities* exist in evolving portability of devices that would enable practitioners to take those devices to locations where young people do not have access (e.g., streetwork, family homes) and use the Cybersystem as a focus of the work. By creating accounts, introducing skills, and helping young people find locations both in cyberspace and the physical world, CYC practitioners can develop and continue relationships and social justice activities in spite of limited financial resources for personally owning the necessary technology.

There is no doubt that a shift has occurred in child and youth care practice, in part enabled by digital technologies, to which we must continue to respond. This includes the democratization of relationships by supporting young people's connection to diverse online social groups; providing opportunities for young people to explore identities and seek meaning in the cyber world; and increasing our openness about how we relate to and connect with others through more adroit and non-hierarchical relational practices in cyberspace.

The potential of the Cybersystem as a location for practice can only be tapped if practitioners accept the importance of influencing policy and practice standards. Rather than ignoring current policy (as in the examples above), young practitioners, conversant and comfortable with digital technology, are in an ideal position to influence policy. We must work to enable new practitioners to challenge existing policies and develop new ones that guide digital interaction. The ethical codes of honesty, respect, truthfulness as well as safety and protection of young people should guide interactions and the policy and practice that arise. With careful consideration and discussion of these challenges, the possibilities of the Cybersystem as a practice setting can be safely and thoughtfully carried forward, rather than our current approach, which has us scrambling to catch up to the young people who are already fully engaged.

REFERENCES

Agyapong, V. I. O., Farren, C. K., & McLoughlin, D. M. (2011). Mobile phone text message interventions in psychiatry—What are the possibilities? *Current Psychiatry Reviews, 7*, 50–56.

BBC News. (2015). Facebook's Mark Zuckerberg pledges refugee camp internet access. Retrieved from http://www.bbc.com/news/technology-34373389

Blanchard, M., Herrman, H., Frere, M., & Burns, J. (2012). Attitudes informing the use of technologies by the youth health workforce to improve young people's wellbeing: Understanding the nature of the "digital disconnect." *Youth Studies Australia, 31*(1), 14–24.

Boydell, K., Hodgins, M., Pignatiello, A., Teshima, J., Edwards, H., & Willis, D. (2014). Using technology to deliver mental health services to children and youth: A scoping review. *Journal of the Canadian Academy of Child and Adolescent Psychiatry, 23*(2), 87–99.

Burns, J., Webb, M., Durkin, L., & Hickie, I. (2010). Reach Out Central: A serious game designed to engage young men to improve mental health and wellbeing. *Medical Journal of Australia, 192*(11), 27–30.

Garner, J., & O'Sullivan, H. (2010). Facebook and the professional behaviours of under-graduate medical students. *The Clinical Teacher, 7*, 112–115.

Gharabaghi, K., & Stuart, C. (2013). *Right here, right now: Exploring life-space interventions for children and youth.* Toronto: Pearson.

Guan, S., & Subrahmanyam, K. (2009). Youth internet use: Risks and opportunities. *Current Opinion in Psychiatry, 22*(4), 351–356.

Henson, B., Reyns, B. W., & Fisher, B. S. (2013). Fear of crime online? Examining the effects of risk, previous victimization, and exposure on fear of online interpersonal victimization. *Journal of Contemporary Criminal Justice, 29*(4), 475–497.

Hinduja, S., & Patchin, J. (2008a). *Bullying beyond the schoolyard: Preventing and responding to cyberbullying.* Thousand Oaks, CA: Corwin Press.

Hinduja, S., & Patchin, J. W. (2008b). Cyberbullying: An exploratory analysis of factors related to offending and victimization. *Deviant Behavior, 29*(2), 129–156.

Howard, J., Friend, D., Parker, T., & Streker, G. (2010). Use of SMS to support parents who experience violence from their adolescence. *Australian Journal of Primary Health, 16*(2), 187–191.

Koutamanis, M., Vossen, H. G. M., Peter, J., & Valkenburg, P. M. (2013). Practice makes perfect: The longitudinal effect of adolescents' instant messaging on their ability to initiate offline friendships. *Computers in Human Behavior, 29*, 2265–2272.

Kross, E., Verduyn, P., Demiralp, E., Park, J., Lee, D. S., Lin, N., ... & Ybarra, O. (2013). Facebook use predicts declines in subjective wellbeing in youth. *PLoS One, 8*, e69841. doi:10.1371/journal.pone.0069841

Lehavot, K., Barnett, J. E., & Powers, D. (2010). Psychotherapy, professional relationships, and ethical considerations in the MySpace generation. *Professional Psychology: Research and Practice, 41*, 160–166. doi: 10.1037/a0018709

MacDonald, J., Sohn, S., & Ellis, P. (2010). Privacy, professionalism and Facebook: A dilemma for young doctors. *Medical Education, 44*, 805–813. doi: 10.111/j.13652923.2010.03720x

Martin, J. (2010). *To be seen ... not heard: Conceptualizing the harms done to children made the subjects of sexual abuse images on the Internet.* Unpublished manuscript.

Martin, J. (2014). "It's just an image, right?": Practitioners' understanding of child sexual abuse images online and effects on victims. *Child & Youth Services, 35*(2), 96–115.

Martin, J., & Stuart, C. (2011). Working with cyberspace in the life-space. *Relational Child and Youth Care, 24*(1/2), 55–66.

Mehta, S., & Chalhoub, N. (2006). An e-mail for your thoughts. *Child and Adolescent Mental Health, 11*(3), 168–170.

Midkiff, D., & Wyatt, W. (2008). Ethical issues in the provision of online mental health services (etherapy). *Journal of Technology in Human Services, 26*(4), 310–332. doi: 10.1080/15228830802096994

Mishna, F., Bogo, M., Root, J., Sawyer, J., & Khoury-Kassabri, M. (2012). "It just crept in": The digital age and implications for social work practice. *Clinical Social Work Journal, 40*, 277–286.

Preziosa, A., Grassi, A., Gaggioli, A., & Riva, G. (2009). Developments in the use of technology in counseling and psychotherapy. *British Journal of Guidance and Counseling, 37*(3), 315–325.

Rafferty, J., & Steyaert, J. (2009). Social work in the digital age. *British Journal of Social Work, 39*(4), 589–598.

Richards, D., & Vigano, N. (2013). Online counseling: A narrative and critical review of the literature. *Journal of Clinical Psychology, 69*(9), 994–1011.

Tunick, R. A., Mednick, L., & Conroy, C. (2011). A snapshot of child psychologists' social media activity: Professional and ethical practice implications and recommendations. *Professional Psychology: Research and Practice, 42*(6), 440–447. doi: 10.1037/a0025040

Whitlock, J., Powers, J., & Eckenrode, J. (2006). The virtual cutting edge: The Internet and adolescent self-injury. *Developmental Psychology, 42*(3), 407–417.

CHAPTER 7

Child and Youth Care Practice with Trans Children, Youth, and Their Families

Julie James

CARRIE'S STORY

Carrie walks into the room for her interview, shy and nervous, yet warm, open, and engaging. Carrie is white, able-bodied, and not easily identifiable as trans. She speaks about her life without too much emotion, revealing hardships and how she dealt with them. She was born in a remote Northern Ontario town and raised with five other siblings by a single mother. She remembers identifying as trans from an early age (about six). She recalls telling her mother repeatedly, "I don't *feel* like a girl; I *am* a girl," and her mother telling her, "It's just a phase." She asked her family to call her by the nickname "Car" (instead of her birthname, Carson; she really wanted to be called Carrie though), and when they did, she felt a little better, a little more seen as herself. At the age of eight, Carrie was placed in foster care because of her mother's issues with addiction. While in care, Carrie was made to identify as cisgender (male). She was also physically and sexually abused by her foster parents. She was verbally harassed by teachers and students when she dressed or acted like herself (a girl). She ran home to her mother a total of eight times and was placed back in care each time. When she told her social worker about her experiences in care and at school, she was not believed.

Carrie left care at the age of 18 and started to socially live her gender identity in an urban location far from her family's home. She attempted to finish school, but going out in public on a regular basis where she was stared at often and called names proved to be too anxiety provoking. She tried to obtain gender-affirmation medical care (hormone therapy and maybe surgery), but the local physicians said they couldn't help, and she did not have the money to travel. She tried to change her legal name, but the process was complicated, involving several forms, numerous trips to various offices, and quite a bit of money. She looked for work and would get as far as the interview stage before her trans identity became apparent and subsequently was told that she was not a good fit. Carrie entered the shelter system where she experienced assault from several residents. She went to the hospital for treatment for her injuries and was outed in the process. She reported the incidents to a shelter staff member who offered emotional support but then recommended that she leave the shelter for her own safety. She found herself on the streets where she experienced verbal harassment—once in front of two police officers who did not intervene to help her. Carrie spoke to me about feeling depressed, anxious, and fearful of public spaces.

Carrie came to our interview with two friends who also identify as trans and whom she refers to as her "family"; one of them secured housing for them by pretending to be cisgender after being rejected by several landlords. They work to support and protect one another. They study together, search for work, and safeguard one another in public. They find further support from other trans youth online, where they co-create understandings about gender, share their journeys, and slip into a world that values and celebrates gender diversity. Carrie talks about wanting things to change: She wants the harassment and violence against trans youth to stop; she wants a world that is gender inclusive; and she wants trans identities to be accepted and honoured.

INTRODUCTION

Carrie's story is a composite that I wrote after completing several interviews with trans or gender-diverse youth for a province-wide study on accessing justice for trans people in Ontario called TRANS*forming* JUSTICE (TFJ). Before taking a faculty position in the Child and Youth Care department at Ryerson University, I had been in the field, working front-line with children and youth for over 20 years. Not much, if anything, still shocked me. My compassion and deep care remained but the visceral impact of taking in stories of abuse had calmed. These interviews changed that. Rarely had I heard tales of violence—in all its forms—so pervasive, across so many contexts, leaving few if any places of safety. At times I, not the interviewee, needed to take a break from the interview. Almost more moving to me than the heartbreaking experiences of these youth were their persistent traits of empathy, warmth, care, and love coupled with their impressive accounts of creating community, advocacy, care-taking, and protection. I present Carrie's story here to ground the concepts presented in this chapter, using this narrative as a guide to think through how child and youth care practitioners (CYCPs) can pervasively challenge the oppression trans children and youth face, be advocates for gender inclusivity, and insist on letting the children and youth lead the way in their own self-determined gender journey.

Over the past few years, mainly while gathering information for the TFJ study, I have had numerous conversations with trans young people, their families, the CYC practitioners who are trying to meet their needs, supervisors of CYCPs, and global leaders in the field. The following chapter is drawn from those conversations and offers an account of how I have come to understand the situation for trans children and youth in Canada. I centrally describe how the field of practice is *transitioning* from conversion practices to *forming* a field of gender-affirmative care (see also Anderson-Nathe, this volume). Unsurprisingly, CYC practitioners are amongst the small army of advocates who are making this type of practice a reality. My experience with this topic is long and varied: It includes being a front-line worker for trans children and youth in care and not knowing how to support them, studying gender at the doctorate level for seven years, writing and reading about gender, listening to trans youth and leaders in the field, attending conferences, giving workshops, and being a researcher for TFJ. I am still eagerly learning. I can barely keep up because the field of supporting trans children and youth has simply exploded within the past five years. I don't doubt that by the time of publication the field will be quite a bit more advanced.

Therefore, what I offer below is an examination of the field of supporting trans children and youth in Canada as it stands in 2018. First, I overview trans-related terminology as it is currently used within professional and academic practice. Second, I set up a context for understanding the struggle that trans people (young and old) face by reviewing Eurocentric notions of gender and the legacy of colonialism with respect to trans individuals. Third, I review the transition that is taking place from conversion practices to gender-affirmative care. Fourth, I look at the gender affirmation movement in Canada. Fifth, I detail how trans youth, their families, and CYC practitioners are leading the way in forming this field of gender affirmative care. Sixth, I summarize my conversations with trans youth and CYCPs in Canada to highlight the key areas of struggle and describe how CYC practitioners are already working to meet these challenges. I also detail how and why I believe this work is so important; I essentially call for a recognition of the work trans youth and CYC practitioners are doing, for further support of their labour, and for all to join in these efforts. I conclude the chapter by revisiting Carrie's story, pretending that I am her worker, following the lead of the impressive trans youth and CYC practitioners from whom I have been fortunate to learn.

TERMINOLOGY

Before delving into a discussion about trans children and youth, it is likely help-ful to define the terms commonly used by practitioners in the field and identify how I am using particular terms in this chapter. First, the term *sex* is often used in relation to the biological physical body. This encompasses, but is not limited to, primary sex characteristics (internal and external organs related to reproduc-tion), secondary sex characteristics (body hair, voice depth, hip width, breast structure, level of musculature, facial features, etc.), hormones, chromosomes, and the physical brain. Within this terminology, one may be born with a body assigned as male, a body assigned as female, or a body with both male and female features assigned as intersex. Second, *gender identity* is often used to refer to the internal sense of oneself as male, female, non-binary, agender, gender fluid, and so on. Third, relatedly, *gender expression* refers to the social expression (dress, hair style, behaviour, etc.) of this identity. Fourth, the terms *sexuality* or *sexual orientation* are often used to refer to whom we are romantically and/or sexually attracted or an absence of this attraction.

There are a few further nuances and terms often referred to within the broader category of gender. The term *cisgender* refers to someone whose *sex* (as-signed biological physical body) linearly aligns with their *gender identity* (i.e., male body and male gender identity), and the term *transgender* refers to some-one whose sex and gender identities are not linearly connected (i.e., assigned male body and female gender identity, assigned female body and non-binary gender identity, etc.). *Non-binary* tends to refer to a person whose gender identity does not fit neatly into either male or female categorizations (one may identify as both, neither, fluid, or something else). In this chapter, I tend to truncate the word transgender to simply *trans*. I also believe that there are numerous configurations of trans identities and these identities should be self-determined. *Gender spectrum* refers to the understanding that gender exists along a continuum and does not fit neatly into two binary boxes (Ehrensaft, 2011, 2016). *Gender inclusivity* refers to practices that are inclusive of all genders—male, female, non-binary, cisgender, transgender, and so on. Finally, the *Gender Affirmation Model* denotes practices that do not pathologize transgender identities but rather celebrate gender diversity.

In the world of trans children and youth, some further terms are deployed. Various terms are used somewhat interchangeably (although with some debate) to denote a child or youth with a transgender identification. These terms include transgender, gender non-conforming, gender variant, gender diverse, and gender creativity (Ehrensaft, 2011, 2016). Within these categories, some children and youth are persistent, insistent, and consistent with their gender creativity, and some are not (Ehrensaft, 2016; Temple Newhook et al., 2018). When practitioners talk about a child's *natal gender* or *natal sex*, they are referring to the child's sex designation as male, female, or intersex at birth. Another way of referring to a child's natal sex or gender is to say "assigned female or male or intersex at birth" (also known as afab, amab, or aiab). Many front-line practitioners from a number of professions (for example, child and youth care, psychology, and social work) have taken the stance that children and youth should lead the way in defining their own gender identities and creating the terms that best describe them. Diane Ehrensaft (2011, 2016), who is considered widely to be the founder of the Gender Affirmation Movement, shares that some of the terms that the children and youth she serves use are gender priuses, gender minotaurs, gender-ambidextrous, and—one of my personal favourites—gender smoothies.

THE LEGACY OF COLONIALISM

To understand the struggles that trans people—young and older—currently face, it is important to comprehend the impact of Eurocentric notions of gender and colonization on trans identities and lived realities. Prior to colonization, in communities around the globe, including Africa, Australia, India, Europe, North

America, and South America, multiple sexes, multiple genders, and multiple sexualities are documented as having existed (Feinberg, 1996; Jacobs, Thomas, & Lang, 1997; Stryker & Aizura, 2013). Treatment of individuals who might be understood by Western frameworks as transgender is noted to vary greatly between communities (Jacobs et al., 1997; Stryker & Aizura, 2013). Non-acceptance, fear, violence, acceptance, reverence, being given a special role, and more in relation to transgender people unfolded in a variety of forms across the pre-colonial world (Jacobs et al., 1997). The period of colonization saw an imposition of European ideas of binary sex, gender, sexuality, and selfhood (Jacobs et al., 1997). This imposition involved various practices of genocide, including the mass killing and attempted social-cultural eradication of Indigenous transgender people, as one of the ways to conquer Indigenous societies (Feinberg, 1996; Jacobs et al., 1997). However, despite these efforts, transgender individuals continue to exist, and because of this colonial past and residual neo-colonial practices, their existence is often fraught with issues of violence, discrimination, and erasure.

Eurocentric notions of gender and colonization impact trans individuals in Canada in multiple and diverse ways. Indigenous trans and Two-Spirit individuals are left to contend with intergenerational trauma, the recovery of cultural knowledge specific to them, anti-Indigenous racism, as well as transphobic neo-colonial practices. Non-Indigenous racialized trans individuals contend with societal transphobia, racism, and possibly transphobia within their communities. Some racialized TFJ participants spoke to me about not being able to go to their communities to help shield, recover, and protect themselves from racism because some members within these communities were transphobic. Non-Indigenous white settler trans people contend with transphobia, have white privilege, and need to grapple or are grappling with white settler responsibility. Further, privilege and adversity within the trans community also exist along the lines of male privilege, heteronormativity, newcomer status, age, access to trans-specific medical care, health status, being identified as trans in public, and ableism.

Awareness of these hierarchies and attempts to address them was evidenced within a trans youth advisory group I assembled to direct me in organizing a trans youth conference. The advisory group insisted on centring the voices of Black, Indigenous, and diversely abled trans youth amongst them. White trans youth members were focused on understanding their privileges, learning to address white settler responsibility, and unpacking effective allyship. They are aware that while they all grapple with transphobia more broadly, they each have various intersections of privilege and oppression, and how transphobia manifests may be quite different for each of them. Wanting the most marginalized among them centred, supported, and focused on was a main driving factor for this trans youth advisory group.

The overarching ways in which transphobia and the enforcement of Eurocentric notions of gender continue currently is through practices of pathology, conversion, erasure, and violence. In 2013, the *Diagnostic Statistical Manual* (DSM) shifted its diagnosis of gender identity disorder to gender dysphoria for trans individuals (Lev, 2013). The criteria for children and youth to receive a diagnosis of gender dysphoria is that they are both persistently identifying as trans and are also experiencing distress (Lev, 2013). Two problems linger: While this new term moves from seeing a trans identification as a pervasive disorder to a mental health condition causing stress, it still remains under a mental health diagnosis; as well, several practitioners argue that the distress does not come from the identification itself, but rather from dealing with a transphobic society. The sticky aspect of the new diagnostic term is that to receive trans-related medical transitional treatment, a diagnosis of gender dysphoria is necessary (Lev, 2013).

Practices of conversion, erasure, and violence tend to be connected to the matter of pathologizing a transgender identification. Somewhat closely aligned with treating transgender identification as a mental health issue are the practices that seek to "remedy" this identification. As will be explicated in further detail below, these practices involve conversion techniques aimed at eradicating a transgender identity and cultivating a cisgender presentation (Ehrensaft, 2011, 2016). Also in line with seeing transgender identities as something beyond what exists within the human spectrum is the reality of erasure (Bauer et al., 2009). Erasure includes the silencing of transgender his/her/their stories, the absence of formal institutional (medical, social, and legal) services that can meet the needs of trans individuals, and the invisibility of trans realities from mainstream contexts (Bauer et al., 2009). Finally, a failure to see trans people as fully human, healthy, and important seems to have resulted in an incredible amount of violence towards this population.

This violence is very prevalent within Canada, and it heavily impacts our trans children and youth. In the 2016 TRANS*forming* JUSTICE study, we found that trans youth (ages 16–24) in Ontario experience discrimination at much greater frequency than does the general Canadian population; further, they rarely receive any formal (medical, social, or legal) support for these issues, and this all has a profound impact on their well-being. Narratives from trans youth whom I interviewed for the TFJ study reveal experiences of discrimination, harassment, and violence across multiple contexts (family, school, public, community, employment, housing, child welfare, online) over many years, leaving few if any places of safety (TRANS*forming* JUSTICE dataset, 2016). The Being Safe Being Me Canada-wide health study of 933 trans youth (Veale et al., 2015) found that two-thirds of the respondents reported experiences of discrimination, 70 percent reported being sexually assaulted, one-third reported being physically harmed, and one half of older youth reported being cyberbullied. Stories about increased hostility towards the trans population, including children and youth, with the onset of the Trump administration both within the United States and across the border in Canada pervade professional in-person and online forums. Overall, even within a terrain of legislative support and small but growing social acceptance, there remains a colonial legacy of violence towards trans people and a backlash against supporting trans children and youth.

The impact of this violence on our young trans people is profound. The Being Safe Being Me results reveal that, within a recent one-year time frame, two-thirds of respondents reported self-harm, two-thirds reported serious thoughts of suicide, one-third had attempted suicide, and one-quarter had run away from home (Veale et al., 2015). This same study advises that trans youth in Canada have low connectedness to school, most feel cared about by their families but 70 percent feel as though their families do not understand them, one in three felt that they did not have an adult in their family they could talk to, and only 15 percent felt very comfortable talking to their family doctors about their trans identities (Veale et al., 2015). Overall, many trans youth are dealing with significant well-being issues and are not receiving social, mental health, or medical support.

TRANSITIONING FROM CONVERSION TO AFFIRMATION

Over the years there has been an increased awareness that particular practices with trans children and youth are harmful. Conversion therapy, also understood as reparative therapy, is better known as a practice that attempts to convert LGBTQ2S+ individuals into becoming heterosexual; it is less known that it is also used as a practice to try and convert transgender people into becoming cisgender. Medical and mental health associations across Canada and the

United States outright denounce reparative practices for both sexually diverse and gender non-conforming children and youth. The Canadian Professional Association for Transgender Health (CPATH), the Canadian Association of Social Work Education (CASWE), the American Academy of Child and Adolescent Psychiatry (AACAP), and the World Professional Association of Transgender Health (PHSA) are clear in their condemnation of these practices (AACAP, 2018; CASWE, n.d.; CPATH, 2015; PHSA, 2018). These professionals assert that seeking to eradicate diverse sexual and gender identities is unethical, does not work, and is harmful for an already very vulnerable group. In June 2015, Ontario passed the Affirming Sexual Orientation and Gender Identity Act, making it illegal to practise conversion therapy in Ontario.

Replacing conversion practices as the predominant framework used for supporting trans children and youth is a focus on promoting overall well-being through the Gender Affirmative Model (Ehrensaft, 2016; Temple Newhook et al., 2018) This model posits that gender variations are healthy, differ across cultures, may involve binary or fluid configurations, are not pathological, and are not disorders (Ehrensaft, 2011, 2016). Further, it asserts that the distress felt by trans individuals is the result of societal transphobia, not the individual's gender identity (Ehrensaft, 2011, 2016). As Ehrensaft (2016) puts it: "If there is a gender pathology, we will find it not in the child but in the culture" (p. 15).

In the Gender Affirmative Model, children and youth are listened to and observed as they lead the way in revealing their own gender identities. Gender-creative children and youth who are persistent in this identification may then be supported in a social transition that can involve changing their names, pronouns, and styles of dress and hair, and expressing more fully their gender identities in a multitude of ways. This expression may vary across different social contexts in accordance with the children's/youths' wishes, needs, and safety concerns. They may also be supported in a medical transition that may include the use of puberty blockers to stave off puberty, reduce acute anxiety related to bodily changes not in line with their gender identities, and buy some time to decide the course of medical action (or inaction) that will best meet their needs. After puberty blockers, trans youth may consider hormone replacement therapy to help transition into bodies that feel more authentic to them. They may then decide later to undergo top and/or bottom surgery. The youth and their care team may choose one, some, or all of these interventions at various stages of their development. Alongside these social and medical transition considerations are front-line people (trans youth, CYC practitioners, parents, etc.)

who are creating services, advocating for access to trans-youth health care, and working to create gender-inclusive environments in all the spaces that children and youth live and play.

THE GENDER AFFIRMATION MOVEMENT IN CANADA

In Canada, it is the grassroots people who are increasingly making gender affirmation a reality for young trans people. These grassroots folks include trans children, trans youth, families, older trans adults, CYC practitioners, and a host of caring professionals. Parents who accept and support their gender-creative children are working to forge a social and cultural world that is inclusive of all genders. They have created online forums, collaborated with researchers to generate a resource database called "Gender Creative Kids" (www.gendercreativekids.ca), organized support groups, and built community-based programs. Parents, families, peers, practitioners, trans children, and trans youth are all advocating for gender-inclusive practices to be instituted in schools, sports teams, recreational facilities, community groups, shelters, and the child welfare system. Medical clinics have been created by passionate and concerned professionals. Family practitioners and endocrinologists are collaborating and trying to understand best practices for this population. Finally, professionals from several disciplines (community, mental health, child welfare, health, and education) are working to make their fields safe and effective for trans children and youth. Often this work is starting off, just where it should, by listening to and centring the voices of trans children and youth.

The legal system in Canada supports the emergence of gender-affirmative care for all trans people. Canada has pervasive laws protecting trans people (adults, youth, and children) from discrimination. There is federal and provincial legislation safeguarding gender identity and expression under human rights codes, the Criminal Code, and in family law. In most provinces, there is no age for medical consent, meaning that trans youth are legally able to access trans-related medical care without parental approval. It is important to note that these laws not only protect trans individuals who have experienced overt violence but also necessitate the provision of services that meet the needs of trans people—including trans children and youth. Therefore, it is important that all services for trans children and youth (medical, educational, social services, foster care, shelters, community services, recreational, etc.) work to incorporate gender-affirmative practices yielding gender-inclusive environments.

FORMING THE FIELD OF GENDER-AFFIRMATIVE CARE

The field of gender-affirmative care for young trans people is small but burgeoning. Grassroots initiatives undertaken by a range of concerned professionals has led to the rise of medical clinics that support trans youth. Canada seems to fall somewhere in the middle of this development in relation to other countries who have clinics and have adopted these practices. The more developed side—the United States, the United Kingdom, and the Netherlands—have interdisciplinary gender identity clinics that include psychiatrists, paediatricians, endocrinologists, nurses, social workers, and community workers. Often these clinics have referral systems of many local psychologists and counsellors to further support families, as well as resources to go into schools and provide education on gender-inclusive practices. Funding issues remain pervasive, but the team of trained support personnel appears strong. On the less developed side is a child psychiatrist named Simon, who represents the entire gender identity clinic in South Africa: He is the psychiatrist, endocrinologist, social worker, family support worker, and community educator in one.

In Canada, we have a handful of part-time, hospital-based, inter-disciplinary gender-identity clinics that serve youth in Vancouver, Toronto, and Ottawa. Typically, these clinics are only open a couple of days each month and none of them have direct funding. Passionate yet very over-worked staff support a growing client base. For example, the Gender Identity Clinic at the Hospital for Sick Children in Toronto was started in 2013 because of the concern of practitioners from its adolescent mental health clinic. The director of the clinic does not have full-time status even though she manages over 500 families (Cathy Maser, personal conversation, 2017). In Canada, approximately 10 part-time, community-based health clinics, as well as some individual family doctors, psychiatrists, and endocrinologists also administer gender-affirmative care to youth; they all use different service-delivery models.

These unfunded, understaffed, and differently modelled clinics do not have an extensive psychologist, counsellor, and community referral base. Rather, trans youth, their families, and concerned youth practitioners continue with the work of providing advocacy, education, support, and training to schools, communities, and health care providers. They are doing excellent work. In Sudbury, local advocates and youth workers are partnering with police and school boards to provide gender-inclusive training. In Kingston, youth workers organized a symposium to have trans youth lead in sharing their stories and detailing their needs. In Ottawa,

Kaeden, a trans youth, led their school in providing gender-inclusive workshops. In Toronto, trans youth groups have sprouted up at several LGBTQ2S+ organizations. At the Children's Aid Society of Toronto, the "Out and Proud" program is working to advocate for gender-affirmative practices for children and youth in care. The 2-Spirit of the First Nations in Toronto has long had extensive and impressive policies and practices regarding Two-Spirit trans-identified youth. Black Cap (www.blackcap.ca), also in Toronto, has similarly worked on behalf of trans-identified Black Youth. The work being done is growing and impressive. It is also under-funded, exhausting, and potentially triggering.

In short, the gender-affirmative care system in Canada for children and youth is small, growing, underfunded, piecemeal, inconsistently administered, and falling on the backs of a few passionate souls. The people doing the demanding work in the field are incredible and deeply committed; they are also tired and need help. This help is important because the number of trans children and youth in Canada is far greater than most people would estimate, and they are dealing with some serious issues. The William's Institute estimates the prevalence of trans identities within the US youth population (ages 13–24) to be roughly 1 in 140 (Flores, Herman, Gates, & Brown, 2016). If we apply that ratio to the 2016 census estimates of the same-aged youth population in Canada, we find approximately 72,000 youth in Canada who identify as trans. This means that in Canada, there are over 70,000 trans-identified youth who face a totally inadequate support system and who may be dealing with multiple and very serious issues. If this ratio applies to children under 13, approximately 41,000 Canadian children can be added to this estimate, equaling a total of over 110,000 young people. When you factor in issues of racialization, sexuality, poverty, rural or remote locations, and diverse abilities, these concerns are further exacerbated.

ROLES AND FUNCTIONS OF CHILD AND YOUTH CARE PRACTITIONERS

CYC practitioners are already taking a lead role in forging a field of gender-affirmative care for trans young people and their families. I have met them. I am learning from them. While gathering information from trans people in Ontario, I engaged with many trans youth and many CYC practitioners who are trying to support them. I also connected with several CYC practitioners and their supervisors across the country. Below I offer an account of the key areas of challenge that trans youth identified in their conversations with me, the known protective factors for young trans people, and how CYC practitioners are already enhancing these protective factors to help address these struggles. I conclude this section of the chapter by calling for this work to be recognized, supported, and increased.

AREAS OF CHALLENGE

The youth who participated in the 2016 TRANS*forming* JUSTICE study identified six key challenge areas: families, identity documents, health care, employment, housing, and school. It is important to note that these challenges often do not exist in isolation; rather, the youth typically experienced multiple issues across most of these areas. Below is a brief overview of these struggles and how they specifically impacted the youth in the study.

Families

Many youth spoke about experiencing abuse and rejection from their families because of their trans identities. They told me stories about being blocked from trans-related medical treatment, being unable to change their identity documents, being made to conform to a cisgender identity, being physically abused, being emotionally abused, and being kicked out of their homes. Some youth had been placed in care and spoke about experiencing these same issues while residing in foster or group homes. Cultural considerations were discussed: Some youth experienced support within their families and communities from people who were knowledgeable about trans histories and/or Two-Spirit traditions; others talked about needing to hide their trans identities from their families and communities as their cultural norms included severe negative treatment of trans people, which left some racialized trans youth without access to their culture and without community support and protection from racism.

Identity Documents

Trans youth reported issues with obtaining a name change and/or gender marker change on their identity documents. They had difficulty navigating the complex name-change system, finding the funds to pay for the process, and/or regarding issues with obtaining parental consent when needed. These issues were intensified for trans youth who had immigrated or had refugee status; in such cases, obtaining consent for a name change through their countries of origin is required and several countries outright deny these requests. Not having identity documents that match their gender identity led to feelings of depression, being outed in various environments (school, health, employment), and a loss of housing and/or employment.

Health Care

Trans youth spoke about having issues with access to medical care. This included having access to physicians who felt knowledgeable and comfortable treating trans youth regarding routine medical check-ups and care, as well as trans-specific medical interventions (e.g., hormone treatment). Sometimes medical care (trans-specific and non-trans-specific) was denied by medical professionals, and/or the professionals advised that they did not have the proper training. Sometimes parents refused to consent to trans-specific medical interventions, and while their consent is not legally needed, because hormone therapy is not covered under public health insurance, their financial support is often required. As well, several physicians involved in gender-affirmative medical care told me that in practice they do not proceed with this type of treatment without parental consent. As a result, youth spoke about not having regular medical care and about obtaining hormones on the street and/or online. In conversations outside of this study, practitioners revealed that trans youth whose families do not support their gender identities are volunteering to come into foster care, so they can acquire trans-specific medical treatment.

Employment

Older trans youth spoke about having issues obtaining and/or retaining employment. Several spoke about being fired, experiencing changes in duties, being treated differently, and not being interviewed once their trans identities were revealed. Often a trans identity was made known to an employer once the youth had to present their identity documents with names and sex markers that did not align with their gender identity and presentation.

Housing

Trans youth revealed issues with being denied housing, being harassed by neighbours, and being evicted once their trans identities were revealed. Some of the youth spoke about not being given the option to be housed in a shelter in line with their gender identities. A couple of youth told stories of being physically and sexually assaulted in these shelter spaces; when they reported the assaults to shelter staff, they were either blamed for the incidents or made to leave the shelter space.

School

The youth spoke about multiple and ongoing negative experiences at school. Many talked about being told by peers and teachers from a very early age to conform to their natal gender identity. Several were not out in their school environments for fear of harassment and violence; some spoke about being harassed and assaulted within their school environments. Most of the youth did not feel connected but rather isolated in their school communities.

MEETING THESE CHALLENGES IN CHILD AND YOUTH CARE PRACTICE

One way to think about addressing these challenges is to understand what factors significantly and positively influence the well-being of trans children and youth. A few such protective factors are known. School connectedness, an empathetic adult, using a young trans person's chosen name, and strong family support are all reported to have a significant positive impact on the mental health of trans youth (Travers et al., 2012; Veale et al., 2015). Trans youth who report school connectedness are twice as likely to have good mental health (Veale et al., 2015). Trans youth with very supportive parents "report higher life satisfaction, higher self-esteem, better mental health including less depression and fewer suicide attempts, and adequate housing compared to those without strong parental support" (Travers et al., 2012, p. 1). Recent research also shows that use of a trans youth's chosen name is linked to reduced depressive symptoms, suicidal ideation, and suicidal behaviour (Russell, Pollitt, Gu, & Grossman, 2018). Finally, "trans youth who had supportive adults both inside and outside their family were four times more likely to report good or excellent mental health and were far less likely to have considered suicide" (Veale et al., 2015, p. 2). Dr. Annie Pullen Sansfacon at the University of Montreal is, at the time of writing, investigating the oppressive factors and the resiliency factors for trans youth in Quebec (http://travail-social.umontreal.ca/repertoire-departement/vue/pullen-sansfacon-annie). Findings from this research will further help inform practitioners in developing supportive and effective care.

CYC practitioners are involved in both forming the field of gender-affirmative care through grassroots labour and working to meet the needs of young trans people by drawing on relational CYC approaches that engage with the known protective factors. In short, CYC practitioners are being those engaged adults, working with families to increase their support of their trans child or youth, and advocating within school systems so that young trans people can be safe and feel included. CYC practitioners are also working as self-taught educators, advising schools about gender inclusivity, informing various social and community service agencies about appropriate practices, and helping families understand the gender spectrum. Some workers are engaging youth and communities to unearth his/her/their hidden stories of trans people within specific locations in Canada. CYC practitioners are also being strong advocates, trying to have intake forms changed, acting to obtain identity documents in line with gender identities, and putting pressure on agencies to develop trans youth programs, including opening a trans-specific youth shelter. They are doing all of this at their own initiative, without formal training, and largely with the absence of supervisory support. As well, throughout this, CYC practitioners are careful to follow the lead of trans youth while they walk with them on this complicated journey.

The CYC practices of relational work, "being with" children and youth, life-space work, and "following" all are important practices for understanding a child or youth's gender identity (Garfat & Fulcher, 2012). Engaged adults are needed to foster environments through which gender explorations can take place and to understand the gender identities being presented to them. CYC practitioners who work from a relational perspective engaged in life-space work following the lead of trans children and youth are exactly those engaged adults. Relational work involves genuinely caring about, being present for, and using one's authentic self in relationship with children and youth (Garfat & Fulcher, 2012). Life-space work, as defined by Gharabaghi and Stuart (2013), is the therapeutic work that takes places in the spaces where children and youth live and play. The notion of "following" comes from Celine Cabral (2017) and involves supporting trans children and youth in cyberspace contexts by having them take the lead in this online engagement (see also Martin & Stuart, this volume). This can also be applied to physical life-space where CYC practitioners follow the lead of trans children and youth as they explore and reveal their inner selves. Taken together, we have practitioners who are engaged alongside trans children and youth in the actual and virtual spaces where they live and play, following their lead as they explore their identities. As is well-understood, this work often does not take place in short spurts but rather in longer and regular intervals. Unlike CYC practitioners, other professionals who meet children and youth in clinical settings for shorter durations are limited in their abilities to both foster gender-inclusive life-spaces and be present for the expressions of various gender identities.

Nurturing gender-inclusive life-spaces and helping to more accurately determine a child or youth's gender identification is incredibly important for several reasons. First, CYC practitioners can be critical in forging avenues and environments within which to explore and generate trans identities specific to them. Second, gender identity clinics spend a substantial amount of time trying to figure out a child or youth's gender identification to determine how to best offer support (Ehrensaft, 2011, 2016; Olson, Durwood, DeMeules, & McLaughlin, 2016). CYC practitioners can be considered key informants and partners in this process, offering the most substantial information. Most vitally, CYC practitioners can then work to support this identification beyond the administration of medical interventions and into possibly all other areas of that young person's life. Third, medical professionals and researchers are currently highlighting the need to promote the well-being of young trans people (Temple Newhook et al., 2018). CYC practitioners' time commitment and active engagement with these young people can provide essential information in this process so that supports can be put in place that are in line with the young person's identity and needs as these needs arise and as their identities are revealed. Finally, in the process of creating gender-inclusive life-spaces, CYC practitioners are also working to support gender-creative expressions and identity explorations for all children and youth. This may be one way of challenging gender hierarchies that also support other forms of oppression (see also Anderson-Nathe, this volume).

It is at this point that I feel the need to reiterate that trans youth, their families, and CYC practitioners have been and continue to be active at the grassroots level in helping to form the field of gender-affirmative care. CYC practitioners are working alongside trans children and youth to help address their struggles. The work that CYC practitioners do can greatly aid trans young people, and they are doing all of this largely in the absence of training, supervisory support, and compensation—and in the presence of a socio-political and systematic context of erasure and backlash. I want to offer my sincere gratitude to the trans youth, their families, the caring professionals, and the fierce CYC practitioners who are making gender-affirmative care a reality in Canada. I believe their work needs to be recognized and further supported, both within the child and youth care field and by other professionals. Finally, I believe we all need to follow their lead.

CARRIE'S STORY REVISITED

Now, I revisit Carrie's story through the lens of following the lead of trans youth, parent advocates, CYC practitioners, supportive professionals, and community change-makers.

Carrie walks into the room for her interview. She is warm, confident, and softly outspoken. Carrie talks about her past with some emotion and reflection. She recounts living in a rural northern Ontario community and being placed in care at the age of eight. When she first went into care, she was assigned Melissa as her worker. Melissa had trained Carrie's foster parents on trans-affirmative care and gender-inclusive practices. Melissa also connected Carrie with Lorraine Gale from the "Out and Proud" program. Melissa and Lorraine have formed a team around Carrie, ensuring that her foster parents are knowledgeable about gender inclusivity and are actively pursuing trans-affirmative care as Carrie directs them regarding her wishes in this process. Carrie has decided to pursue some hormone therapy but no surgery at this time. She is not able to legally change her name as there are issues with her mother agreeing to this process, but her school, health care providers, and community support services use her name and pronouns. She is meeting with other trans youth online and through face-to-face group experiences. Dani, her youth worker from "The 519," an LGBTQ+ organization, is working with Carrie on uncovering the trans his/her/their stories from her mother's area in northern Ontario. Carrie is using the knowledge she is uncovering with Dani to help construct an online trans superhero futuristic world with two other trans youth. Her school had already instituted gender-inclusive practices for all its students, allowing both trans and cisgender youth to be able to more fully express their authentic selves. Carrie continues to experience transphobia in public spaces and from some peers and some providers. Her workers and foster parents have equipped Carrie with tools to cope with these experiences. She also actively reflects in her journal, with her friends, and through online discussions on her privileges and responsibilities as a white settler, able-bodied, young trans person. She works to centre more marginalized young trans people in the programs she attends, in school discussions, and in online forums. At the interview, Carrie talks mostly about being sad about losing her connections with her siblings and her mother through being in care. She is hoping to regain those bonds later on in life as she continues to realize her full and ever-growing authentic self.

. . . .

REFERENCES

American Academy of Child and Adolescent Psychiatry (AACAP). (2018). *Policy statement on conversion therapy.* Retrieved from https://www.aacap.org/AACAP/Policy_Statements/2018/Conversion_Therapy.aspx

Bauer, G. R., Hammond, R., Travers, R., Kaay, M., Hohenadel, K. M., & Boyce, M. (2009). "I don't think this is theoretical; this is our lives": How erasure impacts health care for transgender people. *Journal of the Association of Nurses in AIDS Care, 20*(5), 348–361.

Cabral, C. (2017). *Online relational practice: Following and lugging in with LGBT youth.* Unpublished master's thesis, Ryerson University, Toronto, Ontario, Canada.

Canadian Association of Social Work Education and Canadian Association of Social Workers (CASWE). (n.d.). *Joint statement on the affirmation of gender diverse children and youth.* Retrieved from https://www.casw-acts.ca/en/joint-statement-affirmation-gender-diverse-children-and-youth

Canadian Professional Association for Transgender Health (CPATH). (2015). *Canadian Professional Association for Transgender Health submission to the Standing Committee on Justice Policy Re: Bill 77, Affirming Sexual Orientation and Gender Identity Act, 2015.* Retrieved from http://www.cpath.ca/wp-content/uploads/2016/02/2015-06-03-CPATH-Submission-Re-Bill-77-Affirming-Sexual-Orientation-and-Gender-Identity-Act-2015.pdf

Ehrensaft, D. (2011). *Gender born, gender made: Raising healthy gender-nonconforming children.* New York: Workman Publishing.

Ehrensaft, D. (2016). *The gender creative child: Pathways for nurturing and supporting children who live outside gender boxes.* New York: Workman Publishing.

Feinberg, L. (1996). *Transgender warriors: Making history from Joan of Arc to Dennis Rodman.* Boston: Beacon Press.

Flores, A. R., Herman, J. L., Gates, G. J., & Brown, T. N. T. (2016). *How many adults identify as transgender in the United States? The Williams Institute Public Report.* Retrieved from https://williamsinstitute.law.ucla.edu/wp-content/uploads/How-Many-Adults-Identify-as-Transgender-in-the-United-States.pdf

Garfat, T., & Fulcher, L. (2012). Characteristics of a relational child and youth care approach. In T. Garfat & L. Fulcher (Eds.), *Child and youth care in practice* (pp. 5–24). Cape Town, South Africa: CYC-Net Press.

Gharabaghi, K., & Stuart, C. (2013). Life-space intervention: Implications for caregiving. *Scottish Journal of Residential Child Care, 12*(3).

Jacobs, S. E., Thomas, W., & Lang, S. (Eds.). (1997). *Two-Spirit people: Native American gender identity, sexuality, and spirituality.* Chicago: University of Illinois Press.

Lev, A. I. (2013). Gender dysphoria: Two steps forward, one step back. *Clinical Social Work Journal, 41,* 288–296.

Olson, K. R., Durwood, L., DeMeules, M., & McLaughlin, K. A. (2016). Mental health of transgender children who are supported in their identities. *Pediatrics, 137*(3), e20153223. Retrieved from http://pediatrics.aappublications.org/content/pediatrics/early/2016/02/24/peds.2015-3223.full.pdf

Russell, S., Pollitt, A., Gu, L., & Grossman, A. (2018). Chosen name use is linked to reduce depressive symptoms, suicidal ideation, and suicidal behavior among transgender youth. *Journal of Adolescent Health.* Retrieved from http://www.jahonline.org/article/S1054-139X(18)30085-5/fulltext

Stryker, S., & Aizura, A. (2013). *The transgender studies reader* (2nd ed.). New York: Routledge.

Temple Newhook, J., Winters, K., Pyne, J., Jamieson, A., Holmes, C., Feder, S., … & Sinnott, M.-L. (2018). Teach your parents and providers well: Call for refocus on the health of trans and gender-diverse children. *Canadian Family Physician, 64*(5), 332–335.

Travers, R., Bauer, G., Pyne, J., & Bradley, K., Gale, L., & Papadimitriou, M. (2012). *Impacts of strong parental support for trans youth: A report prepared for Children's Aid Society of Toronto and Delisle Youth Services.* Retrieved from http://transpulseproject.ca/wp-content/uploads/2012/10/Impacts-of-Strong-Parental-Support-for-Trans-Youth-vFINAL.pdf

Veale J., Saewyc, E., Frohard-Dourlen, H., Dobson, S., Clark, B., & the Canadian Trans Youth Health Survey Research Group. (2015). *Being safe, being me: Results of the Canadian Trans Youth Health Survey.* Vancouver: Stigma and Resilience Among Vulnerable Youth Centre, School of Nursing, University of British Columbia.

World Professional Association of Transgender Health (PHSA). (2018). *World Professional Association of Transgender Health: Standards of Care* (7th ed.). Retrieved from http://www.phsa.ca/transgender/Documents/Glossary%20of%20Terms%20-%203%20sources.pdf

CHAPTER 8

Why Should We Care? Reflecting on Child and Youth Care Practice *for, about,* and *with* Autistic Young People

Nancy Marshall

It is unlikely that current child and youth care practitioners (CYCPs) will finish their career without caring for at least a few autistic young people (Gural & MacKay-Chiddenton, 2016). CYCPs support this population in schools, treatment centres, hospitals, private homes, and residential facilities. While doing so, many are asked to collaborate with medical and behavioural models of care that designate autism as a developmental disorder to be treated with the methods of Applied Behavioural Analysis (ABA). Readers might therefore expect the all too common definition of autism according to the *Diagnostic Statistical Manual* (APA, 2013), or the prevalence rate according to Centers for Disease Control (CDC, 2014). As a substitute, I would like to offer a description of autism provided by the Autistic Self Advocacy Network (ASAN):

> Autism is a neurological variation ... Although it may be more common than previously thought, it is not [new] ... and exists in all parts of the world ... The terms "Autistic" and "autism spectrum" often are used to refer inclusively to people who have an official diagnosis on the autism spectrum or who self-identify with the Autistic community. While all Autistics are as unique as any other human beings, they share some characteristics typical of autism in common ... (1) Different sensory experiences ... (2) Non-standard ways of

learning and approaching problem solving ... (3) Deeply focused thinking and passionate interests in specific subjects ... (4) Atypical, sometimes repetitive, movement ... (5) Need for consistency, routine, and order ... (6) Difficulties in understanding and expressing language as used in typical communication, both verbal and non-verbal ... (7) Difficulties in understanding and expressing typical social interaction. (ASAN, 2017)

Readers may be surprised to encounter my preferred definition of autism so eloquently written without the use of the word *disorder*. Autism, as a term, has a young history backed by oppressive language deeming autistic individuals to be "disordered," "disturbed," "dysfunctional," and burdened with "deficits." Leo Kanner (1943) is credited with the first definition of autism through his seminal work classifying young children as severely disordered in social learning and emotional affect, which he hypothesized to be caused, in part, by cold and rigid parenting. A year later, Hans Asperger published similar findings in German, this time with respect to older children with higher intellect and milder "deficits," whose traits he thought to be influenced largely by genetics (Chown & Hughes, 2016; Silberman, 2015; Singer, 2016). Although deficit-based, Asperger's more encompassing perspective on autism was an improvement that remained unpublished in English until 1981 (Chown & Hughes, 2016). As a result, Kanner's (1943) discouraging view of "autistic disturbances" in the ability to love or be loved gained headway in shaping the pathologized view of autism that we know today.

Hans Asperger was not the only researcher to define autistic individuals by more than just their deficits. Two years before his work was published in English, Lorna Wing and Judith Gould (1979) gained recognition for framing autism as a spectrum. Their work, along with Asperger's, made room for a more encompassing view of autism as a heterogeneous condition, which allowed autistic self-advocates to challenge Kanner's narrow view of severe autistic dysfunction (Singer, 2016). Nonetheless, since its inclusion in the DSM III in 1980, Autism Spectrum Disorder (ASD) continues to exist in the mainstream narrative as a symptomatic, deficit-based condition in need of a cure (APA, 2013).

Yet, despite its short history as an official diagnosis, autism is far from new. Before Kanner's, Asperger's, or Wing and Gould's publications came to be, autistic people existed (arguably) in the same numbers as they do today (Silberman, 2015). Throughout history, they were simply labelled with other diagnoses—schizophrenia, brain damage, mental illness, childhood psychosis, and so on (Silberman, 2015; Wing, 1997). Silberman notes that recent research suggests autism has existed for millions of years in the roots of our human DNA, not as a result of modern vaccines, pollution, junk food, or excess videogame play. So there is no need to panic about an increasing "epidemic." Autistic folk have been here for many years, across many global cultures, including people of colour who remain underrepresented in published statistics (Brown, 2017). Despite the traditional child and youth care (CYC) history of supporting "troubled" young people, without much focus on disability (Garfat, 1998, p. 12), it is likely we have been supporting autistic young people far longer than we think.

On that note, it is interesting to mention that autism and CYC share some common early history. Bruno Bettelheim, influenced by Kanner's psychoanalytic approach, is known for his view that "refrigerator mothers" caused autism in their children through cold, rigid parenting (Chown & Hughes, 2016; Silberman, 2015). Bettelheim is also touted as the forefather of milieu therapy (Trieschman, Whittaker, & Brendtro, 1969), commonly believed to be an intervention for troubled children who require some distance from their families (Shaw, 2015). The field of CYC takes pride in its early start in milieu therapy based on the foundational work of Bettelheim and his mentors (Trieschman, Whittaker, & Brendtro, 1969). This is for good reason—milieu residential care provides much needed support to young people globally (see also Gharabaghi & Charles, this volume). The ideas that milieu therapy is best conducted in isolation from family (see also Shaw, this volume) and that autism is created by cold parenting have, however, long been abandoned. It is nevertheless important to recognize our early connections when explaining our practice in relation to autism, especially considering that Bettelheim's psychoanalytic influence shaped professionals' and parents' ideas about autism from past until present (Silberman, 2015).

I would like to explain my own experience with this population, my choice of language when referring to these young people, and my values incorporating a disability rights and advocacy lens to my work. In my 10-plus years working with this population, I have learned that the young people themselves are the experts, as is the global autism community filled with vibrant, energetic self-advocates. As such, I will refrain from using person-first language (i.e., "young people with autism"), despite advice from seasoned CYC practitioners and other professionals to do so (APA, 2010; Gural & MacKay-Chiddenton, 2016).

Instead, I will use the preferred "identity first" choice of the autism advocacy community (i.e., "autistic young person"; Brown, 2012; Dunn & Andrews, 2015). Very simply, many autistic self-advocates prefer identity-first language because they do not believe autism is a shameful disorder to be placed second to their identity (Brown, 2012). They believe autism is a neurological difference to be celebrated as an asset, rather than a hindrance to society (Singer, 2016). The identity-first language has become so common that even psychiatrists are beginning to respect this wish (Dunn & Andrews, 2015). While I align myself with this advocacy movement, CYCPs will meet young people and families who choose otherwise. What is important is to listen to young people and families with respect to their choice of language.

In short, CYCPs work with autistic young people in virtually every CYC setting. There is some debate as to whether it is our place to support developmentally diverse young people or whether we should leave this work to other professionals (Gharabaghi, 2010). I have heard this argument echoed by colleagues who believe they are not qualified to support autistic youth. I firmly believe that this debate must stop. CYCPs absolutely need to involve themselves in the care of autistic young people, no matter where these young people lie within the spectrum of disability. Speaking of CYC practice in relation to the world of developmental disabilities, Gharabaghi asked, "What are the odds that the same theories, concepts and practice principles and strategies are meaningful in the context of such profoundly different worlds?" (para. 17). My answer to this question is, "the odds are very good!" Gharabaghi continued that it is not "useful to try and do one thing [support young people with developmental disabilities] through the perspectives of another [CYC practice]" (para. 17). In contrast to this, I argue that young people with developmental disabilities benefit from CYC's focus on holistic, relational, and strength-based care. I do not believe that these are "profoundly different worlds." Instead, CYCPs can provide an important service for autistic young people who are so often harmed by oppression, maltreatment, and inequities. Throughout this chapter, I will explore our current roles, challenges, and analyses of what CYC practitioners offer to autistic youth. I will conclude with some projections that I hope will inspire more practitioners to join the conversation to unpack relational CYC practice as an authentic support for autistic young people. No matter how "new" we believe we are to the practice of supporting autistic young people, CYCPs are increasingly employed in this area. There is no reason to believe our support will, or should, cease.

CYCP ROLES IN SUPPORTING AUTISTIC YOUNG PEOPLE

When conducting my own research, I found very little written in the area of a CYCP's role in supporting autistic youth. Up until 2015, much of the relevant literature informed practitioners to teach, guide, and encourage autistic young people to overcome their deficits with targeted treatments to improve their "symptoms" of autism (Donnelly, 2001; Fortunato, Sigafoos, & Morsillo-Searls, 2007; Fucilla, 2005; Gural & MacKay-Chiddenton, 2016; Laursen & Yazdgerdi, 2012; Sarahan & Copas, 2014; Successes with Autism, 1999). Within these writings, the authors suggest strategies to teach autistic young people to stay calm, communicate, reduce hand-flapping, make eye contact, build empathy, and become more affectionate in order to mitigate the isolation that they have seemingly caused by way of their own strange and undesirable behaviours. If these publications were truly any indication of what is expected in our role supporting autistic young people, I hope CYCPs feel a little disappointed—if not now, then maybe by the end of this chapter. Of course, the authors of these writings are caring professionals with nothing but the best intentions for helping autistic young people achieve a successful and meaningful life. Yet, while reading these publications, I asked myself, where are the strength-based, relational, and ecological perspectives that CYCPs are trained to practise with young people and their families? Why is it that little attention is given to the external oppressive structures that contribute to their poor outcomes and well-being? Granted, these authors did propose the need for practitioners to tailor their support in response to the needs of the young people. For example, Fucilla (2005) recognized the need for a "dual-change process that recognizes the importance of staff adaptations as well as client adaptations in order to effect positive behavioural choices" (p. 45). Likewise, Sarahan and Copas (2014) discussed the importance of relational connection with practitioners beyond the focus on self-regulation techniques. However, I felt that none of these resources addressed the potential of a complete CYC lens to practice, a lens that addresses human rights, and respect for developmental diversity.

Recently, publications have emerged that incorporate a more specific CYC lens to our role in supporting autistic young people. My own writings (see in particular Marshall & Tragni, 2015; Marshall, 2017a) explain how to apply strength-based approaches and disability rights to practice. These writings were inspired by my direct role in school-based autism programs where I attempted to apply a disability rights lens to my work. Since the first publication, I recognize incredible growth in my learning and admit that, like the aforementioned publications, I too have succumbed to deficit-based assumptions about autism. For example, in our 2015 publication my colleague and I state, "Often, youth on the spectrum have difficulties fostering relationships, let alone maintaining them" (p. 56). Although the article describes in-depth details about the importance of strength-based care, it is apparent that our biases (shaped by the deficit-based assumptions that underlie the medical model of disability—specifically the DSM) permeated our belief system. This belief system ultimately blames young people and their disability for the difficulties they face. Since then, I have come to understand that it is not my place to make general statements about autistic young people's social incapacities without their knowledge. Instead, I have learned to challenge the oppressive societal attitudes that contribute to their isolation. In my more recent publication (2017a), I explain the importance of allowing ourselves to be vulnerable and admit to mistakes made in the past. I believe that this vulnerability is essential to the role of CYCPs supporting any population. Therefore, our role requires us to be active learners in the pursuit of genuine, holistic care for young people. This means we need to do more than simply implement the latest resource in teaching "appropriate" social and self-regulation skills. Such "best practice" resources and philosophies will come and go throughout the course of our career. What is important is that we reflect often, challenge our assumptions, and continue to learn as we move forward (see also Newbury & Vachon, this volume).

In my own role, I submerge myself in disability rights and theory while reflecting on the suggestions made by the young people themselves. In my recent research study (Marshall, 2017b), I incorporated autistic young advocates' advice in comparison to the documented literature:

> "If somebody says, hey, I'm being bullied, don't be just like, 'ignore it'. Ignoring is a load of BS! It doesn't work …" Sarahan and Copas (2014) suggested good practice is to teach autistic young people to be calm and empathetic in their response to bullies. Shauna disagreed: "The victim is not thinking straight … If someone was going up to somebody and deliberately provoking them, teachers need to start doing something … Bullies [are] 'a-holes' who enjoy ticking people off and ignoring is pretty much impossible …"

Advice such as this transforms my practice. Instead of focusing solely on peaceful self-restraint, I realize the importance of appreciating self-confidence and resilience in the face of abuse.

I have further been inspired by Yvonne Bristow (2015, 2017), a school-based practitioner who believes CYC characteristics to be an unequivocal best practice approach for autistic young people. She encourages practitioners to be creative when engaging autistic young people with diverse communication abilities and challenges assumptions that autistic individuals are incapable of forming and sustaining relationships. Instead, she argues that when non-autistic people (known as neurotypical) are creative in their attempts to engage with autistic youth, relationships form naturally. However, it requires practitioners to reflect on normative understandings of connection and relationship. Bristow writes that this reflection requires a foundation in the knowledge of ableism, systemic oppression, and equitable rights of neurodivergent young people. Only with this foundation can our role focus on truly "meeting them where they are at"—an important characteristic of CYC practice (Garfat & Fulcher, 2013).

Almost a decade earlier, another practitioner (Walter, 2008) wrote of the normative assumptions stifling our ability to engage in creative CYC practice with autistic youth. Walter explained, "their [practitioners'] anxiety about the disturbing reactions they often meet in children with autism frequently leads them to adopt a controlling approach" (p. 61). As an example, he described a situation where a practitioner attempted to keep a non-verbal autistic youth from getting up repeatedly from the dinner table, likely assuming this was some kind of maladaptive behaviour. This caused the young person to ultimately scream and self-harm. When Walter suggested that the practitioner allow the young person to get up from the table, the youth simply walked to the kitchen to get peanut butter from the cupboard. Walter explained that practitioners' anxiety about autistic behaviours not only prevents the potential for positive experiences, but also causes maladaptive behaviours to occur. In this situation, the practitioner mistook the young person's behaviour of getting up from the table as a problem, rather than as a solution to meeting her own perfectly reasonable needs. Through a focus on power structures and oppressive societal attitudes, Walter further described how practitioners can reframe their perceptions of autistic behaviours in order to engage with autistic youth in more productive ways. Like Bristow (2015, 2107), Walter described how joining autistic young people with rhythmicity, creativity, and sharing of moments creates a therapeutic exchange that benefits both the practitioner and the young person. He provided a poignant example of joining an autistic young person in his silent, rhythmic activity of pressing repeatedly on a window with his hands. This moment of interaction soon led to a game where Walter connected with the young person through a gentle sensory exchange of push, back and forth with their hands, which both Walter and the boy thoroughly enjoyed.

Without creative efforts to engage in ways that make sense to autistic young people, practitioners run the risk of leaving autistic young people to occupy themselves. I worry that this lack of engagement only perpetuates their isolation. Laursen and Yazdgerdi (2012) discussed the desire for autistic young people to feel connection and belonging with neurotypical people. However, unlike Bristow (2015, 2017) and Walter (2008), the authors described how CYCPs can give "direct instruction on how to relate to others" (p. 47). They do not seem to entertain the idea that practitioners themselves can learn how to relate to autistic individuals (i.e., by showing interest in their intense passions about certain objects or topics of discussion). The dearth of literature on mutual engagement opportunities for autistic youth in CYC, with a focus on disability rights, is concerning. Our role should not be to simply teach autistic young people how to perform better in a neuro-normative world. Our role in their lives needs to incorporate a broader ecological perspective that challenges ableism and societal attitudes immersed in pathology.

CHALLENGES TO RELATIONAL PRACTICE WITH AUTISTIC YOUNG PEOPLE

As evidenced by the literature and my own experiences, a tension exists in current CYC practice supporting autistic young people. Do we consider autism to be a disorder in need of behavioural and medical treatment? Or do we believe it to be a natural neurological difference, too often misunderstood and oppressed by the structures of society? As with most theoretical practice frameworks, the lens CYCPs choose to adopt in practice will depend largely on the education they receive from those holding the power of information. Therefore, it is important to critically examine the dominant deficit-based view of autism in order to provoke thought into possible alternatives.

A recent publication authored by Deborah Gural (psychology instructor) and Dawne MacKay-Chiddenton (CYC instructor; 2016) unconsciously reflects the current tension between deficit-based and strength-based perspectives in relation to autism. Psychology, a practice that often relies on the pathological depiction of disorders within the DSM, is sometimes argued to be antithetical to strength-based CYC practice (Fewster, 2002). Thus, this publication represents an interesting perspective attempting to balance two opposing perspectives. Yet, while the authors acknowledge ableism and the importance of strength-based practice for autistic young people, the overall tone of the writing remains largely deficit-based. For example, they uphold that although inclusive classrooms are a basic human right, they are not advisable for autistic youth who "lack the social skills to navigate their environment" (p. 131) or get bullied in mainstream classrooms. Further, the authors state that "many youth with an ASD can be unaware of their overall deficits and have a tendency to experience the cause of their difficulties as external to themselves (blaming others)" (p. 122). Such bold statements reflect the overarching assumptions in our society that autistic people bring misery upon themselves by way of their disability. In my own experiences, autistic young people thrive in inclusive classrooms when respect, diversity, and non-discrimination are embedded within the school curriculum. Without this environment, they often become acutely aware of the "deficits" people have labelled them with, blame *themselves* for these deficits, and acquire low self-esteem, which further perpetuates stigma and isolation. It seems that practical advice targeting autistic deficits is the norm in current CYC education. I feel that this advice is unfair to both autistic young people and CYCPs, as young people are denied basic human rights and practitioners are denied opportunities to practice holistic support through an anti-oppressive lens.

As a further response to autistic "deficits," Gural and MacKay-Chiddenton (2016) recommend CYCPs use the much-touted, evidence-based practice of Applied Behavioural Analysis (ABA). This represents another tension in our field. The authors endorse ABA as a tool for behaviour management, which targets problematic behaviours in order to devise intervention plans. In Ontario, ABA is considered the best ethical and evidence-based intervention due to results determined by short-term studies that measure a young person's behaviours (i.e., their ability to sit quietly at a desk, speak, make eye-contact, reduce self-harm, etc.; Busch & Koudys, 2017). Although some variable success at improving these behaviours are noted by prominent authors of ABA studies, the results are determined by collecting data on very young participants who receive intensive therapy of 25 to 40 hours per week for up to four years (Flanagan, Perry, & Freeman, 2012; Freeman & Perry, 2010; Perry et al., 2008). In my own recent qualitative study, my research participant, Falon Wilton, expressed concern about the long-term effects of this supposed evidence-based practice: "just because something is evidence-based, doesn't mean that it's ethical or even useful long term. Have we even followed these kids well into adulthood … How are they doing?" (Marshall, 2017b). She has a right to be concerned.

Studies have found that autistic young people are at risk of growing up depressed (Chandrasekhar & Sikich, 2015; Kuhlthau et al., 2010; Mazurek, 2014; Stoddart et al., 2013) and sometimes suicidal (Paquette-Smith, Weiss, & Lunsky, 2014; Storch et al., 2013). It is interesting to note that ABA holds roots in treating feminine behaviours in young boys using rewards and physical punishments (Rekers & Lovaas, 1974). Years after Rekers and Lovaas's study, a family complained publicly that the treatment, which inhibited their son's ability to express his true identity, caused his eventual suicide (Bronstein & Joseph, 2011). Although ABA has discontinued harsh, aversive practices, the lack of long-term follow-up of mental health and well-being in autistic young people is a concern. It is concerning because the treatment is often intensive (25–40 hours per week outside of school), administered without the young person's consent (Dawson, 2004), and can stifle benign autistic behaviours that represent autistic identity (Kirkham, 2017; Mottron, 2017).

In CYC, the lack of long-term measures to identify young people's sustained self-worth and self-esteem has become a recent critique of evidence-based practices (EBPs) (Stein, 2009). Instead, some have turned attention away from EBP to favour practice-based evidence (PBE), which focuses on the importance of lived experiences and "systematic, ongoing feedback on how we are delivering what works" (Brendtro & Mitchell, 2012, p. 10). As such, Brendtro and Mitchell explain that PBE resists scientific methods that quantify human behaviour in rigid manners that objectify young people. Indeed, Bristow (2015) agrees scientific behavioural methods, such as ABA, hinder practitioners' ability to be relational in building rapport with young autistic people. Bristow explains that in practice, CYCPs are asked to adhere to strict regimens of delivering immediate reinforcements when desirable behaviours have been observed in young people. As a practitioner with over eight years of training in ABA in various settings, I can attest to the rigidness of these reinforcement schedules.

Using ABA methods, practitioners reward young people with edibles, tangibles, verbal praise, and other reinforcements in response to the performance of behaviours that are deemed appropriate. For those who may be unfamiliar with ABA, one way to illustrate how this behaviour management approach unfolds in practice is to compare it to that of training animals—reward good behaviours and extinguish (a.k.a. punish) bad ones. Over the years, I too have carried M&Ms in my pouch in anticipation of rewarding desirable behaviours, while simultaneously attempting to "extinguish" undesirable ones through the use of planned ignoring and other consequences. Only recently have I realized that my well-intentioned efforts at "training" young people in such a way was not only futile, but unethical. Twenty years ago, prolific writers in CYC cautioned practitioners away from the harmful use of compliance (Fox, 1994) and behavioural modification tactics (VanderVen, 1999) aimed to control the actions of young people. These authors warned that such practices inhibit resilience while negating the ethical values embedded in empathetic and relational care. Their writings, among others in our field, have inspired a renewed relational practice that intentionally avoids behavioural modification techniques across many CYC settings.

Although we still have some way to go before eliminating misguided behaviour modification in all CYC settings, at least we have come to a place where many practitioners recognize the value of interventions based entirely on relational care (Stuart, 2013). Unfortunately, however, it seems that this recognition applies to every other CYC sector *except* those supporting autistic young people. As exemplified by Gural and MacKay-Chiddenton's (2016) resource, post-secondary institutions instruct CYCPs to collaborate with ABA, despite its emphasis on behavioural control. Assuming that CYC practice continues to support this population, I propose this question: Are there less intrusive ways to help autistic young people self-regulate, focus, sustain relationships, and achieve goals in ways that challenge oppressive practices? Again, I believe the answer to this is "yes."

INNOVATING RELATIONAL, STRENGTH-BASED PRACTICE TO SUPPORT AUTISTIC YOUNG PEOPLE

My current practice supporting autistic young people is influenced by my education in disability rights, anti-oppressive frameworks, and continued self-reflection into holistic and relational care. Some have claimed CYCPs lack the appropriate and specific training needed to support individuals with developmental disabilities, including autism (Gharabaghi, 2010; Gural & MacKay-Chiddenton, 2016). To some extent I agree with this claim, just not in the way that they mean it. I have come to believe that sound training in rights-based practice and relational CYC characteristics is all that is needed to support autistic young people. I also believe a focus on rights-based relational care through an anti-oppressive lens is critically lacking in CYC training to support all young people, not just those with disabilities (see also Stuart, Snell, & Magnuson, this volume). If this focus were firmly in place, CYC practice would be an excellent alternative to what is currently offered as support to autistic young people. I further hypothesize that such an approach will ultimately benefit autistic young people *more* than any specific or targeted interventions (i.e., ABA), which rely on behavioural management techniques. Considering this, I believe CYCPs *are* lacking in proper training, since so few have boldly admitted to the value of abandoning ABA in favour of rights-based relational practice.

So, what are disability rights and how do they apply to our practice? In Canada, disability rights are protected in two significant ways: through the United Nations *Convention on the Rights of the Child* (UNCRC; United Nations [UN], 1990) and the United Nations *Convention on the Rights of Persons with Disabilities* (CRPD; UN, 2006). Both documents hold society accountable for respecting autistic persons' rights to dignity, autonomy, freedom from discrimination, equal opportunities, accessibility, acceptance of diversity, and effective inclusion within all settings. When we apply this lens to practice, we can see how some aforementioned examples negate important and guaranteed human rights. For instance, how can we protect a young person's right to dignity and freedom from discrimination when we constantly refer to them as disordered? Second, how can we guarantee effective inclusion when we recommend they learn in separate classrooms? Third, how can we respect their right to autonomy when we perpetually control their behaviours through rewards and punishments? When we apply a rights-based lens to our work, it becomes glaringly obvious that deficit-based pathologies and behavioural interventions negate autistic young people's rights on various levels.

In response to pathologized and deficit based views of autism, Judy Singer (2016) coined the term *neurodiversity* in her 1999 doctoral research recognizing autism as an important neurological difference along the spectrum of human diversity. Identifying as an autistic woman herself, Singer used her lived experience to challenge the dominant discourse of autism as a disorder. In doing so, she also expanded on important disability theories, particularly the *social model of disability*, that places the onus on society to find solutions to barriers for disabled persons (Oliver, 2013). Oliver explained that his social model relieves disabled persons of the burden and personal blame stemming from the medical model framework. However, critics argue that the social model is much too simplistic, as it ignores the reality of the biomedical challenges that accompany disability to hinder full participation in society (Shakespeare, 2010). Accordingly, Singer's idea of neurodiversity embraces neurological differences as both a challenge and a necessity to diverse human experiences. I believe this view aligns nicely with our practice, as CYC focuses on the individual needs *and* the strengths of young people.

Since I have begun to apply this theoretical framework and rights-based lens to my practice, I have noticed slight shifts in my relationships with and support of autistic youth. For example, I am more relaxed because I spend less time in the office tallying negative behaviours in order to develop targeted interventions. Instead, I focus on relational moments and building rapport with autistic youth so that I can truly understand their unique way of being in the world. My paperwork focuses mainly around a one-sided goal sheet with goals developed in collaboration with the young person. The rest of my support is consumed by mutual engagement and co-development of skills based mainly on *their* needs (not the needs of the institution). Of course, as Bristow (2017) points out, sometimes caring adults need to make decisions for young people to ensure their safety and well-being. These decisions may be difficult for them to accept but we can always involve them in the process of making these decisions. Ultimately, I have found the majority of goal setting and goal achieving is best done by the young people themselves. Much more of my practice is now spent educating colleagues, teachers, families, and peers about neurodiversity and supportive relationship building with autistic young people.

With this in mind, I think it is beneficial to discuss some characteristics of relational CYC practice as outlined by Garfat and Fulcher (2013). Bristow (2017) has begun this work in her article touching on characteristics within the domains of Being, Interpreting, and Doing.[1] First, Bristow poignantly explains how *being* with autistic young people involves flexibility and individuality. Recently, I returned to practice after an educational leave. My return to participating with students as they live their lives within classrooms has enlightened me to just how important this domain of "being" is. Coming back to some very challenging behavioural dynamics, I have had to channel my ability to respect, hang in, and express love for young people who have so often been told they are disrespectful or need to mature. On my second day back, one of my autistic students asked me why I chose to be a CYW when I have to work with "retards" like them. Knowing that this otherwise funny and engaging young person had a history of using self-deprecating language in response to his own low self-esteem, I responded, "I like my job because I meet awesome students like you every day. I think you are great." The student paused for a moment and then responded, "No one has ever said that to me before." For the next week, I spent extra time getting to know this young person through hanging out and connecting. While walking to class one day (counselling on the go), we discussed how words like "retard" did not represent the incredible diversity of him or his classmates.

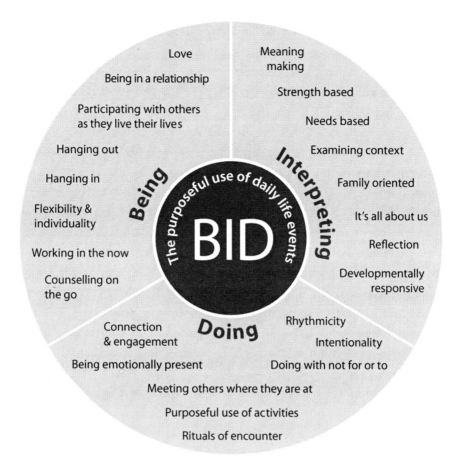

Figure 8.1: Characteristics of a Relational Child and Youth Care Approach

Source: Freeman, J., & Garfat, T. (2014). Being, interpreting, doing: A framework for organizing the characteristics of a relational child and youth care approach. *Child & Youth Care Online, 179,* 23–27. Retrieved from http://www.cyc-net.org/cyc-online/jan2014.pdf. Used with kind permission of the authors.

Within the domain of *interpreting,* Bristow (2017) describes a strength-based CYC approach in supporting resilience, working with families, establishing individual pride, and reflecting on our own personal privilege. To expand even further, "interpreting" allows CYC practitioners to reflect on the underlying *needs* driving behaviours in order to help autistic young people better meet those needs. Coincidentally, a needs-based focus is also considered to be the crux of ABA methods; ABA refers to this focus as defining the "functions" of behaviour (Geneva Centre for Autism, 2015). The distinction between the two approaches is that ABA categorizes the functions of behaviour into four specific groups: (1) attention, (2) sensory, (3) tangible, and (4) escape. Comparatively, I believe the needs-based characteristic of CYC is a more meaningful way to interpret autistic needs. Not only are the ABA groupings rigidly defined using scientific terminology, but I believe they offer a narrow view of the purpose of behaviour. The possibility of alternative reasons for undesirable behaviours is often ignored by ABA practice. For instance, one of ABA's popular responses to address attention-seeking behaviour is planned ignoring and positive praise (praise given when desirable behaviours occur). The philosophy is that undesirable behaviours can be put on "extinction" by ignoring them (Geneva Centre for Autism, 2015). ABA methods do not attempt to discover the deeper systemic reasons autistic young people seek attention, such as a lack of positive attention due to perpetual stigma. A needs-based approach in CYC practice would consider the entirety of a young person's circumstances in order to give *more* attention in response to attention-seeking behaviour in as many positive and creative ways as possible. In this way, a CYC perspective does not consider withholding attention from a young person who so desperately seeks it. Planned ignoring is still widely used in CYC practice. However, I believe that close attention to the BID needs-based approach will become more common as the model gains exposure.

Lastly, Bristow (2017) explains that the domain of *doing* means we connect and engage with autistic young people where they are at by doing things with them, not *for* or *to* them. She explains that this is done through challenging our assumptions as neurotypical adults who do not always know what is best for autistic young people. In the field of psychology, new ideas have emerged that recognize disability as a form of diversity (Dunn & Andrews, 2015). The authors explain that it is the obligation of practitioners to adopt a "cultural competence" when engaging with this population (p. 255). They further explain that respecting a person's choice to view disability as an identity "promotes autonomy, agency, and indicates a decision to exercise choice over one's disability destiny" (p. 257). The same cultural lens fits perfectly within the BID model's realm of "doing." *Rituals of encounter* means that practitioners maintain intentional engagement that acknowledges cultural differences. As Singer (2016) suggests, when we observe autism as cultural difference rather than disorder, mutual encounters become more inclusive of diverse experiences. Through documenting the ideas inspiring CYC rituals of encounter, Fulcher (2003) affirmed that "Conventional wisdom about the care and supervision of young people relies heavily on *normative* theories of child development and interpersonal relations." (p. 19). Thus, the CYC practice of *doing* involves a thorough understanding of one's own cultural biases, including conventional biases related to disability. The surrounding characteristics pertaining to engagement, connection, and rhythmicity depend on this understanding when engaging autistic young people.

LOOKING FORWARD

Although a complete examination of the potential of CYC characteristics, disability rights, and relational practice in supporting autistic youth exceeds the scope of this chapter, I hope this brief introduction inspires practitioners to embrace relational CYC practice as an optimal support for autistic young people across the spectrum. Although we cannot claim that this approach will be evidence-based by scientific behavioural standards, I believe these strength-based approaches will further our research and credibility in practice-based evidence. Looking forward, I would like to see CYCPs adopt a "rights-based" focus to their support of autistic young people. I believe that the incorporation of children's rights and disability rights into the characteristics of CYC would prove to be a valuable advancement of our field. I have heard it argued that this rights-based approach is an overarching lens to our work. However, I believe that this is too easily forgotten in practice.

Furthermore, I would like to see autistic young people's voices amplified in our work. I hope that my recent participatory research (Marshall, 2017b) marks the beginning of this journey, not only for me but for the field of CYC. Listening to young people has allowed me the privilege of transforming my practice over the course of my career. The extent of my continued learning is profound. For example, to conclude my research I stated,

> [My participants'] examples, which spoke to the harmful effects of providing self-regulation and behavioural interventions to autistic youth, caused me to reflect on oppression embedded within my own practices. [The] ability to stand up to bullies, despite adult advice to ignore them, has encouraged me to reflect on the unfairness of teaching emotional restraint to autistic youth versus the benefit of strengthening confident resiliency. In the same way, ... insight into behavioural interventions that negatively impact the physiological and mental wellness of autistic young people, perked my curiosity and skepticism of the touted evidence-based practice of ABA.

So, why should we care to reflect on our relational work *with* autistic young people? Fewster (1990) conceded that "personal vulnerability is the most potent state for all learning" (p. 52). I would have to agree. If it were not for my willingness to admit to and learn from my mistakes, I would not have become the holistic practitioner I am today. I am certain that when CYCPs allow this vulnerability within themselves, compassionate and respectful "autism-informed care" (Wilton, 2017) will form the progressive path to future CYC practice. Autistic young people are here to stay across all CYC sectors. This is what they deserve from us.

I would like to conclude with a special thank you to Falon Wilton for her valuable input into editing this chapter. As an autistic CYC student, Falon's insight was instrumental to both the CYC and autistic perspectives included within.

NOTE

1. The BID diagram can be retrieved from Research Gate: https://www.researchgate.net/figure/308202341_fig1_FIGURE-1-Relational-Child-and-Youth-Care-Characteristics-with-BID-Options-Fulcher.

REFERENCES

American Psychiatric Association (APA). (2013). *Diagnostic and statistical manual of mental disorders: DSM 5*. Washington, DC: American Psychiatric Publishing.

American Psychological Association (APA). (2010). *Publication manual of the American Psychological Association* (6th ed.). Washington, DC: Author.

Autistic Self Advocacy Network (ASAN). (2017). *About autism*. Retrieved from http://autisticadvocacy.org/about-asan/about-autism/

Brendtro, L. K., & Mitchell, M. L. (2012). Practice-based evidence: Delivering what works. *Reclaiming Children and Youth, 21*(2), 5–11.

Bristow, Y. (2015). CYCs and ASDs: A child and youth care approach to autism spectrum disorders. *Relational Child and Youth Care Practice, 202*, 64–66.

Bristow, Y. (2017). BIDing and autism. *CYC-Online, 222*. Retrieved from http://www.cyc-net.org/cyc-online/aug2017.pdf

Bronstein, S., & Joseph, J. (2011). Therapy to change "feminine" boy created a troubled man, family says. *CNN*. Retrieved from http://www.cnn.com/2011/US/06/07/sissy.boy.experiment/index.html

Brown, L. (2012). Identity-first language. *Autistic Self-Advocacy Network*. Retrieved from http://autisticadvocacy.org/identity-first-language/

Brown, L. X. Z. (2017). A note on process. In L. X. Z. Brown, E. Ashkenazy, & M. G. Onaiwu (Eds.), *All the weight of our dreams: On living racialized autism* (pp. viii–x). Lincoln, NE: DragonBee Press.

Busch, L., & Koudys, J. (2017). *Evidence-based practices for individuals with autism spectrum disorders.* Retrieved from http://www.behaviourinnovations.com/sites/default/files/PDF/ONTABA%20OSETT-ASD%20REPORT.pdf

Centers for Disease Control and Prevention (CDC). (2014). *Prevalence of autism spectrum disorder among children aged 8 years—Autism and developmental disabilities monitoring network, 11 sites, United States, 2010.* Retrieved from http://www.cdc.gov/mmwr/preview/mmwrhtml/ss6302a1.htm

Chandrasekhar, T., & Sikich, L. (2015). Challenges in the diagnosis and treatment of depression in autism spectrum disorders across the lifespan. *Dialogues in Clinical Neuroscience, 17*(2).

Chown, N., & Hughes, L. (2016). History and first descriptions of autism: Asperger versus Kanner revisited. *Journal of Autism and Developmental Disorders, 46*(6), 2270–2272.

Dawson, M. (2004). *The misbehaviour of behaviourists: Ethical challenges to the autism-ABA industry.* Retrieved from http://www.sentex.net/~nexus23/naa_aba.html

Donnelly, J. (2001). Reverse mainstreaming: Helps normal children learn about autism. *CYC-Online, 28*. Retrieved from http://www.cyc-net.org/cyc-online/cycol-0501-donnelly.html

Dunn, D. S., & Andrews, E. E. (2015). Person-first and identity-first language: Developing psychologists' cultural competence using disability language. *American Psychologist, 70*(3), 255–264.

Fewster, G. (1990). *Being in child care: A journey into self.* New York: Hawthorn Press.

Fewster, G. (2002). The DSM IV you, but not IV me. *Child & Youth Care Forum, 31*(6), 365–380.

Flanagan, H. E., Perry, A., & Freeman, N. L. (2012). Effectiveness of large-scale community based intensive behavioral intervention: A waitlist comparison study exploring outcomes and predictors. *Research in Autism Spectrum Disorders, 6*(2), 673–682.

Fortunato, J. A., Sigafoos, J., & Morsillo-Searls, L. M. (2007, June). A communication plan for autism and its applied behavior analysis treatment: A framing strategy. *Child and Youth Care Forum, 36*(2–3), 87–97.

Fox, L. (1994). The catastrophe of compliance. *Journal of Child and Youth Care, 9*(1), 1–19.

Freeman, N., & Perry, A. (2010). Outcomes of intensive behavioural intervention in the Toronto preschool autism service. *Journal on Developmental Disabilities, 16*(2), 17–32.

Fucilla, R. (2005). Post-crisis intervention for individuals with autism spectrum disorder. *Reclaiming Children and Youth, 14*(1), 44–51.

Fulcher, L. (2003). Rituals of encounter that guarantee cultural safety. *Relational Child and Youth Care Practice, 16*(3), 20–28.

Garfat, T. (1998). Preparation for the inquiry. *Journal of Child and Youth Care, 12*(1–2), 11–28.

Garfat, T., & Fulcher, L. C. (2013). Characteristics of a relational child and youth care approach. In T. Garfat, L. Fulcher, & J. Digney (Eds.), *Making moments meaningful in child and youth care practice* (pp. 7–29). Cape Town, South Africa: CYC-Net Press.

Geneva Centre for Autism. (2015). *Handouts and transcriptions: Online applied behaviour analysis certificate course for educators.* Toronto: Training Institute, Geneva Centre for Autism.

Gharabaghi, K. (2010). Expansion to what end? *Online Journal of the International Child and Youth Care Network (CYC-NET), 139.* Retrieved from http://www.cyc-net.org/cyc-online/cyconline-sep2010-gharabaghi.html

Gural, D. M., & MacKay-Chiddenton, D. (2016). *Abnormal or exceptional: Mental health literacy for child and youth care.* Toronto: Pearson Canada.

Kanner, L. (1943). Autistic disturbances of affective contact. *Nervous Child, 2*(3), 217–250.

Kirkham, P. (2017). "The line between intervention and abuse"—Autism and applied behaviour analysis. *History of the Human Sciences, 30*(2), 107–126.

Kuhlthau, K., Orlich, F., Hall, T. A., Sikora, D., Kovacs, E. A., Delahaye, J., & Clemons, T. E. (2010). Health-related quality of life in children with autism spectrum disorders: Results from the autism treatment network. *Journal of Autism and Developmental Disorders, 40*(6), 721–729.

Laursen, E. K., & Yazdgerdi, S. (2012). Autism and belonging. *Reclaiming Children and Youth, 21*(2), 44–47.

Marshall, N. (2017a). Child and youth care and disability rights: Listening to young people, challenging our practice. *Relational Child & Youth Care Practice, 30*(2), 55–70.

Marshall, N. (2017b). It's our turn! Autistic young people inform praxis and policy. Unpublished major research paper, Ryerson University, Toronto, Ontario, Canada.

Marshall, N., & Tragni, P. (2015). Successful transitions into mainstreamed high schools for students on the autism spectrum: A child and youth care approach. *Relational Child & Youth Care Practice, 28*(1), 53–62.

Mazurek, M. O. (2014). Loneliness, friendship, and well-being in adults with autism spectrum disorders. *Autism, 18*(3), 223–232.

Mottron, L. (2017). Should we change targets and methods of early intervention in autism, in favor of a strengths-based education? *European Child & Adolescent Psychiatry, 26*(7), 815.

Oliver, M. (2013). The social model of disability: Thirty years on. *Disability & Society,* *28*(7), 1024–1026.

Paquette-Smith, M., Weiss, J., & Lunsky, Y. (2014). History of suicide attempts in adults with Asperger syndrome. *Crisis, 35*(4), 273–277.

Perry, A., Cummings, A., Dunn Geier, J., Freeman, N. L., Hughes, S., LaRose, L., ... & Williams, J. (2008). Effectiveness of intensive behavioral intervention in a large, community-based program. *Research in Autism Spectrum Disorders, 2*(4), 621–642.

Rekers, G. A., & Lovaas, O. I. (1974). Behavioral treatment of deviant sex-role behaviors in a male child. *Journal of Applied Behavior Analysis, 7*(2), 173–190.

Sarahan, N., & Copas, R. (2014). Autism assets. *Reclaiming Children and Youth, 22*(4), 34.

Shakespeare, T. (2010). The social model of disability. In L. J. Davis (Ed.), *The disability studies reader* (pp. 266–273). New York: Routledge.

Shaw, K. (2015). From front line to family home: A child and youth care approach to working with families. In L. Fulcher & T. Garfat (Eds.), *Child and youth care practice with families* (pp. 85–103). Cape Town, South Africa: CYC-Net Press.

Silberman, S. (2015). *Neurotribes: The legacy of autism and the future of neurodiversity* [eBook]. Retrieved from play.google.com

Singer, J. (2016). *Neurodiversity: The birth of an idea* [Kindle edition]. Retrieved from Amazon.com

Stein, J. (2009). Looking beyond evidence-based practice. *CYC-Online, 130.* Retrieved from http://www.cyc-net.org/cyc-online/cyconline-dec2009-stein.html

Stoddart, K. P., Burke, L., Muskat, B., Manett, J., Duhaime, S., Accardi, C., ... & Bradley, E. (2013). *Diversity in Ontario's youth and adults with autism spectrum disorders: Complex needs in unprepared systems.* Toronto: The Redpath Centre.

Storch, E. A., Sulkowski, M. L., Nadeau, J., Lewin, A. B., Arnold, E. B., Mutch, P. J., & Murphy, T. K. (2013). The phenomenology and clinical correlates of suicidal thoughts and behaviours in youth with autism spectrum disorders. *Journal of Autism and Developmental Disorders, 43,* 2450–2459.

Stuart, C. (2013). *Foundations of child and youth care practice* (2nd ed.). Dubuque, IA: Kendall Hunt Publishers.

Successes with Autism. (1999). *CYC-Online, 11.* Retrieved from http://www.cyc-net.org/cyconline/cycol-1299-autism.html

Trieschman, A. E., Whittaker, J. K., & Brendtro, L. K. (1969). *The other 23 hours: Childcare work with emotionally disturbed children in a therapeutic milieu.* New Brunswick, NJ: Transaction Publishers.

United Nations (UN). (1990). *Convention on the rights of the child.* Retrieved from http://www.ohchr.org/EN/ProfessionalInterest/Pages/CRC.aspx

United Nations (UN). (2006). *Convention on the rights of persons with disabilities.* Retrieved from https://www.un.org/development/desa/disabilities/convention-on-the-rights-of-persons-with-disabilities.html

VanderVen, K. (1999). Views from the field: The case against behaviour program point and level systems. *CYC-Online, 3.* Retrieved from http://www.cyc-net.org/cyc-online/cycol-0499-karen.html

Walter, C. (2008). Intensive interaction with autistic children. *Relational Child & Youth Care Practice, 21*(2), 60–70.

Wilton, F. (2017, June). *Autism-informed care: Respecting the spectrum.* Workshop presented at the OACYC Provincial Conference, Toronto, Ontario, Canada.

Wing, L. (1997). The history of ideas on autism: Legends, myths and reality. *Autism, 1*(1), 13–23.

Wing, L., & Gould, J. (1979). Severe impairments of social interaction and associated abnormalities in children: Epidemiology and classification. *Journal of Autism and Developmental Disorders, 9*(1), 11–29.

CHAPTER 9

Queering Gender and Sexuality in Child
and Youth Care

Ben Anderson-Nathe

While gender and sexuality have always been salient features of young people's experiences—and therefore important to relational child and youth care practice—the past 30 years have seen profound shifts in dominant conceptions of each. Increased visibility and social acceptance of both queer sexualities and diverse gender expressions have rendered many old narratives of these phenomena both outdated and limiting in terms of their utility to and for young people. Fixed identity categories are giving way to increased fluidity. Former boundaries around gender and gendered experience are becoming increasingly permeable, and young people employ a new and shifting vocabulary to name themselves and their experiences. Given child and youth care workers' commitment to relational practice and working within the life-spaces of children and youth, CYCs in research and practice would do well to attend to these shifts (see James, this volume; Martin & Stuart, this volume).

   This chapter unpacks trends and themes related to young people's experiences of gender and sexuality over the past 30 years and offers preliminary reflections on how child and youth care workers might respond to some of these transitions. It is not an exhaustive exploration of either sexuality or gender—such is well beyond the scope of any single chapter—and it does not provide a recipe for effective child and youth care practice around gender and sexuality.

Rather, it challenges conventional language and conceptual formulations of gender and sexuality and presents a vision for a more informed and relevant practice in this context.

The proposed vision is one of transformed practice in all the settings and contexts in which CYCs work. Young people's experiences of gender and sexuality are increasingly fluid, yet many CYCs work in institutions and settings that embrace outdated constructions of both (see Gharabaghi & Charles, this volume). This chapter invites CYCs to not only understand the youth with whom they work in ways that might be unfamiliar or challenge some of the orthodoxy with which gender and sexuality have often been presented, but also consider concrete (even if slight) shifts in practice as a result. And practice needs to shift. Youth in residential care continue to state, as evidenced by the Ontario Residential Services Review Panel report (Gharabaghi, Trocmé, & Newman, 2016), that they cannot trust residential facilities to be safe spaces for their gender expressions or queer identities. Queer and trans young people continue to be disproportionately represented among homeless and unstably housed youth. Discipline and therapy referrals in schools continue to follow predictable and problematic gendered patterns. And yet, even in this context, CYCs are positioned to improve practice to be more inclusive of more critical and fluid negotiations of gender and sexuality. CYCs in residential care, for instance, are invited to think more critically about the taken-for-granted (and heteronormative) practice of room assignments based on sex. After-school child and youth care workers can interrogate their use of "boys will be boys" justifications for rowdiness and "girls are just catty" interpretations of relational violence among peers. In their professional documentation, CYCs can ask young people how they choose to be named in terms of pronoun, acronym, and other identity markers—and then push their institutions to allow for this flexibility. The breadth of CYCs' possible critical engagement with young people around gender and sexuality is staggering; this chapter offers a foundation for some of that engagement.

EXPANDING GENDER

Across youth service sectors, there has long been widespread recognition of gender's significance to young people's social experiences and identity. Often, however, this recognition has resulted in grouping young people by gender (male/female) and providing services based on each of these gendered groups' presumed needs. Relying on what Lesko (2001) has called "confident characterizations" of young people, one of which categorically groups young people together and names them as excessively peer-oriented, attention to gender in youth services has often consisted of sweeping generalizations about how boys and girls differ in their interests and needs from one another but share monolithic and hegemonic gendered experiences. Gender has been rendered a fixed demographic characteristic defined by assumedly shared attributes. Put differently, gender-specific programming has attended only marginally to the process or experience of gender *itself* and more to essentialized understandings of what boys need, what girls need, and how these needs differ.

Since the early 1990s, feminist scholarship and activism have attempted to recast gender from an assignment based on sex (male or female) to a set of negotiated interactions with and performances of masculinities and femininities (e.g., Butler, 1990). Lorber (1994) suggested that "individuals are born sexed but not gendered, and they have to be taught to be masculine or feminine" (p. 325) among often shifting social circumstances. Gender is understood in this context not as a fixed identity with assumed characteristics that both are shared within the group and differentiate it from other groups, but rather as an "unfolding performance of social expectation" (Anderson-Nathe, Gringeri, & Wahab, 2013, p. 287). It is a process rather than a status, and the context in which this process unfolds is central to understanding how gendered identities and experiences ultimately take shape. To illustrate, boys raised in environments that prize competition and strength learn early on that they must perform aggressive masculinities in order to be accepted as suitably masculine. By contrast, girls growing up in collectivist cultures where reproductive labour is both praised and expected are likely to perform femininities that celebrate co-operation and relational caregiving over personal desire. Understanding gender as a contextual process or set of negotiations positions those attributes (cooperation or competition, for instance) as responses to environmental demands rather than biologically rooted, sex-linked traits.

Carrie Paechter (2007) has written of these shifting gendered contexts in terms of communities of gendered practice, in which children are both actively and passively taught by more established members of a community how to not only perform their own gender(s), but also interact with people of different genders. Communities of gendered practice employ many mechanisms to teach these gendered expectations, often in rigidly segregated settings, such as Pascoe's (2007) description of how heterosexual boys use "fag" as a tool—almost exclusively among themselves—to regulate performances of masculinity in spite of their assumptions of their peers' sexualities. Armstrong and colleagues (2014) depicted a similar use of "slut" as a practice employed by young women to police gender and sexuality of other women. These communities of gendered practice police gender transgressions and reward conformity.

Mainstream youth-serving institutions and systems, however, have been reluctant to take up this interpretation of gender, working instead from a standpoint in which *gender* and *sex* are effectively interchangeable terms. In this context, *boy* and *girl* are often treated as immutable categories with essential and presumably universal characteristics, and programming then responds to or relies upon the taken-for-granted acceptance of these characteristics. These reified categories, boy and girl, differentiate *between* groups of young people and attribute observed differences to a single characteristic of gender (e.g., boys are competitive, while girls are relational), at the same time that they reinforce dominant and hegemonic attributions *within* those gendered groups (e.g., *all* boys are competitive, and *all* girls are relational, *because* they are boys and girls).

For instance, asserting that schools must take gender into account in their curriculum, instruction, and discipline, Gilliam (2015) invoked a common refrain that relies entirely upon dominant characterizations of gender: "girls like sitting and listening for long periods of time, while many boys feel tortured. Boys need more hands-on activities, with movement and exploration, for their learning to flourish" (p. ix). In this characterization, boys are presented as universally active and explorative, while girls are constructed as passive observers of their environments. It is perhaps no accident, then, that children's conduct on the playground is interpreted in ways that punish non-conformity. Girls who like to direct their friends' activity get called "bossy," where their male peers are rewarded for their "leadership" qualities for the same behaviour.

Likewise, from its inception, the juvenile corrections system has been dominated by similar thinking about the criminal behaviours of boys and girls: Girls' offending behaviour was attributed to immoral sexual behaviour or (primarily relational) mental health concerns, while criminality among boys presumably resulted from individual deviance and oppositional attitudes (Miller, Anderson-Nathe, & Meinhold, 2014). These perspectives allow little room for boys or girls whose experiences do not conform neatly to either interpretation. Further, juvenile corrections and secure placements for young men often, even unintentionally, teach compliance with the very same set of masculine behaviours and ideologies (competition, independence, isolation, stoicism) that contributed to their criminal behaviour in the first place (Abrams & Anderson-Nathe, 2013).

Lastly, considering young people in the mental health system, diagnostic patterns such as greater propensity for depression among girls and conduct disturbances among boys have long been attributed to dominant notions of how boys and girls function differently in the world: Boys simply are active and potentially violent/dangerous (which explains their oppositional or explosive conduct), while girls are principally relational and internally focused (and therefore internalize stressors). Of course, this too translates into practice. Girls are more often assigned to group modalities than are boys, based on a fundamental assumption that girls are relational in a way boys are not. Likewise, practitioners' socialized belief that girls self-harm while boys assault other people may render the boy in care with a (well-hidden) history of cutting or eating disorders even more invisible and underserved. In all these cases, gender as a process, performance, or negotiation between individual young people and their social contexts disappears in favour of adherence to an oversimplified binary and its associated gendered expectations.

The past decade has ushered in important shifts in the social experience of gender. Increased visibility—albeit sometimes problematically sensationalized, such as in the recent media treatments of Laverne Cox and Caitlyn Jenner—of transgender people and others whose gender identities or expressions complicate a male-female binary has sparked broad conversation about the utility of gender as a social organizer. This conversation has emerged across a wide range of contexts, ranging from financial and medical concerns (to what extent does health insurance cover hormone therapies and other medical procedures for transgender people?), to politically and emotionally charged practical considerations (use of restroom facilities in public schools, for instance), to linguistic and philosophical questions of pronoun use and the future of binary gender systems.

The recent case of a University of Toronto professor's stated refusal to use non-gendered or preferred pronouns illustrates how contentious and destabilizing gender can be. In response to Bill C-16, which would amend Canada's Human Rights Act to include gender identity and expression as protected statuses, this professor has remained steadfast in his refusal to adopt gender-neutral pronouns, citing freedom of speech and resistance to what he and others view as a militant movement towards "political correctness." Opposition and support for the professor in this case are equally ardent and striking—as is the larger national conversation around gender Bill C-16 has introduced. These examples, even down to the commonplace but simultaneously controversial practice of inviting people to state the pronouns they use for themselves during an introduction, are active reflections of the depth and salience of gender's changing role. They point not only to conservative efforts to re-entrench gender as a fixed category aligned with sex, but also to the personal and social consequences of failing to embrace gender diversity.

Given this shifting context and the associated tensions, it is more critical than ever before that child and youth care workers begin to reconceptualize gender and gender-specific programming. Clearly, services and interventions designed for hegemonic performances of "boy" and "girl" fail transgender, genderqueer, and gender non-conforming young people altogether. But equally important are the experiences of those young people who may *not* identify as transgender but nevertheless also do not perform their gender congruent with social expectations based on their assigned sex. Thinking back to Gilliam's (2015) depiction of boys as universally active and exploratory, school personnel seeking to respond to these boys must also attend to those boys who do *not* demonstrate these characteristics. Likewise, girls who exhibit strength, confidence, and leadership cannot be sidelined by services that reinforce dominant notions that "good girls" are cooperative, relational, and kind (adjectives that seldom arise in reference to boys' programming). Further, insistence upon essentialized gender constructs fail even those young people who conform to them; by reinforcing a limited range of gendered possibility, hegemonic gender stereotypes restrict exploration, fluidity, and acceptance of alternatives. Taken together, these experiences contradict hegemonic gendered expectations, call into question the male-female gender binary, and open the potential for gender specific programming that focuses on both performances of gender as it is lived by individual young people and the social contexts in which those performances unfold.

QUEERING SEXUAL ORIENTATION

The past 30 years has also been a period of profound transformation in the social and academic attention paid to queer[1] young people. Beginning in the 1980s, research began emerging in the academic literature, seeking to document the existence of queer (then, predominantly gay and lesbian) youth; describe their personal problems, psychosocial development, and peer and family relationships; and offer guidance to professionals seeking to work with them in educational and service settings (D'Augelli & Grossman, 2006). Most of this research and associated practice wisdom, however, presented queer youth as fundamentally vulnerable or at-risk and constructed the queer young person as a work-in-progress rather than a person possessed of self-determination or agency. Indeed, queer young people were painted in the academic literature almost exclusively as victims of misfortune; their experiences were cast in the context of pain and adversity. Literature abounded over the next 20 years to document queer young people's rates of homelessness, substance abuse, familial disruption and rejection, isolation, mental illness, physical and sexual risk-taking, and suicide (Talburt, 2004a).

Also during this time, queer young people's identity formation became of interest in the research and practice communities. Developmental stage models articulated a process for queer identity formation, and while these models were not originally specific to young people, they scaffolded well onto an existing literature base that suggested queer youth were uniquely isolated and at-risk. Perhaps the most well known of these (Cass, 1984; Troiden, 1989) took as a starting point that queer identity development begins with a sense of difference or isolation from one's peers. Moving through that sense of difference and its associated confusion, the models posited that queer people ultimately come to first tolerate and then accept their sexuality in spite of the negative associations it brings (stigma, isolation, and the like). After acceptance comes a period of pride in one's sexual identity, but healthy development within these models is predicated on leaving identity pride and moving into synthesis, in which sexuality is just one (certainly not the defining) feature of a person's total experience. Further, while Troiden in particular stressed that "homosexual identity is emergent: never fully determined in a fixed or absolute sense" (1989, p .68), both models stress that the successful resolution of these developmental milestones is signalled by "commitment to an identity and role" (Talburt, 2004b, p. 118). In this sense, while the meaning of a homosexual identity may shift, commitment to that discrete identity marker is nevertheless central to accomplished development.

Linking together the research literature on queer young people's fundamental at-risk status with models of queer identity development was the cultural trope of coming out of the closet. Coming out was the quintessential coming-of-age experience for queer youth (Talburt, 2004a), essential for eventual healthy development but also fraught with complexity and risk. For many, coming out meant risking rejection and outright violence, and almost uniformly, it reflected an understanding of queer orientation as fixed and immutable. The coming out experience was one of declaration; naming oneself gay or lesbian meant staking a clear claim to identity, not only to attraction or sexual behaviour. This declaration put queer people—youth included—in an untenable situation, wherein they were expected to claim an identity that was understood within the queer community and in the broader conventional wisdom to be characterized by pain, suffering, victimization, and targeting. Still, coming out was the only available pathway to fulfilled adulthood. From Cass's (1984) and Troiden's (1989) developmental standpoints, it was critical to the formation of both identity and community, and paradoxically, it both increased the risk of victimization and, by virtue of a person's willingness to come out in spite of the risks, constituted the opposite of that victimization (Talburt, 2004b).

Taken together, these three constructs (the association between queerness and risk or pain; models that construct healthy development in the context of fixed identities; and a coming out practice that declares adherence to that fixed identity) comprised a narrative of queer young personhood that Rofes (2004) has called the martyr-target-victim model. Over the past 30 years, this model has become the ascendant and dominant narrative structuring queer young people's lives. Youth are either noble martyrs because of their willingness to risk all in order to come out and stake their claims to identity; or targets because of the homophobia and heterosexism they encounter by virtue of that identity marker; or victims of isolation, substance abuse, suicide and the myriad of other "at-risk" conditions. The recently popular It Gets Better Project, in which queer people—generally though not exclusively adults—recorded videos of themselves sharing stories of how life for them improved once they were no longer queer youth, is an example of the dominance of this martyr-target-victim model. The videos presume a condition of loneliness and isolation for queer youth, coupled with a profound lack of agency on the part of the young people themselves; the best wisdom most videos offer is the recommendation that young people simply hold on and wait until their conditions change. In essence, they are told they should endure the condition of their victimization as noble martyrs, with the understanding that things will, in time, "get better."

Contrasting the characterization of queer youth as fundamentally at-risk or victimized, a new construct of the queer young person has emerged over the last decade. Drawing on the popularity of positive youth development and a nascent emphasis in the research literature on resilience rather than risk alone among queer youth (Russell, 2005), researchers and practitioners are now paying a new type of attention to queer young people who thrive despite all odds. This new queer young person is significant in a number of ways. First, the young person who thrives in spite of the at-risk status and "issues" confronting queer youth becomes noteworthy for refuting the taken-for-granted association between queer

youth and suffering. In other words, the resilient youth is the remarkable excep-
tion to the rule; they do not, in general, call the rule into question. And second,
the markers of resilience, of queer youth having "made it" out of the martyr-
target-victim frame, render young people more like their (straight) peers than
different from them. Driver (2008) attributes this to liberal notions of tolerance,
suggesting that far from asserting the agency of self-determination, for queer
youth, "empowerment becomes a sign of fitting into familiar and nonthreaten-
ing models of identity and belonging.... Within such paradigms, queer youth
become valued and supported as long as they don't challenge the status quo by
looking or acting too queer" (p. 50).

In both cases, whether constructed as victims or conversely as remarkable
survivors of former victimhood, queer youth are considered by the literature and
practice communities as a largely homogenous group, linked together by their
claimed identity as queer and the associated assumed experiences of marginalization and pain (even as they may develop different responses to those experiences).
Practice interventions and approaches to queer youth reflect this homogenous
grouping and acceptance of the taken-for-granted conditions of isolation and
pain that accompany it. Forming youth support groups, for instance, is a common
refrain among youth serving organizations—often with the stated premise that
queer youth experience such profound isolation that what they need more than
anything else is other queer people with whom to belong. Gay/Straight Alliances
(GSAs) are the common response to experiences of victimization and harassment
in school settings, in which young people transform themselves from victims or
targets into youth leaders. Common across Canada and the US, GSAs have in
fact become so ubiquitous that in 2015, Alberta's Progressive Conservative government passed legislation requiring all schools in the province to allow such a
club if even a single student requests it. However helpful these responses may be
to individual young people, what they miss overall is an appreciation that young
people's experiences of sexuality are shifting in ways that complicate both notions of sexuality as a fixed marker of identity and the existing tropes of queer
young personhood.

Savin-Williams (2005), for instance, has suggested that contemporary queer
youth may be moving away from a limited range of fixed identity categories
related to their sexualities. Instead of staking immutable identity claims, young
people may be more inclined now than in previous generations to articulate their
attractions and sexual behaviours as just those: attractions and behaviours. The
need for finite identity markers may be fading for young people, as gender and

other binary categories come under greater public scrutiny. Just as young people are increasingly comfortable transgressing cultural norms related to gender (challenging the male-female gender binary, embracing genderqueer and transgender identities, and the like), so are they complicating conventional understandings that same-sex attractions or behaviour must result, ultimately, in a same-sex oriented identity. As Robertson (2014) articulates, however, being less attached to discrete "mono-sexuality" does not suggest that queer youth have detached from identity or from labels. Instead, she argues that identity may matter to young people even more than before, as evidenced by a proliferation of sexual identity labels (e.g., queer, pansexual, demisexual, open, and others, among the more conventional and traditionally legible gay, lesbian, straight, and bisexual). What has shifted, however, is the rigidity of boundaries surrounding these identities and their presumed fixed status; queer youth continue to adopt identity labels to name their genders and sexualities, but these labels are increasingly flexible in significance and durability.

Perhaps due to this increased flexibility and permeability in the labels queer youth choose and what those labels do (and do not) signify for them, the lives of contemporary young people contradict the superstar-or-victim tropes that have dominated their representations in the past. In her (2009) ethnography of rural queer cultures, for instance, Gray relates the experiences of rural queer youth, whose social circumstances certainly predispose them to the trope of the isolated, victimized queer young person, but instead routinely host unsanctioned late night drag shows at the local Walmart. Far from the monolithic victim presented in the literature, but equally far from the GSA community organizer and youth leader, these young people are simply carving out new spaces and ways in which to negotiate sexuality.

RECOMMENDATIONS FOR RESEARCH AND PRACTICE

Given that much contemporary child and youth care practice, and possibly even more the institutional contexts in which CYCs work, relies on outdated conceptualizations (gender-specific programming that reinforces essentialized characterizations of boys and girls, and queer-specific interventions that reinscribe either the martyr-target-victim or GSA superstar tropes for queer young people), the time has come for a shift in approach for child and youth care workers. Conceptions of gender and sexuality are in flux, trending towards less fixed constructions of immutable identity categories (e.g., of male and female, of gay and straight) and instead towards greater attention to how young people navigate fluid interpretations of gender and sexuality within and across their social contexts (Horn, Kosciw, & Russell, 2009).

Here, I join others (Horn, Kosciw, & Russell, 2009; Rofes, 2004; Russell, 2005) in calling for increased research into the normative experiences of queer young people, destabilizing the traditional emphasis on individual pain and pathology on the one hand and young gay superstardom on the other. It is, of course, critical that scholars and practitioners understand and appreciate how stigma and harassment lead many queer youth to negative behavioral, social-emotional, and mental health outcomes. But it is equally important that we focus scholarly attention on those features of queer young people's lives that are affirming, or at least simply normative. This shift in perspective is essential, lest we continue to restrict the range of viable self-images for queer young people to those illustrated by Rofes' (2004) martyr-target-victim model. Further, expanding the range of queer youth "issues" to include romance and dating, falling in love, experiences of supportive family and peers, social media, and recreational or extracurricular activities provides child and youth care workers seeking to support queer youth with a broader perspective of what those youth might be bringing to the therapeutic relationship. In other words, research literature that paints a picture of queer youth beyond simply pain and pathology may help child and youth care workers to see the queer youth in their programs with greater complexity and nuance than they might previously have done.

Similarly, child and youth care practice must also expand, placing young people's lived experiences of gender and sexuality in the foreground. This new approach calls for an intersubjective orientation to work with young people, such that youths' complex lived experiences of gender and sexuality—rather than or before the taken-for-granted dominant narratives of each—guide intervention and professional response. Gharabaghi (2008) has written of the pitfalls child and youth care workers encounter when they attempt to apply what he refers to as "objective" approaches to their practice. While applying interventions that "ought to work" based upon some pre-existing interpretation of a young person's demographics, group memberships, age, or other characteristics may be grounded in research and therefore defensible (on the surface), the unintended consequence is that these approaches negate the specific young person's individual experiences. In contrast, an intersubjective orientation to practice recognizes that the young person's interpretation of self and need are as central to the relationship as are the worker's taken-for-granted interpretations or biases. Holding both worker and young person in complex interaction with one another invites CYCs to inquire about the young person's experience before—and possibly rather than—moving forward with practice interventions that seem "obvious" based on our (often partial or flawed) professional knowledge.

Working from a relational practice perspective requires no less; young people must be supported to name and negotiate their identities on their own terms. In order to support this navigation, child and youth care workers will do well to approach their work with young people from a phenomenological orientation—attentive less to the (limited) tropes of "queer youth" or "boy" or "girl" and more to the nuance and subtlety of how each young person in their care names their own experiences of gender and sexuality. Relational practice requires that child and youth care workers interrupt their own hegemonic interpretations or expectations related to gender and sexuality and instead roll with young people's identity fluidity. Illustrating this fluidity, Regales (2008) relates how one young person, Izz, articulated the complexity of gender and sexuality:

> "I've concluded that my identity is fluid as fuck. Sometimes I feel like a femme fag, sometimes like a butch dyke, sometimes like a cocky teenage boy, sometimes like a girly girl. And those are only the binaries I inhabit, there are so many more feelings I can't yet articulate." (p. 88)

Izz's depiction of fluidity presents an invitation for child and youth care workers to lean in, seeking the interpersonal in-between (Garfat, 2012) of relational practice. Where traditional practice with queer youth might have resulted in Izz being encouraged to stake a clear and fixed identity claim (both to gender and orientation), it may be more useful for youth workers to resist their impulse to label and instead seek to understand more from Izz about the fluidity and complexity itself.

The practical implications are vast. If Izz were in residential care, embracing this fluidity would likely require re-evaluation of a program's policies related to sex-segregated room assignments. The assumptions nested in such practices (e.g., of assumed heterosexuality or fixed and binary gender expectations) are called into question by gender expressions that so directly contradict them. In schools, CYCs might need to be particularly vigilant to observing how Izz's gender expressions may be both, or subsequently, stigmatized and embraced by peers. In this description, Izz defies coming out and developmental narratives that position fixed identity as the hallmark of developmental maturity; it stands to reason, then, that Izz may benefit from school staff and peers who are willing to hold space for this exploration and flux rather than implicitly expecting conformity and stability in gender or sexual identity. In health and sexual health settings, Izz's presentation of fluidity may require workers to ask more questions about health concerns and associated behaviours without making assumptions about physical anatomy or sexual health risks.

In all cases, Izz's gendered experience and gender identity demand of CYCs that they position themselves interrogatively, inviting Izz to name a location in a galaxy of gendered expressions at any given time and with full recognition that one expression may exist today and shift tomorrow. In complicating orthodox binary gender constructs, CYCs and others must be careful not to simply rein-scribe "trans" or "gender non-conforming" as another fixed point on a hypothetical continuum.

What holds these recommendations together is an urgent call for CYCs (in research and practice) to interrupt hegemonic binaries and taken-for-granted characterizations of gender and sexuality. I have written elsewhere (Anderson-Nathe, Gringeri, & Wahab, 2013) that categorization itself is not problematic; humans are capable of taking in stunning amounts of stimulus, and we need systems of categorization to help us make sense of all that data. Categories and grouping of like observations help us make quick interpretations of our experiences and are useful in shaping future action; this is the heart of the hermeneutic cycle. But it is critical to keep these categories tentative and their resulting interpretations or expectations partial. Once-fixed binaries of gender (e.g., male/female or masculine/feminine) and characterizations of queer youth (martyr-target-victim) have come under increased scrutiny in recent years, and young people's lived experiences have revealed these constructs to be fragile, unreliable, and limiting. As Rasmussen (2004) has suggested, historical conventions for reading these binaries and the labels that signal them must be revised and held open for future revision. As child and youth care workers, in order to fully embrace our commitment to relational practice and walking respectfully alongside young people, we must dedicate ourselves to interrogating these categories for their fit, hearing the experiences and self-identifications of the young people with whom we work, and being willing to replace or reject our taken-for-granteds altogether.

NOTE

1. I use *queer* throughout this chapter in two deliberate ways. First, queer has emerged since the 1990s as a broad marker of those sexual orientations, identities, and expressions that do not benefit from the "normalized" status of heterosexuality. In this spirit, and because queer is increasingly the term used by many lesbian, gay, bisexual, Two-Spirit, trans, and other youth to name themselves, I use queer as well. Further, as articulated by RECLAIM, a Minneapolis-based mental health support program for queer and trans youth, "for many youth in our communities, the term LGBTQ … is a label that has been put on them, while the terms 'queer' and 'trans' are chosen and preferred" (www.reclaim.care/). Second, I use queer as a verb, to indicate the act of deliberate transgression of status quo and taken-for-granted assumptions: queering the gender binary, for instance, or queering conventional characterizations of lesbian and gay youth as fundamentally at-risk and fraught.

REFERENCES

Abrams, L., & Anderson-Nathe, B. (2013). *Compassionate confinement: A year in the life of Unit C.* New Brunswick, NJ: Rutgers University Press.

Anderson-Nathe, B., Gringeri, C., & Wahab, S. (2013). Nurturing "critical hope" in teaching feminist social work research. *Journal of Social Work Education, 49*(2), 277–291.

Armstrong, E. A., Hamilton, L., Armstrong, E. M., & Seeley, J. L. (2014). "Good girls": Gender, social class, and slut discourse on campus. *Social Psychology Quarterly, 77*, 100–122.

Butler, J. (1990). *Gender trouble.* New York: Routledge.

Cass, V. (1984). Homosexual identity formation: Testing a theoretical model. *The Journal of Sex Research, 20*, 143–167.

D'Augelli, A., & Grossman, A. (2006). Researching lesbian, gay, and bisexual youth: Conceptual, practical, and ethical considerations. *Journal of Gay & Lesbian Issues in Education, 3*, 35–56.

Driver, S. (2008). *Queer youth cultures.* Albany, NY: State University of New York Press.

Garfat, T. (2012). The inter-personal in-between: An exploration of relational child and youth care practice. In G. Bellefeuille, D. Jamieson, & F. Ricks (Eds.), *Standing on the precipice: Inquiry into the creative potential of child and youth care practice* (pp. 7–34). Edmonton: Grant MacEwan Press.

Gharabaghi, K. (2008). Values and ethics in child and youth care practice. *Child & Youth Services, 30*, 185–209.

Gharabaghi, K., Trocmé, N., & Newman, D. (2016). *Because young people matter: Report of the Residential Services Review Panel.* Toronto: Ministry of Children and Youth Services.

Gilliam, L. (2015). *The seven steps to help boys love school.* Lanham, MD: Rowman & Littlefield.

Gray, M. (2009). *Out in the country: Youth, media, and queer visibility in rural America.* New York: New York University Press.

Horn, S. S., Kosciw, J. G., & Russell, S. T. (2009). Special issue introduction: New research on lesbian, gay, bisexual, and transgender youth: Studying lives in context. *Journal of Youth and Adolescence, 38*(7), 863–866.

Lesko, N. (2001). *Act your age!: A cultural construction of adolescence.* New York: Psychology Press.

Lorber, J. (1994). "Night to his day": The social construction of gender. In M. Adams, W. Blumenfeld, C. Castañeda, H. Hackman, M. Peters, & X. Zúñiga (Eds.), *Readings for diversity and social justice* (3rd ed., pp. 323–329). New York: Routledge.

Miller, K. M., Anderson-Nathe, B., & Meinhold, J. (2014). Gender, racially, and culturally grounded practice. In W. T. Church, D. W. Springer, & A. R. Roberts (Eds.), *Juvenile justice sourcebook* (2nd ed., pp. 581–603). New York: Oxford University Press.

Paechter, C. (2007). *Being boys, being girls: Learning masculinities and femininities.* Maidenhead, UK: Open University Press.

Pascoe, C. J. (2007). *Dude, you're a fag: Masculinity and sexuality in high school.* Berkeley, CA: University of California Press.

Rasmussen, M. (2004). "That's so gay!": A study of the deployment of signifiers of sexual and gender identity in secondary school settings in Australia and the United States. *Social Semiotics, 14*, 289–308.

Regales, J. (2008). My identity is fluid as fuck: Transgender zine writers constructing themselves. Albany, NY: State University of New York.

Robertson, M. (2014). "How do I know I am gay?": Understanding sexual orientation, identity and behavior among adolescents. *Sexuality & Culture, 18*, 385–404.

Rofes, E. (2004). Martyr-target-victim: Interrogating narratives of persecution and suffering among queer youth. In M. Rasmussen, E. Rofes, & S. Talburt (Eds.), *Youth and sexualities: Pleasure, subversion, and insubordination in and out of schools* (pp. 41–62). New York: Palgrave Macmillan.

Russell, S. (2005). Beyond risk: Resilience in the lives of sexual minority youth. *Journal of Gay and Lesbian Issues in Education, 2*, 5–18.

Savin-Williams, R. (2005). *The new gay teenager.* Cambridge, MA: Harvard University Press.

Talburt, S. (2004a). Intelligibility and narrating queer youth. In M. Rasmussen, E. Rofes, & S. Talburt (Eds.), *Youth and sexualities: Pleasure, subversion, and insubordination in and out of schools* (pp. 17–40). New York: Palgrave Macmillan.

Talburt, S. (2004b). Constructions of LGBT youth: Opening up subject positions. *Theory into Practice, 43*, 116–121.

Troiden, R. (1989). The formation of homosexual identities. *Journal of Homosexuality, 17*, 43–73.

CHAPTER 10

Child and Youth Care Practice in the Context of Deaf Communities

Shay Erlich

In this chapter, I will explore some of the core themes and issues relevant to child and youth care practice in Deaf communities. At the outset, it is important to state that while the chapter will not highlight intersectionality as a central focus, Deaf young people must of course be approached with an intersectional lens. Aside from Deafness, young people may identify as Trans (see James, this volume), autistic (see Marshall, this volume), or LGBTQ2S+ (see Anderson-Nathe, this volume). Furthermore, there is a high correlation between Deafness and additional disabilities (Gallaudet Research Institute, 2011), so approaches that incorporate both a disability justice as well as Deaf culture lens may be required.[1] Their racial and migration backgrounds may further add to their intersectional identities and social locations.

Child and youth care practice often sees itself as a "talking profession," with emphases on relational practices, life-space interventions, and mutual engagement. Such concepts and ideas are as relevant when working in the Deaf community as they are in the hearing community, but there clearly are themes and issues to account for when trying to bring child and youth care concepts to life in work with Deaf young people, their families, and their communities. In this chapter, I will provide both cultural and logistical contexts that child and youth care practitioners must consider, and I will explore ways in which the barriers associated with Deafness can be understood as largely socially constructed and embedded in societal structures and processes. In this way, I will highlight the challenges associated with thinking about child and youth care practice in Deaf communities, while also presenting a hopeful and encouraging framework for being with Deaf young people and supporting their development.

THE DEAF COMMUNITY

The Deaf community is a diverse group of people with a wide range of experiences, united by the common experience of hearing loss. Deaf community members can have hearing loss anywhere on the audiological spectrum from mild to profound, as these labels are typically only used by medical professionals rather than the Deaf community. Deaf community members may use hearing technology such as hearing aids, cochlear implants, or FM systems in order to make use of whatever hearing they have, or pick up on environmental cues, whereas others may choose not to use these technologies. Some members of the Deaf community may use sign language (such as American Sign Language or ASL in English-speaking North America), whereas others may use Signed English systems, and others still may prefer to speak, lip-read, and make use of captioning to communicate. Members of the Deaf community may choose to identify in several ways. Some may identify as Deaf, which is often used to signify an identification with Deaf culture and a preference for sign language use. Others may identify as Oral Deaf, which is often used to signify a person who prefers to lip-read, use captioning/notetaking when necessary, and speak or write to communicate. Others still may identify as Hard of Hearing, which is often used to signify less severe levels of hearing loss (though not always) or a partial identification with Deaf culture, and communication preferences within this group can vary widely. Many people in the Deaf community reject terms such as hearing impaired or deaf-mute and consider them derogatory; however, some people continue to use these terms for their identity, and that should be respected. The Deaf community also includes family members of those who have hearing loss. CODA/KODA refers to Child/Kid of a Deaf Adult, and describes a person who has a Deaf parent or parents, and SODA refers to a Sibling of a Deaf Adult.

It is difficult to estimate exact numbers of the Deaf community in Canada (Canadian Association of the Deaf, 2015). Globally, approximately 5 percent of the world's population is impacted by hearing loss (du Feu & Chovaz, 2014).

Within developed countries that number can be significantly higher, reaching up to 16 percent of the population with any kind of identifiable hearing loss (including mild hearing loss) (Barclay & Yuen, 2017; du Feu & Chovaz, 2014). In Ontario, the Infant Hearing Program (2016) estimates that approximately 4 in 1,000 babies are born Deaf or Hard of Hearing, and further numbers of young people lose their hearing after birth, due to a variety of causes. Therefore, the Deaf community makes up a significant subset of the population in Canada.

DEAF CULTURE

Members of the Deaf community may also identify themselves as being culturally Deaf. Culturally Deaf individuals understand Deafness as a cultural and linguistic difference rather than a disability (Anderson, Wolf Craig, & Ziedonis, 2017a). While medical models of deafness ascribe the challenges that the Deaf community faces to their hearing loss, the Deaf community instead attributes these challenges to a society that utilizes oral/aural communication systems, rather than visual communication systems (Barclay & Yuen, 2017; Lane, Hoffmeister, & Bahan, 1996). The Deaf community believes that when communication is provided accessibly through visible means such as sign languages, there are no barriers to their participation in society (Lane et al., 1996). Furthermore, Deaf culture is distinct and different from hearing (non-Deaf) culture. Within Deaf culture, sign language is the preferred form of communication. Deaf culture has particular cultural value systems and behaviour norms, including the behaviours that one uses to get another's attention (Lane et al., 1996; Leigh, 2009). For example, in non-Deaf culture, most of the time when we wish to get someone's attention we speak their name or attempt to speak louder than the noise in a room to gain the occupant's attention. Within Deaf culture one might tap the person they wish to speak to on the shoulder if they are close by, or wave their hand up and down gently in their direction if they are farther away. A room full of people might be addressed by flicking the lights on and off slowly. Within the Deaf community, urgency is expressed through speed—the faster a gesture, tap, or light-flicking, the more urgent the situation. Deaf culture also has behavioural norms, such as prioritizing face-to-face contact (including the use of video technology) over other forms of communication, and prioritizing information sharing. Deaf culture also has its own unique art forms such as De'VIA (Deaf View Image Arts), ASL poetry, and

ASL rap (Anderson et al., 2017a; Lane et al., 1996). For many Deaf people, including Deaf young people, a strong association with the Deaf community and Deaf culture is one of the most important aspects of their identity.

Unlike many other marginalized communities that child and youth care practitioners may encounter, the Deaf community does not have a particular geographical area of origin; Deaf young people and Deaf family members of young people may be encountered anywhere. While historically many Deaf young people were sent away to residential schools for the Deaf (which existed in nearly every province in Canada; SDHHS, 2018), in recent years registration at these schools has declined and many schools in North America have shut their doors due to low enrollment as more parents choose to educate their children in neighbourhood schools or partially self-contained programs for Deaf and Hard of Hearing students in their local school board (Lane et al., 1996; Leigh, 2009). However, to this day, residential schools for the Deaf continue to exist, and in many cases thrive throughout the world. It is important to note that the Deaf community has a different relationship to residential schooling than the Indigenous community does. As the Deaf community lacked a geographical hub for their community and a Deaf young person may have been the only Deaf person they knew before attending school, residential schools became both a site of cultural oppression and abuses as well as a space for cultural transmission (Lane et al., 1996). In 1880, there was an international gathering of Deaf education professionals in Milan, Italy, which has come to be known as the Milan Conference (Lane et al., 1996). At this conference, primarily hearing educators (there was one Deaf delegate among more than 160 attendees), who were known to favour oralist methods (preferring speaking and listening), determined that the best way to educate Deaf young people was through oral methods rather than sign language, which was a decision that would impact Deaf education internationally for the next 100 years (Lane et al., 1996). Subsequently, the vast majority of schools for the Deaf, which in North America had previously been using sign language, converted to oral teaching methods, and signing was banned for students (Lane et al., 1996). However, while students were banned from using sign languages in the classroom, peer-based learning continued unabated (Lane et al., 1996). Therefore, while students experienced oppression and distance from their cultural identity in their daily experiences of education, schools for the Deaf were also the place where they learned about their culture and experienced a sense of belonging. As a result, many Deaf people remember their experiences at schools for the Deaf fondly, rather than as a site of violence and harm (Lane et al., 1996). Currently, schools for the Deaf teach using a bi-lingual, bi-cultural (bi-bi) model. This was adopted in the mid-1990s and refers to a teaching style that prioritizes fluency in sign language and Deaf culture, while also focusing on written literacy in the hearing community language and understanding differences between Deaf and hearing cultures (Lane et al., 1996). However, ongoing issues of hearing paternalism exist within Deaf schools, where there is a continued fight for Deaf leadership within schools and at the superintendent level (Stevenson, 2015).

COMMUNICATION

Working as a child and youth care practitioner with a Deaf young person or Deaf family member(s) requires paying particular attention to communication. Central concepts in child and youth care practice such as relationships, engagement, and caring cannot be present in the absence of communication. Practitioners must be aware of the range of communication needs within the Deaf community. Early communication choices for Deaf young people are made primarily by their parents. Ninety percent of Deaf young people are born to hearing parents who have often had no exposure to the Deaf community prior to the birth of their child (du Feu & Chovaz, 2014; Edwards & Crocker, 2008; Lane et al., 1996). These parents often depend on guidance from a medical system that emphasizes cures, interventions, and "normalcy" (Lane et al., 1996; Humphries et al., 2016). Often parents are encouraged to attempt to utilize a child's residual hearing through hearing aids or cochlear implants, along with specialized supports for speech and listening as a first attempt to address a child's hearing loss (du Feu & Chovaz, 2014; Lane et al., 1996). Even today, many cochlear implant programs oppose, and even ban, the use of sign language with young people who have cochlear implants, due to the fear that it may cause delays in spoken language acquisition (Hall, 2017; Humphries et al., 2016). However, much research shows that having early access to an accessible (signed) language can in fact facilitate spoken language and second language development (du Feu & Chovaz, 2014; Hall, 2017; Humphries et al., 2016).

Many professionals in the Deaf community advocate for a sign language–first environment, where Deaf young people are exposed to sign language as their first language, and sign is then used to teach additional languages such as written English (du Feu & Chovaz, 2014). Often times audism—a word which describes the barriers and discrimination that Deaf people face on both an individual and systemic level (Lytle, Oliva, Ostrove, & Cassady, 2011)—creates a situation where a young person may be struggling with language acquisition for many years in an oral/aural environment before the young person is allowed to use sign language (du Feu & Chovaz, 2014; Edwards & Crocker, 2008; Humphries et al. 2016). This can result in a young person missing the critical language learning window and suffering from language delays, which can impact their development and mental well-being throughout the lifespan (du Feu & Chovaz, 2014; Edwards & Crocker, 2008; Hall, 2017; Humphries et al., 2016). du Feu and Chovaz (2014) point out that while neither speech and listening nor the use of sign language are inherently better than the other, one is much more likely (sign language) to be consistently accessible to a Deaf young person. Ultimately the most important thing to consider in communication choices for a Deaf child is the appropriateness of the fit of the chosen approach with a particular child. This means that whether spoken language or sign language is chosen, the child's language acquisition should be measured against age-appropriate developmental benchmarks, and if the child is not meeting these milestones intervention should begin early, including a switch in language modality if necessary (du Feu & Chovaz, 2014). Humphries and colleagues (2016) recommend that social service practitioners become adept at recognizing signs of linguistic neglect and recognize it as a form of child maltreatment due to the severity of the consequences that can result from this form of neglect.

When young people utilize ASL or another sign language as their preferred form of communication, it is essential that they are not the only ones in their family or school who are able to use ASL (du Feu & Chovaz, 2014). Often, young people are the only ones in their family to become fluent in ASL, while their parents may have some rudimentary ASL skills. These skills are not enough for the young person to develop meaningful relationships within their families due to communication barriers (du Feu & Chovaz, 2014). This can lead to increased stress and strain on familial relationships (Brown & Cornes, 2015; Zaidman-Zait & Dotan, 2017). In fact, Lytle and colleagues (2011) estimate that only 4 percent of Deaf young people have access to a consistent communication model at home or at school. Young people who do not have access to consistent communication are particularly at risk of isolation and depression and increased stress due to communication difficulties (Lytle et al., 2011; Zaidman-Zait & Dotan, 2017). This further underscores the need for ensuring not only that young people have access to the language modality that is the best fit for them, but also that their entire community is able to communicate with them using that modality. For example, Sheridan (2011) suggests that schools be responsible for providing opportunities for students and staff alike to learn sign language so that a Deaf young person attending can be included in the social life of the school.

Therefore, CYC practitioners must be aware of the context that communication and language preferences will have on every aspect of interaction with a Deaf young person. Care must be taken to determine a young person's communication preferences at first contact (or prior to the first in person contact if possible) and develop a plan to ensure that a young person's preferred approach to communication is possible at all times during work with them. Without clear, consistent communication, any intervention attempted with a young person will fail (du Feu & Chovaz, 2014). Additionally, any attempt at assessment must be carried out using a young person's preferred communication methods, otherwise the results of such assessment will be invalid, as it will be difficult to discern whether the issue is with a communication mismatch or if there are other underlying difficulties the young person is experiencing (du Feu & Chovaz, 2014). Additionally, an understanding of how cultural differences between Deaf and hearing young people will impact a clinician's assessment is important (Barclay & Yuen, 2017). Once communication has been established, relationships can form where a young person can be engaged in deciding how to move forward.

ECOLOGICAL RESPONSES

When working within the Deaf community, it is important to differentiate between situations that require an individual response with the young person or when an ecological response that recognizes the systems a young person exists within as a site of intervention is required. Society views Deafness as a "disadvantage, deficit or risk" (Sheridan, 2011, p. 230). Deaf people are often asked to overcome this deficit by being able to adapt to hearing norms, customs, and behavioural standards, rather than asking settings to reframe Deafness as a natural part of the human experience, and helping the setting to become inclusive of Deaf people who may be present (Sheridan, 2011). This ought to be recognizable to child and youth care practitioners who are familiar with working from an ecological perspective, recognizing the value of identifying the environment as a site of change, rather than the child.

The notion of resilience in the Deaf community being defined as a young person being able to adapt to hearing norms is challenged by Young and colleagues (2008, as cited by Lytle et al., 2011): "For deaf children and young people, the successful navigation of being deaf in a world that faces them with countless daily hassles and which may commonly deny, disable or exclude them, is a key definition of resilience" (p. 255). Sheridan (2011) extends this even further, contending that the majority of systems that Deaf young people interact with lack a fundamental literacy in the Deaf community, and instead expect Deaf people to adapt to their norms. Sheridan (2011) posits that when systems become literate in the needs of Deaf young people to best support their development, Deaf young people are able to thrive in environments that are respectful of their cultural, social, and emotional well-being and needs.

This means that CYC practitioners must challenge themselves to look to the environment first for clues about interventions for a Deaf young person. For example, a practitioner doing family work with a Deaf young person and their family would want to look for opportunities to observe natural communication between family members and determine whether family members are able to communicate with each other effectively (if the family uses sign language and the practitioner is not fluent, this will need to be done with input from interpreters, which will be covered later in this chapter). Families may communicate using a non-standardized language system, or have minimal communication without having an interpreter present. This could provide several clues about potential interventions with this family to better support the young person.

For example, one potential intervention would be arranging for the family to have an opportunity to improve their signing skills so that there could be better communication between family members on an ongoing basis. Another potential intervention that could take place within school, community, or other group settings would be to have a class learn about Deaf people who have made significant contributions to the areas they are studying. An ongoing commitment to ensuring that Deaf content is represented in the curriculum allows Deaf young people to see people like them as successful and making important contributions to society. This is a stark contrast to the societal messages they receive that Deaf people are less than non-Deaf people. Another intervention may be ensuring that educators have appropriately high standards for the Deaf students that they work with, rather than assuming that their hearing loss precludes high academic achievement (Sheridan, 2011).

With the many systemic barriers that Deaf young people face, it is important that CYC practitioners are constantly aware of the need to act as advocates for the young people that they work with. Deaf young people are particularly vulnerable to having their human rights violated. For example, Deaf young people experience significantly higher rates of abuse than hearing young people (Anderson, Wolf Craig, Hall, & Ziedonis, 2016; Anderson et al., 2017a; du Feu & Chovaz, 2014; McDonnall, Crudden, LeJeune, & Steverson, 2017). Deaf young people with developmental disabilities experience the highest rates of abuse and neglect (du Feu & Chovaz, 2014). This places an onus on practitioners to ensure that appropriate supports and care are provided when a young person discloses experiences of abuses or violations of their rights.

Additionally, having access in all areas where Deaf young people live their lives is a continual challenge. With a lack of accessible communication in the Deaf community there is significantly reduced access to incidental learning (Anderson et al., 2017a; Anderson, Wolf Craig, & Ziedonis, 2017b; Brown & Cornes, 2015). Lytle and colleagues (2011) discuss the difficulties that Deaf young people have in having access in "fourth" environments, which are places where people go outside of school or work to hang out and socialize. Within the Deaf community there is a sign for the experience of being surrounded by hearing people and being completely left out of the conversation, which is described as follows:

> Imagine two Pac-Man icons; made with your two hands facing each other, snip, clip, chomping away but not going anywhere. They just face each other and chomp. Now, take those Pac-Man-facing-each-other chomping hands and move them around in a stirring-the-cauldron kind of movement. There, you have—"people blabbing and blabbing all around and as usual I don't have a clue what they are talking about." (Lytle et al., 2011, p. 257)

This sign is often used to describe things such as big family gatherings or school, work, or social events where the majority of people attending are hearing. It is a sign that often expresses feelings of frustration and isolation. One key role that CYC practitioners can take as an advocate when working with the Deaf community is working to increase access to social and recreational spaces where a Deaf young person wants to participate and support these spaces in becoming truly inclusive.

INDIVIDUAL RESPONSES

While interventions with systems will always be an important component to working with Deaf young people, often a combination of systemic and individual interventions will be required. There are high rates of identified mental health difficulties in the Deaf community, with prevalence rates ranging from 40 to 60 percent depending on the study (du Feu & Chovaz, 2014; Edwards & Crocker, 2008). It is estimated that in the United States, over 5 million people who are Deaf require mental health services each year, yet only 2 percent of this population are able to receive appropriate mental health care (McDonnall et al., 2017). One difficulty of determining accurate rates of mental health difficulties in the Deaf community is that those who are assessing mental health difficulties must be aware of the variation in normative behaviours between the Deaf and hearing communities (Barclay & Yuen, 2017; du Feu & Chovaz, 2014). For example, a common grammatical marker in ASL is furrowing one's brow, which can have several meanings based on context. It can be used as a question marker, or even to indicate that one is confused or uncertain about the information they just received. However, to non-signers a furrowed brow can be a sign of anger, displeasure, or aggression. Therefore, when practitioners are unfamiliar with the Deaf community, it is crucial that they involve others who do have familiarity with the Deaf community as part of the treatment team to help determine when a young person is behaving in normative ways for a Deaf young person or if there is potentially a concern that needs to be addressed.

Individual responses to concerns that Deaf young people have will often look similar to responses to concerns that non-Deaf young people have, but they must occur within a context of Deafness. This requires working to understand the ways in which Deafness contextualizes both the identified problem as well as potential pathways to solutions. For example, a Deaf young person reports that they feel anxious in social situations. Upon investigating this anxiety with the young person, it is discovered that they feel particularly anxious when they interact with hearing people, but this anxiety is also present when they are interacting with Deaf people. In this situation, there are multiple pathways to intervening both systemically and individually. The young person may individually require psychoeducation about anxiety to understand what they are experiencing. In fact, the Deaf community has reduced health literacy due to little health care information being available in sign language, and often requires psychoeducation as a starting point for mental health care (Anderson et al., 2017a; Anderson et al., 2017b). They may also require support in developing their confidence.

The Deaf individual should not be the only point of intervention in this example. The groups of hearing people that they are interacting with may also require interventions to become more Deaf-literate and remove some of the burden of communication from the Deaf young person. These types of interventions are described above.

Finally, the young person may want to first work on addressing their social anxiety with the Deaf community, where it may feel safer, before working on it with their hearing peers. This is an example of how an intervention takes into account the role that Deafness plays in both forming the difficulty the young person has as well as providing potential avenues for addressing this difficulty.

A strength-based, resiliency-focused approach recognizes that Deaf young people require a solid sense of their Deaf identity and a social group of peers who have similar lived experiences (Listman, Rogers, & Hauser, 2011; Lytle et al., 2011). Therefore, when working with a Deaf young person who is struggling with identity formation, one essential intervention may be to ensure that they have access to a peer group of Deaf young people, where they can see themselves, and where there is the chance to work on developing an identity as a Deaf young person. This may require that organizations develop the capacity to host such a group if one does not currently exist within their local community. Additionally, providing opportunities for mentorship and for Deaf adults to be used as role models can be another critical intervention to support Deaf identity development.

PRACTICAL CONSIDERATIONS

A central point repeatedly stressed throughout this chapter is that when working with Deaf young people, it is essential to create an environment where there is constant access to communication before expecting any intervention plan to be successful. Therefore, CYC practitioners and agencies must be proactive in determining their approach to providing support to Deaf young people before there is a request to provide accessible services. There is a shortage of mental health practitioners who sign, as well as a lack of policy that creates provision for access for Deaf and Hard of Hearing clients (Anderson et al., 2017a; Anderson et al., 2017b; McDonnall et al., 2017). It is essential that practitioners and agencies recognize that it is not enough to provide sign language interpretation upon request, nor is it sufficient to consider accessibility at points where a client or family member may come into contact with an agency (Barclay & Yuen, 2017). In fact, Barclay & Yuen (2017) suggest:

> To work with Deaf and hard of hearing people, a practitioner should be (a) linguistically competent in American Sign Language (ASL) or the preferred language or communication modality of their client, (b) culturally competent on Deaf culture and Deaf community issues, and (c) trained in clinical assessment, diagnosis, and intervention with this very unique population. (p. 182)

Furthermore, there is a need for both Deaf and hearing practitioners who are fluent in sign language as some Deaf people prefer to work with Deaf practitioners, and others prefer to work with practitioners who are not members of the Deaf community due to concerns about confidentiality and gossip (Anderson et al., 2017b).

Additionally, in child and youth mental health, it is a common practice in North America for agencies to list only a phone number as the contact information for potential clients to contact the agency due to concerns about digital communications. However, for a Deaf parent who is concerned about their child's well-being or a Deaf young person who wishes to self-refer, this kind of contact information is not very useful and they would be unable to access the agency for information about services or to initiate a referral. This could be remedied by having a monitored general email where Deaf clients were able to get in touch with the agency. Another example would be to consider the experience of an in-patient hospital stay through the eyes of a Deaf young person, who may not be provided an interpreter at all or only have one for a small portion of the day.

Consider the experience of being in a significant crisis that required hospitalization and having minimal access to communication while being in a setting that is supposed to provide support and stabilization. This is particularly absurd for a young person whose experiences of being isolated and having few people they can communicate with easily are a contributing factor to the crisis they are experiencing (which is a common source of stress for Deaf people; Anderson et al., 2016; Zaidman-Zait & Dotan, 2017). In providing inaccessible services, practitioners run a significant risk of re-traumatizing young people that they are working with. In fact, Anderson and colleagues (2016) suggest that for the Deaf community, a severe lack of communication at home, school, or in medical settings, and physical/verbal punishment for signing at oral Deaf schools and bullying were all significant sources of trauma. In this case, at a minimum a young person in an in-patient unit would require access to sign language interpretation at all times during their stay. The best accommodation in this situation would be to utilize staff who were fluent in sign language and familiar with Deaf culture and to encourage others staying on the unit and non-fluent staff to learn some basic sign language so that there is the opportunity to have some communication with others beyond one or two staff who may have been brought in temporarily and are not completely familiar with how the unit operates.

These examples demonstrate that while interpreters are likely to be the first accommodation that practitioners think of when working with a Deaf young person, there are in fact multiple approaches to creating accessible environments and that creating an environment that is accessible and welcoming often requires more thought than simply working with interpreters. Organizations and individual practitioners need to carefully think through every step that a young person or family must go through in order to access or participate in services, identify potential barriers for Deaf young people, and work proactively to resolve them. It is important not to assume that this work is not required by an agency because they have never had (or have very few) requests to provide accessible services. In fact, given the prevalence of Deafness, having few requests to provide accessible services can be an indication that there are barriers that are preventing young people/families from requesting access to services that they need.

WORKING WITH INTERPRETERS

Another practical consideration for CYC practitioners working within the Deaf community is learning how to use sign language interpreters effectively. This requires both an understanding of sign language interpretation as a process as well as understanding the role of a sign language interpreter in child and youth care settings. A sign language interpreter is a hearing person who is professionally fluent in both the spoken language as well as the sign language that is being used in the conversation. Sign language interpreters attend to what is being said (orally or visually) and translate from the language of the original message into the other language (Humphrey & Alcorn, 2007). This allows a Deaf person and a hearing person who would not ordinarily be able to communicate with each other to communicate clearly. Interpreters aim for message equivalency between the two languages they are interpreting rather than aiming for word equivalency (Humphrey & Alcorn, 2007). This means that whatever is said in the source language might be a little different than what the interpreter produces in the target language but the message should be the same. This is done because spoken and signed languages have vastly different sentence structures and grammar. Interpreters will interpret everything that is said and everything that is signed in their presence. This is done to ensure that everyone has full access to all the communication that is going on in their presence.

When working in CYC practice settings, it is best to consider the interpreter as a member of the service provision team with an important role and the ability to offer significant insight into what is occurring with a Deaf client (du Feu & Chovaz, 2014). While assessment, intervention, and ongoing service provision fall outside the scope of an interpreter's expertise, working in partnership with an interpreter can help a clinician gain a fuller understanding of a Deaf client, which will support them in their role. Interpreters can help provide context for any culturally relevant information for a practitioner, such as any context regarding a client's affect (Humphrey & Alcorn, 2007). Non-signing practitioners are not likely to have an understanding of what a depressed affect can look like in a young person's signing and how that differs from typical sign language. Interpreters can also help to ensure there is no miscommunication or misunderstandings about cultural norms in the Deaf community that could potentially impact assessment or understanding of the client.

Additionally, CYCs are encouraged to meet with an interpreter in advance of each contact with the Deaf young person to review the goals of each encounter and address any particular interpreting concerns (du Feu & Chovaz, 2014). For example, if the practitioner intended to assess a young person's self-harming behaviour, the practitioner might wish to share the exact questions that they intend to ask with the interpreter prior to their meeting, especially if there are particular reasons for the wording they are utilizing, as the practitioner and interpreter should work together to determine the best way of presenting this information to the client to ensure the most equivalent interpretation. As practitioners, the language choices that are made with clients are often quite intentional to uncover particular pieces of information or to avoid bias or leading people to particular responses. Therefore, care must be taken to ensure that an interpretation accomplishes the same goals, even if they are approached differently.

Finally, after the meeting with the young person, practitioners and interpreters are also encouraged to debrief the encounter jointly (du Feu & Chovaz, 2014). Interpreters can provide the practitioner with any culturally relevant observations or any struggles they had with interpreting particular portions of the meeting. If it was a particularly intense meeting, practitioners may wish to check in with the interpreter afterwards as well. It is important to note that the interpreter is considered part of the team, so the client could experience a transference relationship with the interpreter as well that would need to be addressed (du Feu & Chovaz, 2014).

Additionally, as practitioners it is important to be aware of situations where a Deaf interpreter would need to be utilized with Deaf clients. A Deaf interpreter is a culturally Deaf person who is fluent in sign language and works with Deaf people who have non-standard language use (du Feu & Chovaz, 2014). Deaf interpreters are used in a variety of situations. Deaf interpreters are frequently used when a person has an additional disability that interferes with their ability to produce signs in a standard way, or when their cognitive abilities require more simplified or concrete language, or when someone is a newcomer and has not yet learned the local sign language (Humphrey & Alcorn, 2007). Deaf interpreters may also be used when a Deaf person has been language deprived and uses non-standard sign language to communicate (Humphrey & Alcorn, 2007). Deaf interpreters are also often used with children and in situations where the accuracy of the information is of vital importance (e.g., health care settings, court or legal interpreting, or child abuse investigations; Humphrey & Alcorn, 2007). Deaf clients report that having a mental health practitioner who is willing to work with Deaf interpreters when necessary is a facilitator to accessing mental health treatment (Anderson et al., 2017b).

Deaf interpreters often work in teams with hearing interpreters. The hearing interpreter will convert the spoken language message into sign language, and the Deaf interpreter will attend to the message and create a signed message that is understandable to the Deaf person who requires a Deaf interpreter. They then will attend to the response from the Deaf person, translate that message into standard sign language, and the interpreter will translate that message into the spoken language. This process can take considerably more time than standard interpretation and is often done consecutively rather than simultaneously. Unless all persons in the situation are fluent in standard sign language, Deaf interpreters must work with hearing interpreters as otherwise they are unable to access the spoken language messages.

CONCLUSION

The Deaf community is a cultural and linguistic minority group, much like many other marginalized communities that CYC practitioners may encounter over the course of their careers. While Deafness adds another layer of context to the difficulties that young people are experiencing, it is not always the primary concern that young people have and it is important that a young person's cultural identity as Deaf not overshadow other important concerns such as abuse, neglect, depression, or anxiety. While Deafness can play a role in many of those concerns, it is up to individual practitioners to determine the role that Deafness plays in the particular issues a young person is experiencing at that point in time in partnership with the young person, being aware that the role of Deafness may ultimately be minimal or profound. However, despite the need for this analysis, working within the Deaf community does not require a fundamental shift away from CYC practice principles. When working within communities that include Deaf young people, practitioners need to ensure that their work with these communities is inclusive, not only from a practitioner to young person perspective, but also from the perspective of striving to create an optimal developmental environment. This means that as much attention needs to be paid to how young people are able to interact with each other in a practice setting as is paid to how a young person might benefit from the activity that the practitioners were initiating. The Deaf community often lacks spaces where the fourth environment is accessible, and providing access to peers and support for peers and family members to become fluent in sign language to foster relationships can be a profoundly powerful intervention. Creating communities where Deaf people are represented, respected, and included is a fundamental part of ecological practice with Deaf young people. Furthermore, CYC practitioners, consistent with CYC principles, are encouraged to recognize Deaf young people as the experts in their own lives, respecting their preferred approaches to communication and their perspective on how Deafness impacts their lives and the difficulties that they are facing. Practitioners ought to work in partnership with young people in developing the approach they will take in addressing the difficulties that young people experience, as young people are powerful guides in what will and won't work for them and how they would like to be included in various interventions. Ultimately, practitioners must remember that within the Deaf community, resilience is demonstrated by maintaining a strong sense of identity and pride in one's self as a Deaf individual. This is the case in spite of the dominance of the audist world that presents barriers and seeks to discredit or render this identity invisible (Lytle et al., 2011). The focus of CYC practice with Deaf young people ought not to be on "overcoming" their hearing loss. Taking a resiliency-based approach to work with Deaf young people includes ensuring they are connected to Deaf peers and the broader Deaf community, including Deaf adults who can act as role models. Practitioners must act as advocates and networkers to ensure these necessary supports are in place. With appropriate supports and developmental opportunities, Deaf young people will become confident and capable, able to advocate for themselves and prepared to take on the challenges they will continue to face throughout their lives.

NOTE

1. The Deaf community typically identifies as related to but separate from the disability community, despite human rights laws pertaining to disability classifying it as such. This paper utilizes the term *additional disability* to signify the dual recognition of Deafness as connected to but separate from other disabilities.

REFERENCES

Anderson, M. L., Wolf Craig, K. S., Hall, W. C., & Ziedonis, D. M. (2016). A pilot study of Deaf trauma survivors' experiences: Early traumas unique to being Deaf in a hearing world. *Journal of Child & Adolescent Trauma, 9*(4), 353–358.

Anderson, M. L., Wolf Craig, K. S., & Ziedonis, D. M. (2017a). Barriers and facilitators to Deaf trauma survivors' help seeking behavior: Lessons for behavioral clinical trials research. *Journal of Deaf Studies and Deaf Education, 22*(1), 118–130.

Anderson, M. L., Wolf Craig, K. S., & Ziedonis, D. M. (2017b). Deaf people's help seeking following trauma: Experiences with and recommendations for the Massachusetts behavioral health care system. *Psychological Trauma: Theory, Research, Practice, and Policy, 9*(2), 239–248.

Barclay, D., & Yuen, F. (2017). Introduction: Clinical and community practice with Deaf and hard of hearing people. *Journal of Social Work in Disability Rehabilitation, 16*(3/4), 181–185.

Brown, P. M., & Cornes, A. (2015). Mental health of Deaf and hard of hearing adolescents: What the students say. *Deaf Studies & Deaf Education, 20*(1), 75–81.

Canadian Association of the Deaf. (2015). *Statistics on Deaf Canadians.* Retrieved from http://cad.ca/issues-positions/statistics-on-deaf-canadians/

du Feu, M., & Chovaz, C. (2014). *Mental health and Deafness.* New York: Oxford University Press.

Edwards, L., & Crocker, S. (2008). *Psychological processes in deaf children with complex needs. An evidence-based practical guide.* London, UK: Jessica Kingsley Publishers.

Gallaudet Research Institute. (2011). *Regional and national summary report of data from the 2009–10 annual survey of Deaf and Hard of Hearing children and youth.* Washington, DC: GRI, Gallaudet University. Retrieved from http://research.gallaudet.edu/Demographics/2010_National_Survey.pdf

Hall, W. C. (2017). What you don't know can hurt you: The risk of language deprivation by impairing sign language development in deaf children. *Maternal and Child Health Journal, 21*(5), 961–965.

Humphrey, J., & Alcorn, B. (2007). *So you want to be an interpreter?* (4th ed.). Seattle, WA: H & H Publishing Company.

Humphries, T., Kushalnagar, P., Mathur, G., Napoli, D. J., Padden, C., Rathmann, C., & Smith, S. (2016). Avoiding linguistic neglect of deaf children. *Social Services Review, 90*(4), 589–619.

Infant Hearing Program. (2016). *Hearing.* Retrieved from http://www.children.gov.on.ca/htdocs/English/earlychildhood/hearing/index.aspx

Lane, H., Hoffmeister, R., & Bahan, B. (1996). *A journey into the DEAF-WORLD.* San Diego, CA: Dawn Sign Press.

Leigh, I. W. (2009). *A lens on deaf identities.* New York: Oxford University Press.

Listman, J., Rogers, K., & Hauser, P. (2011). Community cultural wealth and deaf adolescents' resilience. In D. H. Zand & K. J. Pierce (Eds.), *Resilience in Deaf children—Adaptation through emerging adulthood* (pp. 278–298). New York: Springer New York.

Lytle, L. R., Oliva, G. A., Ostrove, J. M., & Cassady, C. (2011). Building resilience in adolescence: The influences of individual, family, school, and community perspectives and practices. In D. H. Zand & K. J. Pierce (Eds.), *Resilience in Deaf children—Adaptation through emerging adulthood* (pp. 251–277). New York: Springer New York.

McDonnall, M. C., Crudden, A., LeJeune, B. J., & Steverson, A. C. (2017). Availability of mental health services for individuals who are Deaf or Deaf-Blind. *Journal of Social Work in Disability & Rehabilitation, 16*(1), 1–13.

Saskatchewan Deaf and Hard of Hearing Services (SDHHS). (2018). *Canadian Deaf schools.* Retrieved from http://sdhhs.com/list-of-resources/canadian-deaf-schools/

Sheridan, M. A. (2011). Whose literacy is it, anyway? Strengths-based guidelines for transforming the developmental environments of Deaf children and adolescents.

In D. H. Zand & K. J. Pierce (Eds.), *Resilience in Deaf children—Adaptation through emerging adulthood* (pp. 229–249). New York: Springer New York.

Stevenson, V. (2015, November 9). Protestors say school appointment is tone deaf. *Toronto Star.* Retrieved from https://www.thestar.com/yourtoronto/education/2015/11/09/ protesters-say-school-appointment-is-tone-deaf.html

Zaidman-Zait, A., & Dotan, A. (2017). Everyday stressors in deaf and hard of hearing adolescents: The role of coping and pragmatics. *Journal of Deaf Studies and Deaf Education, 22*(3), 257–268.

CHAPTER 11

Post-Secondary Education as a Crucible for Learning Practice

Carol Stuart, Heather Snell, and Doug Magnuson

Post-secondary education is very much a part of the evolving landscape of practice in the field and, conversely, has had a significant influence on shaping that landscape. The experience of post-secondary education in child and youth care (CYC) would ideally immerse students in the values, relationships, activities, and purposes of child and youth care practice as an everyday experience. Students would be engaged in transformational learning guided by relational practice values and integrated with traditional academic purposes. Implementing these ideals in higher education is as challenging as it is in CYC practice (see Gharabaghi & Charles, this volume). While aspiring to these ideals, faculty members become part of the field of practice and education becomes one of many possible settings for a career in child and youth care. As with many other settings described in these chapters, post-secondary education is fraught with challenges and there is great potential for change. This chapter begins with a brief exploration of the historical context of professional programs generally and child and youth care particularly, followed by a discussion of the characteristics of some CYC post-secondary programs and the challenges that exist within the setting. We then consider the potential of post-secondary education as a practice setting.

HISTORICAL CONTEXT OF PROFESSIONAL EDUCATION

In the late 19th and early 20th centuries, professional education in social work, education, and nursing was usually located in professional schools. For example, the early teachers' colleges had only one purpose, to educate teachers, and they were also functioning elementary and high schools in which teacher/students immediately began the practice of teaching. The experience of learning to teach and the experience of being a student in post-secondary education were woven together. During the first half of the 20th century, as professional education became more specialized, professional schools were integrated into universities and colleges, and as higher education focused increasingly on research, learning the theory of teaching was separated from the experience of teaching (Sarason, 1986, 1997).

In the mid-20th century, social work in Canada and the US increased efforts to professionalize, and one consequence was that post-secondary education in social work adopted management, casework, and clinical counselling as professional tracks and gradually abandoned group work and some training in direct practice. By the 1960s, group work was a rare discipline in social work (Carson, Fritz, Lewis, Ramey, & Sugiuchi, 2004). This created a vacuum and an opportunity for youth work and child and youth care. CYC practitioner training moved into colleges and universities in the late 1960s and early 1970s as a result of lobbying by professional associations and employers who desired a stable workforce with consistent knowledge and skills capable of caring for young people with significant emotional and behavioural concerns. Academics, often from a professional background, began to explain the work of CYC and define its identity as well as create a framework for career progression that included faculty members as both members of the child and youth care profession and as academics.

In Canada, several important historical events/trends originated in the early 1970s. The Child Care Workers Association of Ontario (CCWAO) was active in both petitioning for a regulatory college in 1974 and creating the first college programs in "child care work" in 1976. In British Columbia, a degree program in Child and Youth Care was established in 1972 at the University of Victoria, and in Alberta the college system began to establish "youth development" programs in 1972. In the United States, programs were established in several states with titles that were recognizably youth work.

Some common themes in these early efforts were that (1) the impetus for education came from the practice arena, (2) the question of vocation (college-based skills and knowledge) or profession (university-based theory and knowledge) was constantly present, and (3) in the absence of a clearly articulated theoretical foundation for the field of practice, the philosophies of social pedagogy[1] and therapeutic science struggled against each other. Further, educators and leaders in the field made decisions about the scope of practice that are still debated. Where one is located may determine what one thinks about the work and whether practice includes children, youth, adults, persons with disabilities, and all young people or only those with emotional or behavioural concerns (see, for example, Marshall, this volume; Erlich, this volume). It also determines which professional settings are included and excluded.

On moving into higher education, child and youth care shared a perspective on children, youth, and families with other disciplines in the social sciences, arts, and humanities. The philosophical struggle between the orientation of the pedagogue and the applied science of human behaviour made theories of education and psychology most relevant to child and youth care. In Canada programs were usually established with a unique identity and departmental title.

Early faculty in the post-secondary institutions came from management and the research and evaluation arms of agencies. Early theoretical influences included the humanistic personal growth movement of the time, such as the t-group and humanism—including Carl Rogers (Rogers, 1961), Lewin's ideas about life-space (Bargal, Gold, & Lewin, 1992), and applied behavioral science (Skinner, 1953; Bandura, 1977). The practice-based orientation to changing the behaviour of young people that faculty brought to the educational institutions emphasized self-reflection, self-awareness, experiential education, and transformational learning for students.

In 1990 the North American Consortium of Child and Youth Care Education Programs was formed and worked on defining core content for programs in both the United States and Canada. Initially, this consortium was interested in accreditation of educational programs; however, defining a philosophy and set of theoretical perspectives within the field as a basis for practice and education became a priority. The orientation they developed moved away from behavioral science and used an interactional/interpersonal perspective to educating child and youth care practitioners that considered the work to have at least four elements: caring as an interpersonal process; the importance of context and the interactions within the milieu; therapeutic interventions; and indirect elements (Krueger, 2002). Further work by this group defined a scope of practice statement, an international code of ethics, and a set of competencies expected of graduates from an educational program. The influence of other disciplines was added as theory and perspective changed and included ecological perspectives (Bronfenbrenner, 1979) from psychology; social justice and cultural competence from social work; and critical, political perspectives from around the world (e.g., Banks, 1990; Davies, 1976; Freire, 1990).

As the struggle for legitimacy and identity went on amongst practitioners and academics in the field, the faculty in college and university programs attempted to create and maintain a unique learning environment that focused on praxis: the integration of theory and application to practice through reflection on self and action. The goal of most CYC programs was that the core principles of change and methods of working with young people and families in practice became the basic tools of educating young people into the profession. In this respect, CYC in higher education was returning to principles of professional schools in the 19th century, integrated with more modern understandings of how to learn to do professional work that were touted in allied fields, like education.

HOW POST-SECONDARY *IS* A PRACTICE SETTING

Since CYC post-secondary programs were originally created in response to the demands of professional practice, it is not surprising that these programs are steeped in the characteristics of CYC practice. Contemporary student experience is still shaped by historical values such as an emphasis on qualities of relationships, with the goal of transformational learning. Whether college or university based, most CYC programs seek to be intentional, relationship based, developmentally responsive, reflexive, contextual, and strength-based (Garfat & Fulcher 2012). These qualities match the widely shared, if not universal, characteristics of CYC practice.

Educational programs aim to support student learning through scaffolded experiences with guided praxis (reflection, learning, and action) as a strategy linking self, knowledge, and practice from one course to the next. CYC education seeks to be congruent with the practice principle of meeting others where they are at (Krueger, 2000). Furthermore, CYC program standards (Ministry of Training, Colleges and Universities, 2014) include outcomes that "give conscious thought to the ways in which [students and faculty] engage with [one] another" (Garfat & Fulcher, 2012, p. 8). Many CYC course learning outcomes are reflexive rather than content-focused in an effort to focus on the transformational nature of the learning. This means many CYC faculty teaching courses directly related to practice are actively engaged with their students much in the same way practitioners engage *with* young people "through the process of their own growth and development—walking alongside them as a guide" (Garfat & Fulcher, 2012, p. 12). It should be noted that the disagreement about emotional and relational factors goes back to Thorndike (1921) and Dewey (1916) in the early 20th century, and the interest in relational factors is an old one. Contemporary writing on education (Loreman, 2011; Määttä & Uusiautti, 2012) is again stressing the role of emotion, relationship, and love as factors in the learning process for young people (Vincent, 2016). Late 20th-century approaches to education emphasized the academic and cognitive abilities of the learner. In post-secondary university education where, initially, critical thinking and academic critique defined program and graduate excellence, approaches to CYC education aspired to a more holistic approach intended to support students as they began their professional maturation. The result was that many early CYC programs aspired to the creation of relational spaces that support reflexive learning and personal change, and thus these original programs are consistent with the more student-focused approach to education today.

Consistent with this more inclusive and relational approach is the commitment to experiential and transformational learning. Experiential education has become more mainstream in universities as government funders look for ways to ensure that university education is relevant to future employment. The standard for experiential education in Child and Youth Care and other professional programs that serve vulnerable populations is different from the vision of experiential education as an essential component of preparing young people for the work force. When students are placed in CYC field practicum experiences, they often work with vulnerable populations. The commitment to relational and transformational education in CYC then suggests that faculty members should also participate by helping students in practicum through the personal challenges they experience. As a result, CYC field practicums are less about being a student "work term" and more about a way to connect the theory and practice learning through praxis.

Field practicum experiences in community settings are extensive in all CYC post-secondary programs. Here is where students, faculty, and practitioners should integrate theory and practice "being with and participating with people" (Garfat & Fulcher, 2012, p. 8). The majority of CYC faculty teams include a field practicum coordinator who works directly with community agencies to secure placements that best match student learning needs (Keough, 2016). Student learning in practicum is evaluated, ideally through a collaborative process involving agency, student, and CYC faculty input. Most CYC practicum experiences require students to set individual learning goals and to regularly reflect on their personal and professional development (Snell, 2016). This type of reflexive and individualized evaluative process is one that "focuses on strengths and supports learners to use those strengths to demonstrate learning outcomes rather than expecting [students] to demonstrate learning in a way that makes sense to us—but not to them" (Shaw, 2011, p. 164).

A review of CYC program curriculum and practicum structures both at the university and the college level demonstrate an underlying belief in transformative learning as praxis (White, 2007). This process of observing and reflecting, of growing individually through experience, is central to CYC practice and a core tenant of the education programs. Indeed, the nature of practitioner development is consistent with one of the core characteristics of the field: the experiential nature of self and relationship as a forum for learning (Fewster, 1990; McMahon & Ward, 1998; Stuart, 2013). This is the crucible for learning CYC practice.

INTEGRATING THEORY AND PRACTICE: CHALLENGES FROM THE ACADEMIC CONTEXT

While it may seem obvious and indeed desirable that CYC education be delivered in a way that is congruent with CYC practice, such congruence is not without challenge. In post-secondary institutions there exists a tension between, on the one hand, the teaching of applied science and critical/analytic theories and, on the other hand, qualitative, intuitive, experiential approaches often referred to as practice wisdom. CYC education, with its grounding in relational, reflexive, and experiential learning, more often embraces practice wisdom over highly differentiated discrete epistemologies. Additionally, in universities and increasingly in colleges, research experience and a track record of external funding are important criteria for hiring faculty, and research experience may be given greater priority than experience in the field. In short, the culture of child and youth care is occasionally at odds with the culture of traditional academia. The nature of these challenges is found in the clash between the relational, transformational, and contextual approach of CYC and the organization of academic traditions.

Challenges to Defining Relationship(s)

The traditional professor–student relationship in formal academic culture has been one of knowledge "provider" and knowledge "receiver." Shaw, however, suggests that CYC faculty need to be comfortable engaging with students in a journey, and "providing them with the opportunity to experience their faculty hanging in" (2011, p. 164). Although "hanging in and hanging out" (Garfat & Fulcher, 2012) may be quintessential characteristics of CYC practice, they are not exemplary of typical academic relationships where a faculty member assumes a position of authority with respect to matters such as course evaluation, teaching, supervising, or advising. Establishing and maintaining boundaries that are congruent with CYC relational practice *and* appropriate to the academic setting then can be a challenge. Shaw (2011), herself a CYC practitioner and an educator, admits, "One of my struggles as I have transitioned from front line residential practice to CYC education has been translating *therapeutic* into the learning environment. Learners are not here to be in treatment—yet engaging in relational practice means that we are reflective on our practice and our relationships with others" (p. 165). In the post-secondary setting, faculty and students must work to explicitly define boundaries that are fluid.

The reflexive nature of CYC teaching and learning values the wisdom found in reflecting on emotion and action in addition to the knowledge gained through critical analysis and cognitive performance. This valuing of wisdom found through life reflection is embodied in undergraduate CYC programs that generally begin with interpersonal and relational dynamics courses. Most CYC programs use the first-year classroom experience as an opportunity for students to form and experience the dynamic nature of different types of relationships in the moment. A review of Ontario CYC curriculum (Stuart & Carty, 2006) indicates students are expected to engage in personal reflection, and most often these reflections are shared with faculty for the purpose of student assessment. This teaching/learning strategy is based on the premise that attachment styles and previous personal relationships can affect the student's ability to form relationships in practice. In the academic arena, sharing first-person narratives that might include personal disclosures about health, family, or personal experiences may run counter to institutional policies and may indeed conflict with principles of trauma-informed care. Certainly, having to evaluate student writing of such a personal nature seems at odds with CYC standards of practice, since grading appears to place a value on the content of the personal disclosure. Moreover, while student writings about existing mental health challenges or disclosures about lifestyle choices may provide for excellent reflective learning opportunities, this content may create an ethical dilemma for faculty when decisions are made about placing students in practicum settings. CYC educators often struggle to balance their ethical commitment to manage risk to agencies and vulnerable persons, while also respecting established legal expectations regarding student privacy and human rights.

Challenges to Protecting the Standard of Care

The balance between risk and privacy also arises in the debate about the role of academic preparation as professional "gatekeeping" (Gibbs & Blakely, 2000). Activities and requirements that make judgments about a student's personal suitability for practice and that screen students into the program or screen students out, either at admissions or before they graduate, may be in conflict with the principles of Canadian federal and provincial human rights legislation and with the interests of the post-secondary institution. At admissions, colleges and universities are interested in academic competence and not professional suitability, and some do not allow screening of any type.

As a student progresses through the program, issues, behaviours, values, and attitudes that faculty see as worrisome or harmful to young people arise for a small number of students. This is a challenge for faculty, because these students of concern may have acceptable academic grades, and yet they demonstrate injurious or unsafe behaviours associated with their own health struggles, behaviours that could put the student or the young people in the communities where they may work at risk. Here, the obligation of a post-secondary institution to accommodate a student with a manifest disability and/or legislation guaranteeing the student's right to privacy for their personal information may create a dilemma for faculty who feel obligated to follow due diligence and standards of practice to protect vulnerable children.

While advocating for students, CYC faculty and program standards must also respect the necessity to do no harm—either to young people serviced by field practice agencies or to vulnerable students themselves. CYC faculty are often thrust into inappropriate clinical roles requiring them to "assess" or "advocate" for students and make decisions that are often beyond the scope of their teaching responsibilities. It should be further noted that such roles often reproduce the stigmatization of mental health and trauma that impacted people deal with in general society—stigma that is antithetical to CYC philosophy and intent. As universities and colleges seek to better support students managing mental health and other challenges, CYC educators will need to continue to manage and negotiate congruence with practice principles and the implied expectation of the field that educational programs function as gatekeepers to the profession.

The ethics of gatekeeping are important, and CYC programs—and the field—have considerable work to do in this regard. To take just one example, some believe that educational programs should work to redirect those students whose personal history of trauma would compromise their relationships and work. This type of action is in contrast to the humanistic principles of accepting people for who they are, focusing on strengths, and believing in the power and possibility of change. "Many people who work in the helping professions have a prior history of what could be considered 'woundedness'" (Vachon, 2011, p. 56). Vachon suggests that although there is little explicit discussion examining the lived histories of youth workers, there is considerable "implicit suggestion that it may have an impact" (p. 57). Past or current trauma experiences with the child welfare or mental health system may well be disclosed in either reflective journaling or assignments and may challenge faculty who receive the disclosure to remain true to their belief in strength and capacity. Vachon suggests that there is insufficient data specific to CYC practice to claim a relationship exists between professional practice efficacy and previous trauma. Any student could make a mistake and violate a standard of care; the difficulty arises when there is limited reflection or learning about the potential harm to young people in their care.

Challenges to Principles of Diversity

As noted in the previous discussion about gatekeeping, the ethical obligation to the field felt by faculty and programs may manifest itself in opinions about the suitability of personal or health characteristics such as age or disability. Acting on such opinions is contrary to human rights legislation, which sets out prohibited grounds of discrimination and requires the accommodation of differences to provide inclusive environments.

Students in Canada are now entering post-secondary studies at a younger age. In some provinces, "dual credit" programs allow high school students to register in post-secondary courses and obtain credit in both institutions. They may graduate and work with young people of a similar age whereas, at one time, students admitted to CYC programs were required to be at least 19 years of age. As legislation providing more universal access to public institutions for people with disabilities becomes more prevalent across Canada and post-secondary institutions recognize the range of supports that can enable learners, students who previously faced insurmountable institutional barriers to success in post-secondary education are now graduating. CYC has attracted students with a variety of challenges and who are interested in "giving back," based on their life experiences.

Further, the articulation between college and university programs has led to greater numbers of students with learning challenges who enter through college open access programs and are now able to continue their studies in pursuit of additional academic credentials. Often, these students benefit from an individualized program and more time to complete program requirements. While the requirement to support learners with various challenges is clear within a classroom setting, it is less clear when the student enters CYC field practicum. While employers are also obligated to accommodate illness or disability for paid employees, there is still confusion about who is obligated to provide individualized accommodations in student field practicums. Unfortunately, there remains trepidation on the part of field practicum supervisors and CYC faculty with respect to the capacity of people with particular kinds of disabilities to actually do CYC practice. The ethics of such a position often takes backstage to arguments about risk management and economics. Agency providers whose resources are already stretched challenge post-secondary institutions about whose priority takes precedence: Their priority is to manage resources to support services to young people in their care, and they may not want to deploy additional resources of their own to support adaptive student learning. Consequently, accommodating individual student learning plans in CYC field practicum remains a challenge, impacting the student's ability to fulfill the graduation requirements.

While accepting and appreciating diversity is a core value within the field, and incorporating a diversity lens is a component of CYC curriculum, it may be difficult for faculty to enact this value within their practice environment (post-secondary education) relative to the CYC students that they are teaching. Faculty may feel ethically compromised and worried about their responsibility to protect young people from harm in contrast to their responsibility to develop student capacity for the care and protection of young people. Societal beliefs about the capacity of those with mental health concerns, disability, and even certain cultural or religious beliefs or ways of being can be deeply embedded in the curriculum and in faculty worldviews. This can further challenge the practice environment in post-secondary education.

Challenges to Credentialing

CYC educational programs have played a strong role in codifying emergent CYC knowledge and practice wisdom and defining standards of competency. There exists a unique relationship between CYC educational pedagogy and professional practice, and yet, although legislation and employer practice varies across Canada, it is rare to find employment settings that require CYC practitioners to have a specific credential or to register as part of a professional college or to become certified through a professional exam process. Most professional associations are voluntary membership organizations, though several provincial associations are actively advocating for legislation to regulate the profession in order to ensure employers hire qualified people. While some argue there is a "cry for" professionalism within child and youth care, others contend that traditional models of professionalism promote values of power, privilege, and exclusivity, which are contrary to the core values of child and youth care (Phelan, 2009; Vachon, 2011). The crux of the debate about professional standards is that child and youth care does not espouse exclusivity or power through expertise, and there are benefits to not being exclusive. Indeed, Dunlop (2004) claims that our "lack of recognition as an established profession" is not "our greatest weakness," but rather "our greatest strength" (p. 263). Vachon too writes about the importance of inclusivity. While advocating for a place for educating people to work effectively with children and youth, Vachon warns against honouring a post-secondary credential as the exclusive eligibility criteria for entrance into professional practice.

Many CYC educational programs that provide leadership to the field are leading or supporting the development of standards and structures for certification and professionalization. On some campuses, faculty are assisting provincial associations to solicit members and to encourage students to write professional certification examinations, while at the same time they advocate for a holistic, interdisciplinary approach that is "highly portable and cuts across disciplines" (Dunlop, 2004, p. 262). CYC in higher education will have to make some decisions about how to encourage professionalism without creating artificial, unnecessary boundaries. Still, there is better and worse work in all practice settings, and higher education ought to be able to explain what good work is and how to learn to do it.

Challenges are situated not only in the educational program's relationship with service providers and their relationship with professional membership organizations but also in how programs are situated within their own educational context.

The shifting landscape of post-secondary education today puts the impetus for vocational training and job readiness against the traditional undergraduate focus on liberal education and critical thinking. Many CYC programs have responded to this challenge by designing innovative curriculum pathways that enable students to integrate theory, practice, and liberal arts electives through the completion of a final capstone project. These projects are often driven by student practicum experiences and can involve research and applied practice within community settings.

In addition, there is a creeping pressure on students towards higher academic credentials leading to a focus on preparing students for graduate school as well as the field of practice. Graduates, proud of their identity as CYC practitioners, have applied pressure for field-specific masters and doctoral programs. The educational institutions have been slow to respond, hampered in part by the lack of doctoral faculty with a strong CYC identity. As a result, many graduates of BA (CYC) programs by default enter other post-graduate programs in Social Work, Education, and Psychology.

FUTURE OPPORTUNITIES

The situated practice of CYC and its uneasy relationship to and within higher education that we describe is analogous to concerns about the "fit" of CYC in many practice settings. In group care, CYC's interest in everyday life development and care was undervalued by many clinicians and psychiatrists, though the field began to professionalize through the writings of Redl, Wineman, Maier, Polsky, and Bettleheim, who recognized the critical role of daily life experiences in residential treatment centres (see Gharabaghi & Charles, this volume). In elementary and secondary education, where CYC has made inroads, educators often expect CYC practitioners to manage problems so that they do not interfere with teaching. In child welfare, CYC practitioners cope with systems of investigation and control, and exert power over families' lives. In community settings, there is pressure on practitioners to teach "things" rather than provide rich, engaging experiences (see Newbury & Vachon, this volume). The challenges of "fit" are not unusual or unique to higher education, and we have similar conflicts and similar temptations to adapt to and imitate the system within which our practice occurs. Doing so has consequences and implications for the future.

First, we can help ourselves by being more articulate about our educational practices and more multi-lingual, interpreting our practices in languages that make them more accessible to those who do not have our frame of reference.

What happens to us is often out of our control, but we have agency and the capacity to influence the dynamism and sophistication of our self-presentation. If our relational and equitable pedagogy is as effective as we hope, we might have something to offer higher education and other institutional systems about how to create rich, dynamic, open-ended, experiential, and diverse learning experiences and relationships.

There is pressure on us from higher education, but higher education itself is under pressure, and we have some expertise that could respond to these pressures. For example, CYC educators have developed exemplary models of strength-based evaluations, including rubrics that provide students with feedback expressed in positive rather than deficit language and approaches to whole person strategies that support both affective and intellectual learning. CYC field educators are becoming well-versed and skilful in methods of authentic evaluation, which could evolve into trial long-term consideration of how CYC graduates actually work with and influence young people. Becoming more articulate about and presenting evidence of effectiveness of our own educational practices would help improve quality in CYC education, and it could shape post-secondary educational communities into life-spaces that are more caring and tolerant.

Second, we proposed that much of the current context of Canadian CYC is shaped by our unique history, often tied to specific work contexts such as residential care. The challenge of responding to diversity in post-secondary education and the diversity of the world of work with youth, as demonstrated in other chapters, poses an opportunity. Practice is more diverse in pedagogy, values, curricula, relationship, goals, intensity, context, age of participant, identity, culture, and history than may be recognized in many CYC programs. It is unrealistic to think that any one program can adequately prepare students for every context, and it is unrealistic to think that only one way of doing things is the right way. We now face interesting new opportunities related to the scope of the field and the need for both specificity and universality in our curriculum. For the most part these are opportunities, and it may mean that CYC programs will evolve in ways that begin to substantially differ from each other.

Valuing of diversity and respect for context are essential CYC values. As CYC programs evolve to reflect regional priorities, it is hoped that CYC approaches to teaching and learning will continue to explore ways to perceive, encourage, and value alternative voices. The academic voice is often that of the dominant culture—patriarchal and ethnically nonrepresentational. This monophonic source of information does not sound like the voices heard in CYC settings, and yet it can often be the dominant voice of academic reading and the taught model of academic writing. Thaiss and Zawacki (2006) describe this voice as that of "an intellectual a thinker and a user of reason"—a voice from which "the senses and emotions must always be subject to control by reason" (p. 6). Many CYC educators are turning their ears and attuning their teaching practices to welcome "other" voices and forms of expression—ways of knowing and communicating that are more embodied, less subject to rational domination, more local, diverse, and honest about privilege and power. The future of academic writing could well be shaped by these CYC pioneers who, together with students, are taking risks with form and ideas while earnestly working to legitimize alternative assumptions about discourse (Royster, 2002).

A third future opportunity for CYC education is the potential offered with the challenge of credentials and professionalism. The self-identity of CYC has often been as "outsider," and the movement of CYC into higher education was a highly desirable development for the credibility of CYC, which continues to nurture anxiety and critique. Often these are related to the aspiration to *be* "professional." CYC will want to continue to work on articulating ideals of professionalism (Sercombe, 2004) that motivate better, more accountable work but do not distance practitioners from young people and their communities and that maintain an emphasis on service rather than our own self-interest. We want to be careful to avoid "mystification," claiming control over practice domains that properly belong in communities. We want to explore ways to realize professional and academic credibility without dishonouring our community vocational roots. We need to find ways to continue authentic field practicum learning and advocate for its parity with educational funding priorities that may favour information dissemination over experiential learning. And we need to remain engaged with communities of young people and their families in order to find ways for these communities to inform CYC curriculum, teaching practices, and, perhaps, even student and faculty evaluations.

Finally, CYC is uneasy about expectations of scientific rigour, and associated with this are now the almost universal expectations of outcome-based practices and evaluation. There are good reasons to be concerned and critical, and yet it is not a credit to us that we resist expectations that we be accountable. Further, in the 20 years we have complained about these expectations, theorists in other fields have moved in our direction and, to our surprise, some of them have begun talking like us—even neuroscientists. CYC educational practice must continue to engage in and teach systematic research methods, while also making space for less traditional praxis-informed research. The intuitive relational experience of practice may be where insight is located, but it can also be where bias and distortions are located. Methods courses taught in CYC programs offer a unique place for students and faculty to apply both intuitive and rational approaches to research—recognizing the value of both rather than placing them in opposition.

Ideally, CYC practice wisdom tells us that CYC education needs to prepare graduates to view issues of child and youth care through the lens of more than one discipline and to continually challenge and revise assumptions in much the same way that applied science does rather than adopting more traditional assumptions about the certainty of knowledge. Bellefeuille (2014) refers to course-based creative modes of inquiry that "address the interconnection between creative inquiry and the meaning making process so central to relational CYC practice … [in order to] … to express understanding in ways that represent different ways of knowing" (p. 30). Future CYC education programs are an opportunity to situate our practice as a "reflective and dialogic engagement with our knowledge and with the people served through it" (McKee-Sellick, Delaney, & Brownlee, 2002, p. 493). We can begin these processes in higher education by evaluating our own pedagogical practices—and by involving students in these efforts. These self-evaluative and self-critical efforts will be part of the ongoing maturing of CYC in higher education.

NOTE

1. Social pedagogy comprises the view that practitioners are educators of young people in the skill and art of socializing within the norms of society, whereas behavioural science follows a more scientific approach that specifically shapes behaviour by identifying and modifying the conditions that surround it.

REFERENCES

Bandura, A. (1977). *Social learning theory*. Englewood Cliffs, NJ: Prentice Hall.

Banks, S. (1990). Youth work, informal education, and professionalization: The issues in the 1990s. *Youth and Policy, 54*, 13–25.

Bargal, D., Gold, M., & Lewin, M. (1992). Introduction: The heritage of Kurt Lewin. *Journal of Social Issues, 48*, 3–13.

Bellefeuille, G. (2014). A course based creative inquiry approach to teaching introductory research methods in child and youth care undergraduate education. *Conference Proceedings: 11th International Academic Conference, International Institute of Social and Economic Sciences (IISES), Reykjavik, Iceland* (pp. 30–40). Retrieved from http://proceedings.iises.net/index.php?action=proceedingsIndexConference&id=3&page=1

Bronfenbrenner, U. (1979). *The ecology of human development.* Cambridge, MA: Harvard University Press.

Carson, C. J., Fritz, A. S., Lewis, E., Ramey, J. H., & Sugiuchi, D. W. (2004). *Growth and development through group work.* New York: Haworth Press.

Davies, B. (1976). *From social education to social and life skills training: In whose interests?* London, UK: National Youth Board.

Dewey, J. (1916). *Democracy and education.* New York: The Free Press.

Dunlop, T. (2004). Framing a new and expanded vision for the future of child and youth care work an international, intercultural and trans-disciplinary perspective. *Journal of Child and Youth Care Work, 19,* 254–267.

Fewster, G. (1990). Growing together: The personal relationship in child and youth care. In J. Anglin, C. Denholm, R. Ferguson, & A. Pence (Eds.), *Perspectives in professional child and youth care* (pp. 25–41). New York: Haworth Press.

Freire, P. (1990). *Pedagogy of the oppressed.* New York: Continuum.

Garfat, T., & Fulcher, L. C. (2012). Characteristics of a child and youth care approach. In T. Garfat & L. C. Fulcher (Eds.), *Child and youth care in practice* (pp. 5–24). Retrieved from http://cycnetpress.cyc-net.org/samples/CYCiP.pdf

Gibbs, P., & Blakely, E. H. (2000). *Gatekeeping in BSW programs.* New York: Columbia University Press.

Keough, M. (2016). Sailing through the fog: Practicum in child and youth care education. *Relational Child and Youth Care Practice, 29*(3), 123–137.

Krueger, M. (2000). Central themes in child and youth care. *Child and Youth Care Online, 12.* Retrieved from http://www.cyc-net.org/cyc-online/cycol-0100-krueger.html

Krueger, M. (2002). A further review of the development of the Child and Youth Care profession in the United States. *Child and Youth Care Forum, 31*(1), 13–26.

Loreman, T. (2011) *Love as pedagogy.* Rotterdam, the Netherlands: Sense Publishers.

Määttä, K., & Uusiautti, S. (2012). Pedagogical authority and pedagogical love— Connected or incompatible? *International Journal of Whole Schooling, 8*(1), 21–33.

McKee-Sellick, M., Delaney, R., & Brownlee, K. (2002). The deconstruction of professional knowledge: Accountability without authority. *Families in Society: The Journal of Contemporary Human Services, 83*(5/6), 493–498.

McMahon, L., & Ward, A. (1998). Helping and the personal response: Intuition is not enough. In L. McMahon & A. Ward (Eds.), *Intuition is not enough: Matching learning with practice in therapeutic child care*. New York: Routledge.

Ministry of Training, Colleges and Universities. (2014). *Child and youth care program standards*. Toronto: Government of Ontario. Retrieved May 27, 2017, from www.tcu.gov.on.ca/pepg/audiences/colleges/progstan/humserv/60701e.pdf

Phelan, J. (2009). The wounded healer as helper and helped. *CYC-Online, 121*. Retrieved from http://www.cyc-net.org/cyc-online/cyconline-mar2009-phelan.html

Rogers, C. (1961). *On becoming a person*. Boston: Houghton Mifflin.

Royster, J. J. (2002). Academic discourses, or small boats on a big sea. In C. Schroeder, H. Fox, & P. Bizzell (Eds.), *Alternative discourses and the academy* (pp. 23–30). Portsmouth, NH: Heinemann.

Sarason, S. (1986). *The preparation of teachers: An unstudied problem in education*. Cambridge, MA: Brookline.

Sarason, S. (1997). *How schools might be governed and why*. New York: Teachers College Press.

Sercombe, H. (2004). Youth work: The professionalisation dilemma. *Youth Studies Australia, 23*(4), 20–25.

Shaw, K. (2011). Child and youth care education: On discovering the parallels to practice. *Relational Child and Youth Care Practice, 24*(1/2), 163–167.

Skinner, B. F. (1953). *The possibility of a science of human behavior*. New York: The Free Press.

Snell, H. (2016). *A preliminary investigation into field work models in Canadian Child and Youth Care education*. Report prepared for the Canadian Child and Youth Care Accreditation Board. Retrieved from http://www.cycaccreditation.ca/docs/FWM.pdf

Stuart, C. A. (2013). *Foundations of child and youth care*. Dubuque, IA: Kendall Hunt Publishers.

Stuart, C., & Carty, W. (2006). *The role of competence in outcomes for children and youth: An approach for mental health*. Toronto: Ryerson University.

Thaiss, C. J., & Zawacki, T. M. (2006). *Engaged writers and dynamic disciplines: Research on the academic writing life*. Portsmouth, NH: Boynton/Cook Publishers Inc.

Thorndike, E. L. (1921). *Educational psychology*. New York: Teachers College Press.

Vachon, W. (2011). Honouring the wounded: Inviting in our successes and mistakes *Relational Child and Youth Care Practice, 23*(2), 54–62.

Vincent, J. (2016). Perspectives on love as a component of professional practice. *Scottish Journal of Residential Child Care, 15*(3) & *International Journal of Social Pedagogy, 5*(1), Joint special issue: Love in Professional Practice.

White, J. (2007). Knowing, doing and being in context: A praxis-oriented approach to Child and Youth Care. *Child and Youth Care Forum, 36*(5/6), 225–244.

CHAPTER 12

Child and Youth Care in Quebec

Varda R. Mann-Feder[1]

Child and youth care (CYC) has long been a respected vocation in Quebec, domi-
nating services for troubled and troubling youth since the 1950s. Understanding
the evolution and the status of the field in Quebec is a complex task for many reasons. There are, and have always been, completely separate systems of service delivery for the Anglophone and Indigenous minorities and the Francophone majority
in Quebec. Consequently, the models of CYC practice evolved independently, although they share common roots and espouse similar concepts. All CYC agencies
and services in Quebec are publicly funded and they are unique in North America,
both for the degree to which they are regulated by the government and having
been influenced by a long history of unionization (Vanglois, Baillargeon, Caldwell,
Frechet, Gauthier, & Simard, 1992). While there are some workers in private practice, the overwhelming majority of CYCs are subsumed under three job titles in
the public sector: "Educateur Specialise," "Educateur," and "Psychoeducateur."
The latter has been a licensed profession since 2000 (Ordre des Psychoéducateurs
et Psychoéducatrices du Québec, n.d.). All three of these occupational groupings
are lifespan practices, and as a consequence, all but one educational program in
Quebec prepare CYC practitioners in the context of lifespan care. Lastly, the state
of CYC work as a whole, encompassing English and French models, has never
been documented in a single publication. This chapter represents a first attempt to

do so, and as such is the first iteration, which by its very nature provides an overview and a degree of speculation by the author. It is hoped that this can provide a starting point for future analysis and debate. What follows is based on a review of scholarly literature, government documents, and in-house reports from agencies, professional associations, and educational institutions, many of which were accessed through the Internet. This research was supplemented by interviews with key informants, who were consulted to fill in gaps in information and validate the conclusions of the author.

A detailed discussion of the status of CYC models and services for Indigenous youth is beyond the scope of this chapter, given the depth of the cultural and historical issues. However, Indigenous young people remain an underserviced population in Quebec, because of a lack of equitable and culturally sensitive services (Canadian Child Welfare Research Portal, 2011), including a shortage of trained Indigenous CYC workers. For treatment of this issue, see Sinha and Kozlowski (2013); Simpson, Fast, Wegner-Lohin, and Trocmé (2014); and the Canadian Child Welfare Research Portal (2011).

THE EVOLUTION OF CYC IN QUEBEC

Until the mid-20th century, the clergy managed and staffed all sectors of the health and social service fields in Quebec (Pigeon & Marquis, n.d.). Hospitals, orphanages, and services for neglected, abused, and delinquent youth were run by religious communities, much as they were in the rest of North America (Charles & Garfat, 2009; also see Gharabaghi & Charles, this volume). Service delivery was seen as charity, and institutions for children and youth stressed correction through punishment, protection, and education (Gregoire, 2012). Staff were untrained and residential programs were overcrowded, with one adult managing anywhere from 40 to 90 young people (Gregoire, 2012). A long history of dominance of the political and social structures by the Anglophone minority resulted in marked inequities in access to these services. These conditions persisted well into the 1950s, although by then, fewer Quebeckers were joining the clergy, and increasingly laypeople had been hired to fulfill staff functions in the institutions for children and youth (Gregoire, 2012). These staff were untrained and, despite good intentions, did not have the skills to provide anything beyond basic custodial care (Landry, 2007).

Following World War II, Quebec experienced a surge in prosperity and the emergence of a new Francophone middle class (Linnteau, 2006) that favoured secularization and modernization of the health and social service sector. The advent of the Quiet Revolution, a series of reforms under the Lesage Liberal government, aimed to "redefine the role of Francophone society ... and resulted in the liquidation of the political and ideological heritage" (Gregoire, 2012, p. 1), notably through the redefinition of the role of the Catholic Church (Durocher, 2013). This resulted in the creation of centralized systems of health and social services for both the Francophone and Anglophone communities (Pigeon & Marquis, n.d.). School boards were created, and the orphanages and reform schools came under government control.

During this same period, the provincial government established a new department of education, which in turn built a system of "Colleges D'Enseignment Generals et Professionels" or CEGEPs (Greenwald, 1993). The curriculum for these public post-secondary colleges was developed by the provincial government, and included both two-year pre-university programs and three-year technical career programs. Among the latter were programs to train "Educateurs Specialises" (Special Care Counsellors in English) (Vanier College, n.d.), who could take on roles with a wide range of clientele, including disadvantaged and disruptive children and youth.

The initial impetus for the establishment of the Educateur Specialise programs was the work of two French Canadian priests, Father Albert Roger and Father Noel Mailloux, who were inspired by European models in their work with youth in placement. Their pioneering efforts were consolidated by two laypeople who were recruited to work in their respective centres, Gilles Gendreau and Jeannine Guindon (Arsenault, Begin, Bluteau, & Pronovost, 2012). Gilles Gendreau had been recruited in the 40s by Father Roger to work at Boscoville with young offenders. After the president of the Association Nationale des Educateurs Specialises in France visited Boscoville in 1953, Gendreau began to work on the creation of a model of residential care built on models of re-education (Arsenault et al., 2012). His work on a structural model of psychoeducation utilized theory from Piaget and Erikson to outline steps in the treatment process. Gendreau's model was subsequently extended by Jeannine Guindon. Guindon was hired as the Director General of the Centre D'orientation et Readaptation de Montreal in 1957. She was a former teacher from Ottawa who pursued a doctorate in psychology at the University of Montreal as part of her search for principles to guide work with young people (Université de Montréal, 2002). The three models that significantly influenced her thinking were the "Educateur Specialise" model in France, the work of Redl and Winemen at Pioneer House in Detroit, and the psychoanalytic writings of Bruno Bettelheim from the Orthogenic School in Chicago. She built on these theoretical frameworks and Gendreau's earlier work as the basis for a unique Quebecois model of CYC work, psychoeducation, that quickly gained prominence in the French sector. Gendreau had made use of notions of accommodation and assimilation to understand the impact of intervention strategies, and he espoused the notion of a "total milieu" where activities were used to foster adaptation and positive development (Ordre des Psychoéducateurs et Psychoéducatrices, n.d.). All of these important influences contributed to the psychoeducation model, so named because it blended elements from psychology and education (Arsenault et al., 2012).

Psychoeducation has continued to evolve since this early work (Chenard, 2013), while playing a major role in the evolution of CYC overall in Quebec. While it was never adopted in the Anglophone system as a treatment model, it became the basis for the ways in which job titles and job status are assigned because it provided a model of CYC practice in Quebec early on, coinciding with the creation of public services.

By 1968, Educateurs Specialises were graduating from both French and English CEGEPs and were populating schools and residential programs for children and youth. In 1976, Manny Batshaw, an Anglophone social worker and well-known activist in Montreal, was appointed by the provincial government to review the status of services for young people in Quebec (Batshaw Youth and Family Centres, n.d.). Batshaw recommended lighter measures for delinquent youth, shorter stays in residential placement, and the development of community-based services to support deinstitutionalization (Landry, 2007). As a result, a continuum of care was developed in both the French and English sectors, administered by large youth centres (Centres Jeunesse) that were created for each region of the province. All of the youth centres operated foster care, group homes, residential care, day centres, and community services for youth and families (Cosgrove, 1975). The CEGEP programs adjusted accordingly, and family intervention became a strong component of education and training for Educateurs Specialises (see Modlin & Legett, this volume, for comparable developments in English Canada).

It is important to note that, since its inception, the system of services for children and youth in Quebec have undergone successive reorganizations, with an emphasis on streamlining and centralizing services in favour of efficiency and cost-effectiveness (Martin, Pomey, & Forest, 2010). In fact, at the time of writing, the system has recently undergone another major amalgamation, this time integrating youth centres with adult services and health providers (Linnteau, 2006). The end result is the reduction of 182 institutions in Quebec to 34 large, integrated health and social service establishments (Martin et al., 2010). Throughout these processes, and since the time of the Quiet Revolution, unions have played a major role in determining the status of CYC workers in Quebec. The strength of unions in the province has translated into an ability to negotiate advantageous working conditions for CYC practitioners, especially when compared with those in the rest of North America (Mann-Feder & Savicki, 2003).

CURRENT STATUS OF THE FIELD AND EMPLOYMENT PROSPECTS

As mentioned earlier, three distinct job titles exist in the public sector in Quebec for CYC practitioners: "Educateur," "Educateur Specialise," and "Psychoeducateur" (Ministère, 2015). Currently, only the latter, Psychoeducateur, is considered a professional designation, with a formal licensing structure and roles in client evaluation that are "reserved" as defined by provincial legislation (Ordre des Psychoéducateurs et Psychoéducatrices du Québec, n.d.). This distinction between professional CYC workers and those who are considered paraprofessionals also influences salary scales and ascension to management. The legislation that differentiated professional from paraprofessional CYC practitioners, Bill 21, was implemented in 2012 and is controversial because it changed the responsibilities and job prospects of many CYCs who were not eligible to be licensed by the Order of Psychoeducaters. Psychoeducation is a model of practice unique to French Canada, and there are no dedicated education and training programs in English. In addition, the provincial government has decreed that professional licensing will only be available to individuals with a master's degree and that, for the time being, it will not accredit any additional licensing bodies. Currently, licensing is only readily available to CYC graduates from one of the six Francophone universities that house master's programs in psychoeducation. The vast majority of CYCs in Quebec, in both linguistic sectors, are CEGEP graduates. This is further complicated for Anglophone CYC workers, as only one English graduate program in CYC currently exists in Quebec, the Diploma in Youth Work at Concordia University. The program began in 2013, but a proposal to add another graduate degree, an MA in Youth Work and Psychoeducation, is currently under review with the Ministry of Education. It is hoped that this will bring psychoeducation to the Anglophone community and create more synergy between all the universities that prepare CYC professionals in the province. It will also nurture a new sector of the Anglophone workforce, that of licensed Psychoeducateur CYCs.

Educateur Specialise and Educateur are CYC job titles that require either a three-year CEGEP diploma in Special Care Counselling for the former or a relevant undergraduate degree for the latter. Educateurs Specialises are seen as having intensive preparation for practice and, accordingly, higher salaries. This is in recognition of the specificity of their training in 26 competencies defined by the Ministry of Education for all the CEGEP programs for CYC workers (see Box 12.1). The job description for Educateurs Specialises and Educateur reads as follows (translated by the author):

> A person who insures the education and rehabilitation of users according to in-tervention programs established in collaboration with the team of professionals onsite, in consideration of both the rehabilitation needs of the individual and social reinsertion. This person applies educational and rehabilitation strategies using everyday life events, and by organizing, coordinating, and animating planned activities to promote learning and the acquisition of new attitudes and behaviours. They observe and analyze the behaviour of service users, partici-pate in evaluating their needs and their capacities, and note their progress in relevant documents. They also provide program descriptions of the activities. (Ministère de la Santé et Services Sociaux: Direction des relations de travail du personnel, 2015; trans. V. R. Mann-Feder)

Psychoeducateurs, Educateurs Specialises, and Educateurs are all defined as lifespan practitioners according to provincial norms. Their sectors of employ-ment include residential care for children, youth, and seniors; youth protection; elementary and high schools; psychiatric and medical programs in hospitals; and social service work in community settings. Recent reports state that there is a virtually 100-percent employment rate for graduates of Psychoeducation and Educateur Specialise programs in Quebec, and workers in these job positions are more educated than the labour force overall (Service Canada, 2014). However, the majority of these job positions are part-time or contract positions. There are upwards of 18,000 Educateurs and Educateurs Specialises in Quebec, and approximately 3,000 Psychoeducateurs (Ratel, personal communication, 2015). The overwhelming majority of Psychoeducateurs work in social services, resi-dential programs for youth, or schools (Begin, Bluteau, Arsenault, & Pronovost,

Box 12.1: Twenty-Six Specific Competencies for the Special Care Counselling (Educateurs Specialises) Programs in CEGEPs in Quebec

1. To examine the job functions of a special care counsellor
2. To become familiar with community resources and services
3. To communicate with clients and members of a work team
4. To examine biopsychosocial adjustment issues
5. To gather information about the client's behaviour
6. To design development activities and clinical tools
7. To evaluation the ability of the client's living environment to provide appropriate support
8. To assist a client in need of help
9. To associate approaches, objectives, and techniques with specific adjustment problems
10. To abide by the code of ethics of the profession
11. To establish a helping relationship
12. To carry out adaptive and rehabilitative activities for clients with an intellectual disability
13. To carry out adaptive and rehabilitative activities for clients with learning or language difficulties
14. To carry out adaptive and rehabilitative activities for clients with a physical impairment or neurological disorder
15. To act as a facilitator for groups of clients or work teams
16. To carry out activities for older individuals who are no longer autonomous
17. To carry out adaptive and rehabilitative activities for young people with adjustment difficulties
18. To protect their personal well-being
19. To analyze the relationship between social phenomena and adjustment problems
20. To carry out rehabilitative activities for clients with mental health and drug addiction problems
21. To carry out adaptive and rehabilitative activities for clients who are socially excluded or who are perpetrators or victims of violence
22. To develop an intervention plan
23. To interact with clients from cultural and ethnic communities different than their own

24. To carry out adaptive and rehabilitative activities for clients who are re-entering society or the workplace

25. To intervene in a crisis

26. To draw up and carry out an integrated intervention project

---

Source: Ministère de L'Education, Loisir et Sport, 2005, p. 11

2012), while most Educateurs Specialises work in schools, health settings, or social services (Service Canada, 2014). A large percentage of both these groups work with children, youth, and families. There are currently 31 post-secondary institutions that provide college and university education in the province, 7 universities and 24 colleges. Four of these programs are delivered in English (one in a university and three in the college system). In 2009, Charles and Garfat cited Quebec as one of the leaders in specialized education in the CYC field.

MODELS OF PRACTICE: DIFFERENCES AND COMMONALITIES

CYC in Quebec incorporates a number of models of practice, varying along linguistic lines and levels of educational preparation. The post-secondary institutions that prepare CYC practitioners have had a huge impact on practice from the beginning, as services for youth in the province and the educational programs developed side by side from their earlier inception.

In French Quebec, the psychoeducation model developed by Father Mailloux, Gilles Gendreau, Jeannine Guindon, and others has significantly influenced practice for all categories of CYC practitioners (Ratel, personal communication, 2015). As mentioned earlier, the initial roots of this model were the Educateur Specialise model in France and a series of models from the US: Redl and Wineman's life-space model, Bettelheim's psychodynamic model of treatment, and Erikson's model of ego psychology. The other major influence on psychoeducation was the cognitive-developmental model of Jean Piaget from Switzerland (Gregoire, 2012). As stated by Begin and colleagues (2012):

> The pioneers of Quebec Psychoeducation in conceptualizing a re-education process based on the presence of self-consciousness and self-empowerment were predominantly influenced by Piaget and Erikson's Epigenetic theories. (p. 4)

In essence, psychoeducation was built on a foundation of developmental and psychodynamic theory, using lifespan techniques (Begin et al., 2012). Gendreau and Guindon created a highly structured model of milieu treatment that stressed ongoing assessment of a young person's progress and the promotion of psychological development and adaptation through therapeutic activities. Psychoeducation emphasizes careful planning, sequencing, and execution of therapeutic activities, which must be constantly re-evaluated in light of the evolving treatment needs of the "subject" (Arsenault, Begin, Bluteau, & Pronovost, 2012). This intervention process is conceptualized as a continuous loop involving eight "professional processes" (Arsenault et al., 2012): observing, pre-assessing, planning, organizing the treatment context, running activities, utilizing experiences for therapeutic purposes, and assessing post-intervention (Arsenault et al., 2012, p. 11). The last process, communication, runs throughout the other seven processes, and is both "formative" (feedback to the client) and functional (sharing of information with other professionals and important others in the client's life; Arsenault et al., 2012).

In addition, psychoeducation's "structural psychoeducative model" identifies 13 components of the treatment environment that must be taken into consideration when engaging in the professional processes. These 13 components specify the people involved, the environmental considerations, and the features of an intervention that require attention before engaging with a young person. The 13 components are the client, the peer group, the psychoeducators themselves, the parents, other professionals, the objectives of treatment, the means of generating interactivity, time, space, the code of conduct and procedures, roles and responsibilities and measurement, evaluation, and recognition (Arsenault et al., 2012, p. 4). In this way, psychoeducation is deeply rooted in an ecosystemic perspective and clearly enunciates all the features of the life-space and of an intervention that must be addressed in working with young people. The model is associated with "a sense of thoroughness in clinical practice" (Arsenault et al., 2012, p. 8) as it is highly prescriptive and structured in providing guidelines for CYC intervention. However, it is also clear that the alliance between a psychoeducator and a young person is central to the work, and that psychoeducative methods are "brought to life by means of the relationship" (Arsenault et al., 2012, p. 4), and by "dyadic interaction" (Chenard, 2013).

The basic model was conceived in the 60s, but it is in constant evolution (Chenard, 2013). Most recently, psychoeducation has incorporated elements of cognitive behavioural and behavioural approaches, as well as biosocial models of intervention and emerging knowledge in developmental psychopathology

(Begin et al., 2012). It is important to note that psychoeducation was first developed in the context of residential care for youth, but later broadened to include applications that involved infants and young children and adults of all ages (Ratel, personal communication, 2015). Despite the fact that psychoeducation is a uniquely Quebecois model, it is not a focus of education and training or practice in the English sector. The Youth Work Diploma at Concordia University represents the first formal foray into the integration of psychoeducation with other models of CYC practice by an English post-secondary institution (Ranahan, Blanchet-Cohen, & Mann-Feder, 2015).

Several factors may have contributed to the apparent absence of psychoeducation in the Anglophone CYC sector in Quebec. The model developed in the French residential care agencies was pioneered at Boscoville and the Centre d'Orientation through the integration of American models with earlier work in France and Belgium (both Francophone countries). The Anglophone and Francophone service sectors were separate right from the start and historically, there has been little crossover, with a totally distinct clientele and totally distinct staff. The Batshaw Report of the 1960s, mentioned earlier, had a profound effect on the structure of services for children and youth in the province but had its most significant influence in the Anglophone sector. The report questioned models of treatment that required long stays in residential care and cited psychoeducation as an example. Batshaw also recommended that service providers in the province look to models from psychology and sociology such as transactional analysis, guided group interaction, positive peer culture, and reality therapy (Gregoire, 2012). Early on in the evolution of the Anglophone youth centre, key union and association leaders reached out actively to the National Organization of Child Care Workers of America (NOCCWA) to adopt models of practice from the US (Maciocia, personal communication, 2015). Some of the program managers in the Anglophone system were imported from across the border to bring models from both the juvenile justice sector and child welfare to Quebec, among them Phillip Harris (Welsh & Harris, 2013), Gale Burford (Ainsworth & Fulcher, 2006), Marge Reitsma-Street (Reitsma-Street & Leschied, 1988), and Thom Garfat (Garfat, n.d.), all of whom have contributed to the field as a whole. As pointed out by Burford and Fulcher (2006, p. 178):

> The 70s and the 80s were of considerable influence for those of us caught up
> in the excitement of the many discoveries and innovations in the treatment of
> young people who came into conflict with the law. And the Canadian province

of Quebec was an exciting place in which to be engaged in Child and Youth Care practice … the treatment discoveries were mainly originating in the U.S.A., especially in the California Youth Authority.

Among the earliest models to be implemented in the Anglophone care system were two that relied heavily on classification systems and client-worker-environment matching: interpersonal maturity or I-Level, from California (Sullivan, Grant, & Grant, 1957), and the conceptual level model, which was first conceived in Toronto (Reitsma-Street & Lescheid, 1988). Historically, CYC agencies in Quebec have kept in close touch with developments from across North America and have consistently invited experts from the field beyond Quebec to provide in-service training on the newest approaches.

No one model dominates CYC in the Anglophone sector in Quebec, although responding to relational needs and providing personal connections are broadly recognized as the hallmark of the work, both by the college programs and the organizations that provide services. The lifespan programs at the college level emphasize a mastery of the 26 government dictated competencies in the context of an eclectic mix of theoretical models or the "greatest hits of CYC" (Carpanzano, personal communication, 2015). At the time of writing, there was a strong focus in the largest Anglophone college program on the island of Montreal on trauma-based intervention and resilience theory (Carpanzano, personal communication, 2015). Students are also exposed to attachment theory, accountability case management, and cognitive behavioural models. An emphasis on strength-based approaches runs through the college system, and is also represented by the recent adoption of the "Circle of Courage" as an intervention model in the largest Anglophone youth centre in Quebec (Batshaw, n.d.; see also Stuart, Snell, & Magnuson, this volume). The "Circle of Courage" is an American model based on First Nations principles of child rearing (Brendtro, Brokenleg, & Van Bockern, 1990). Four essential needs of young people are at the centre of the model: belonging, mastery, independence, and generosity. Strategies for working in residential care are aimed at positive encouragement of these four areas of functioning (Brokenleg & Van Bockern, 2003). As before, trainers from outside the province were brought to Quebec in recent years to provide in-service training to Educateurs and Educateurs Specialises, among other helping professionals in the Anglophone network.

Beyond the obvious cultural and linguistic differences, Anglophone and Francophone approaches to CYC are characterized by different theoretical models and different jargon. The dominant Francophone model developed in concert with models of practice in France and Belgium, and comparisons with these countries still serve as a basis for research and scholarly writing in Quebec (for an example, see Grevot & Lacharite, 2009). The Anglophone system, on the other hand, responded to developments in the US and other parts of Canada. On closer examination, however, there are some important commonalities. In both contexts, there is an emphasis on relationships, where the foundation of all intervention is shared experience (*vecu partagee* in French) in the young person's life-space (Chenard, 2013). Also evident is a focus on the promotion of positive strength and adaptation. As stated in the Champlain College program description, "The essence of the role … is to develop relationships that provide support and guidance to enhance client's development, adaptation and quality of life" (Champlain College, n.d.). Lastly, there is a universal appreciation of the importance of ecosystemic intervention, in which multiple levels of influence on a young person are understood and become a focus of intervention. This is expressed most directly in both the Francophone and Anglophone CYC programs through the importance of family work, and a preoccupation in both linguistic sectors with providing culturally sensitive services.

PROFESSIONAL ASSOCIATIONS AND THEIR ROLE IN THE FIELD

Two professional CYC associations exist in Quebec, and are each dominated by one linguistic community. The Quebec Association of Educators (QAE), a primarily Anglophone group, was created in 1985 by front-line workers who had attended their first Child and Youth Care conference in Little Rock, Arkansas. These workers were warmly received by the National Organization of Child and Youth Care Associations, and were also inspired by opening remarks by Hillary Clinton, then the First Lady of Arkansas, who emphasized the important role that CYC plays in the lives of children, youth, and families (Maciocia, 2010). With a small initial membership and the support of local agencies, the QAE went on to adopt a code of ethics, organize conferences, provide advocacy for the field in the local youth serving institutions, and foster networking among members of the field (Maciocia, personal communication, 2015). The Association participated in the creation of a national consortium of professional child and youth care organizations, the Canadian Council of Child and Youth Care Associations, and is still an active member. The QAE distributes a newsletter to all its members, which features articles on current developments in the field along with writing by the membership on a range of practice issues. QAE Annual Awards of

Excellence recognize the important contributions of individual association members to enhancing services for children, youth, and families (Maciocia, 2010).

The Association des Educateurs Specialises du Quebec (AEESQ), a primarily Francophone association, was created in 2006 to further the interests of CEGEP graduates in the field, and was, in part, a response to Bill 21, which was seen as overlooking Educateurs Specialises and excluding them from consideration for professional status (AEESQ, 2015). The AEESQ has a newsletter, a code of ethics, and is constantly updating its membership on developments around the province and the ongoing implications of Bill 21 for its members (AEESQ, 2015). The current president of the association participated in the leadership for a bilingual group that banded together to take up an opportunity to participate in national hearings on Bill 21 in 2009 (Maciocia, 2010).

OPPORTUNITIES AND CHALLENGES

Child and youth care, as practised by Educateurs Specialises, Educateurs, and Psychoeducateurs, is a respected field in Quebec. It has a rich history and a long tradition of professionalization, along with a well-established tradition of intentional CYC practice guided by a range of theoretical models, including the psychoeducation model. All the approaches currently practised in the province stress relationships, positive adaptation, and an ecosystemic approach to children, youth, and families. CYC education is well developed, and there are options to pursue college-level technical education, relevant bachelor's degrees, and field-specific MAs and PhDs, although more so in French than in English. Educational institutions, professional associations, and youth-servicing organizations are segregated along linguistic lines. While this provides autonomy, self-regulation, and culturally sensitive services for the Anglophone and Francophone communities, it is also potentially divisive, reducing possibilities for shared resources and collaboration in advocating for the field. Both the recent advent of Bill 21 and the current reorganization of the health and social service sector in Quebec are important issues that will deeply impact the future of CYC practice in Quebec. In the case of Bill 21, the CYC communities lobbied together for the future of the field. The "Regroupement Quebecois des Associations Professionelles en Education Specialise," or Consortium of Special Care Counsellor Associations of Quebec, has by now disbanded (Maciocia, personal communication, 2015), but it serves as a model of cooperation and collaboration between the Francophone and Anglophone CYC communities. It is an apt demonstration of the extent to which the two communities have common interests. Another challenge, one that is being taken up by the AEESQ (Ratel, personal communication, 2015), is to bring together Psychoeducateurs, Educateurs Specialises, and Educateurs to lobby for the continued professionalization of all CYCs.

LOOKING FORWARD: ANTICIPATED CHALLENGES

CYC practitioners, educators, and trainers in Quebec share the preoccupations of the field that are expressed worldwide. There is an awareness of the increased complexity of the social environment in which children, youth, and families may either flourish or flounder and there are consistent efforts in the educational programs, the agencies, and the professional associations to update practice knowledge given the ever-changing environment. Recent concerns include the impact of technology and social media (see also Martin & Stuart, this volume), the increased economic pressures and associated shifts in the job market, contemporary issues in the transition to adulthood, and the importance of learning and relearning how to work in a multicultural context (Carpanzano, personal communication, 2015). Unique to Quebec, however, are the demands of a significant reorganization of services in the public sector occurring at the time of writing, which will significantly alter the availability of resources and the career prospects of CYC professionals, as well as access to services for marginalized populations in Quebec. The advent of Bill 21, legislation that provided new guidelines for licensing and a redefinition of the tasks of different categories of CYC practitioners, is a subject of ongoing concern, and will, without a doubt, continue to be at the centre of preoccupations in the field for some time. Lastly, given patterns of immigration to Quebec, there is an ever-increasing need to provide services to members of cultural communities who are not only displaced, but function as what is referred to in Quebec as "Allophones," speaking neither French nor English. It is hoped that the CYC community can continue to come together across the linguistic divides that still exist in Quebec to share expertise; to continue to lobby for the benefit of children, youth, and families; and to advance recognition of the field as a whole.

NOTE

1. The author wishes to acknowledge the invaluable contributions of Rick Carpanzano, Tony Maciocia, Dayna Morrow, Julia Pare, and Sylvain Ratel.

REFERENCES

Ainsworth, F., & Fulcher, L. (2006) About the contributors. In F. Ainsworth & L. Fulcher (Eds.), *Group care for children and young people revisited* (pp. xvii–xviii). New York: Haworth Press.

Arsenault, C., Begin, J., Bluteau, J., & Pronovost, J. (2012). Psychoeducation in Quebec: A psychoeducational intervention method. *Journal of Theories and Research in Education, 7*(1), 1–22.

Association des Educateurs Spécialisés du Québec (AEESQ). (2015). Retrieved from http://aeesq.ca

Batshaw Youth and Family Centres. (n.d.). *Our history.* Retrieved from www.batshaw.ac.ca/who-we-are/our-history

Begin, J., Bluteau, J., Arsenault, C., & Pronovost, J. (2012). Psychoeducation in Quebec: Past to present. *Journal of Theories and Research in Education, 7*(1), 1–16.

Brendtro, L. K., Brokenleg, M., & Van Bockern, S. (1990). *Reclaiming youth at risk: Our hope for the future.* Bloomington, IN: National Educational Service.

Brokenleg, M., & Van Bockern, S. (2003). The science of raising courageous kids. *Reclaiming Children and Youth, 12*(1), 22–27.

Burford, G., & Fulcher, L. (2006). Group influences on team functioning. In F. Ainsworth & L. Fulcher (Eds.), *Group care for children and young people revisited* (pp. 175–185). New York: Haworth Press.

Canadian Child Welfare Research Portal. (2011). *Aboriginal child welfare in Quebec.* Retrieved from cwrp.ca/sites/default/files/.../quebec% fact%20/sheet%2011-doc

Champlain College. (n.d.) *Special care counselling.* Retrieved from https://champlainconted.com/programs/aec/special-care-counselling

Charles, G., & Garfat, T. (2009). Child and youth care in North America: Historical roots and current challenges. *Relational Child and Youth Care Practice, 22*(2).

Chenard, G. (2013). *Psychoeducation (definition).* Retrieved from http://www.unipsed.net/index.php/articles/433def

Cosgrove, G. (1975, 22 December). Batshaw report on juvenile system: Map for reform or con game. *The Gazette,* 3.

Durocher, R. (2013). The Quiet Revolution. *The Canadian Encyclopedia.* Retrieved from www.thecanadianencyclopedia.ca/en/article/quiet-revolution

Garfat, T. (n.d.). Biography. Retrieved from www.cyc-net/People/people-garfat.html

Greenwald, M. (2003). Curricular initiatives: A generalist approach to training lifespan practitioners at Vanier College. *Journal of Child and Youth Care, 8*(1), 21–24.

Gregoire, J. C. (2012). A propos de la psychoéducation, un bref aperçu historique. *Revue Canadienne de la Psychoéducation, 41*(2), 121–136.

Grevot, A., & Lacharite, C. (2009). Familles et des positifs de protection de l'enfance, des relations marquées par let contextes nationaux: Mise en perspective France-Quebec. *Sante, Société, et Solidarité, 8*(1), 109–117.

Landry, M. (2007). Historique de la profession. In *Processus clinique en éducation spécialisé* (7th ed., pp. 5–8), trans. Vanier College, Department of Special Care Counselling. Montreal: Les Editions Saint-Martin.

Linnteau, P. (2006). Quebec since Confederation. *The Canadian Encyclopedia*. Retrieved from http://www.thecanadianencyclopedia.ca/en/article/quebec-since-confederation

Maciocia, T. (2010). QAE celebrates silver anniversary. *Quebec Association of Educators Newsletter*, (Fall–Winter), 1–3.

Mann-Feder, V., & Savicki, V. (2003). Burnout in Anglophone and Francophone child and youth workers in Canada: A cross-cultural comparison. *Child and Youth Care Forum, 32*(6), 337–354.

Martin, E., Pomey, M., & Forest, P. (2010). One step forward, one step back: Quebec's 2003–2004 health and social service regionalization policy. *Canadian Public Administration, 53*(4), 467–488.

Ministère de L'Education, Loisir et Sport. (2005). *Special care counselling: Technical training programs.* Quebec: Gouvernement du Québec.

Ministère de la Santé et des Services Sociaux, Direction des relations de travail du personnel salarie. (2015). *Nomenclature des titres d'emploi, des libelles, des taux, et des échelles de salaire du recherche de la santé et des services sociaux.* Quebec: Government of Quebec.

Ordre des Psychoéducateurs et Psychoéducatrices du Québec. (n.d.). *Historique.* Retrieved from www.ordrepsed.qc.ca/fr/lordre/historique

Pigeon, M., & Marquis, D. (n.d.). Quebec in the second half of the twentieth century. Collections and Research, McCord Museum. Retrieved from www.mccord-museum.qc.ca

Ranahan, P., Blanchet-Cohen, N., & Mann-Feder, V. (2015). Moving towards an integrated approach to youth work education. *International Journal of Child, Youth and Family Studies, 6*(4), 516–538.

Reitsma-Street, M., & Leschied, A. (1988). The conceptual level matching model in corrections. *Criminal Justice and Behaviour, 15*(1), 92–108.

Service Canada. (2014). *Educateur specialise.* Retrieved from www.servicecanada.qc.ca/fr/emploi/4215.shtml

Simpson, M., Fast, E., Wegner-Lohin, J., & Trocmé, N. (2014). Quebec's child welfare system. *Canadian Child Welfare Portal, Information Sheet #136E.*

Sinha, V., & Kozlowski, A. (2013). The structure of Aboriginal child welfare in Canada. *The Indigenous Policy Journal, 4*(2).

Sullivan, C., Grant, M. Q., & Grant, J. (1957). The development of interpersonal maturity: Applications to delinquency. *Psychiatry: Interpersonal and Biological Processes, 20*(4), 373–385.

Université de Montréal. (2002). *Hommage à Jeannine Guindon*. Retrieved from http://archive.wikiwix.com/cache/?url+http%A%2F

Vanglois, S., Baillargeon, J., Caldwell, G., Frechet, G., Gauthier, M., & Simard, J. (1992). *Recent social trends in Quebec 1960–1990*. Montreal, QC: McGill-Queens' University Press.

Vanier College. (n.d.). *About the CEGEP system*. Retrieved from www.vaniercollege.qc.ca/about/cegep.php

Welsh, W., & Harris, P. (2013). *Criminal justice policy and planning* (4th ed.). New York: Routledge.

ABOUT THE CONTRIBUTORS

Ben Anderson-Nathe is an associate professor and the program director of the Child, Youth, & Family Studies program at Portland State University. He began his career with young people in the mid-1990s, working in short-term and crisis residential care. He has also worked with youth in therapeutic foster and group care, community mental health, juvenile corrections, homeless and street settings, community education, sexuality education and sexual health, and recreation/camping. His teaching and scholarship draws from this practice experience and focuses primarily on youth work and professional development of youth workers, social justice, and gender/sexuality. Ben also provides training, consultation, and program reviews for youth serving organizations and educational institutions. Correspondence can be directed to banders@pdx.edu.

Emily Carty began her career as a child and youth care practitioner working in the outdoor adventure field. She has over 16 years of experience working alongside children, youth, and families in various roles such as outdoor educator, outreach worker, and residential care worker. Emily completed an MA in Child and Youth Care at the University of Victoria, where she wrote her thesis on bridging outdoor adventure and child and youth care. Emily is a part-time instructor at Georgian College in the Child and Youth Care Program. She also coordinates services for Bartimaeus Specialized Behavioural Support Services, and is a Service Director for Brayden Supervision Services in Muskoka, Ontario. Correspondence can be directed to emilycarty@hotmail.com.

Grant Charles is an associate professor in the School of Social Work and an affiliated associate professor with the Division of Adolescent Health and Medicine in the Department of Pediatrics at the Faculty of Medicine at the University of British Columbia. He is also an adjunct professor with the School of Child and Youth Care at the University of Victoria. He is a past editor of *Relational Child and Youth Care Practice*. Grant served for many years as special adviser to the first British Columbia Representative of Children and Youth and to the Aboriginal Healing Foundation. His areas of specialty are child and youth mental health and child welfare. He is currently involved in research on historical institutional abuse. Correspondence can be directed to grant.charles@ubc.ca.

Shay Erlich is a Hard of Hearing, multiply disabled, and genderqueer child and youth care practitioner. They have spent the last ten years advocating for better inclusion and services for young people with disabilities, and currently work as an independent consultant assisting front-line service organizations in creating more accessible programs for the diverse young people that they work with. Shay strongly believes in a social justice and disability rights approach within a child and youth care relational context. Shay holds an MA degree in Child and Youth Care from Ryerson University and their research interests include Deafness and disability in a child and youth care context, gender identity, as well as Social Circus. They are interested in expanding the definition of child and youth care practice to include the therapeutic benefit of physical expression through the arts (such as circus) rather than understanding child and youth care as a solely talking profession. Correspondence can be directed to shay@shayerlich.com.

Kiaras Gharabaghi is the Director of the School of Child & Youth Care at Ryerson University in Toronto. He spent 25 years working directly with young people and their families in child and youth mental health, child welfare, and youth homelessness sectors. Kiaras has published seven books and many articles on issues and themes related to child and youth care practice, and he is a regular columnist for the International Child and Youth Care Network (www.cyc-net.org). Most recently he has published *A Hard Place to Call Home: A Canadian Perspective on Residential Care and Treatment for Children and Youth*, also through Canadian Scholars. Correspondence can be directed to k.gharabaghi@ryerson.ca.

Nevin Harper has more than 25 years' leadership experience in outdoor adventure education as a guide, youth counsellor, administrator, and researcher. He is an associate professor in the School of Child and Youth Care at the University of Victoria and the national research coordinator for Outward Bound Canada. Nevin founded the Canadian Adventure Therapy Symposium series and is co-chair of the Adventure Therapy International Committee. His research examines the role of natural environments and adventure experiences in human health and development. Nevin maintains field qualifications and trainer status with the Outdoor Council of Canada and Paddle Canada. Correspondence can be directed to njharper@uvic.ca.

Julie James has worked with young people for over 25 years across multiple sectors. Most of her front-line work, and where her heart remains, is with young people in care. Julie also focuses on supporting resurgence practices as they emerge through youth-led activism particularly for Indigenous, Black, trans, and other LGBTQ2S+ individuals. Her PhD dissertation explored the power of Indigenous youth activism for disrupting the white Canadian settler state. Her research work centres on supporting young trans people and their families. Her current project is a province-wide study that explores the social and legal service needs of trans Ontarians with a large youth representation. She is also part of a national research project examining the advocacy work of parents of young trans people. Finally, Julie aims to help build capacity for gender/trans affirmative care across community service sectors (education, child welfare, housing, and youth services) through research and advocacy. Correspondence can be directed to julie.james@ryerson.ca.

Andy Leggett is the clinical director and owner of Broken Arrow, a private foster care agency in Ontario. Andy has been working in foster care and with foster parents, both privately and in the public sector, for almost 30 years. Andy is a published author and a contributor to journals, and can be found at most conferences promoting the work of foster carers and child and youth care practitioners worldwide. Andy is married and a proud father of three now adult children, whom he hopes to be just like when he grows up. Correspondence can be directed to aleggett@barts.ca.

Doug Magnuson is an associate professor at the University of Victoria in the School of Child and Youth Care. He is the co-author of the forthcoming book *I Feel Like I've Really Grown Up: The Experience of Emerging Adulthood among Street-Involved Youth* and is the co-author of other recent and forthcoming publications about street-involved youth and sex workers. He teaches courses about research methods and data analysis, and his work experience includes outdoor education, group homes for youth and adults, and community centres. His degrees include a BA in Philosophy, an MA in Outdoor Education, and a PhD in Educational Psychology, Social Psychology of Education. More information can be found at http://web.uvic.ca/~dougm. Correspondence can be directed to dougm@uvic.ca.

Varda R. Mann-Feder is a professor of Applied Human Sciences at Concordia University and the founding director of the Graduate Diploma in Youth Work. She is known for her research on aging out of care and her advocacy on behalf of youth in placement. She worked for many years as a consulting psychologist in the Anglophone child welfare system in Montreal, where she provided intervention training to front-line workers across a range of domains. She is the adult mentor to the newly formed Care Jeunesse, the first alumni of care organization in Quebec. At the international level, she is an active member of INTRAC and a member of the Editorial Board of FICE. Correspondence can be directed to varda.mann-feder@concordia.ca.

Nancy Marshall has been working as a classroom and community-based CYCP for over ten years, supporting young people with diverse disabilities. Nancy recently completed an MA in Child and Youth Care at Ryerson University in Toronto, with a research focus on autism, social justice, and disability rights. Correspondence can be directed to marshall.nancy@gmail.com.

Jennifer Martin is the associate dean of the Faculty of Community Services and an associate professor in the School of Child and Youth Care at Ryerson University. Her program of research and scholarship focuses on trauma, child sexual abuse images and online exploitation, and implications of digital technology in child and youth care practice. An integral component of her research entails collaboration with community agencies and organizations. Her research interests include practitioner self-care and the pedagogical role of mindfulness in the "caring" classroom. Student engagement and mentorship of new faculty are important components of her scholarship. Correspondence can be directed to jjmartin@ryerson.ca.

Heather Modlin has worked with young people in residential care for 30 years. She is currently provincial director of Key Assets Newfoundland and Labrador, an organization providing residential and family-based care to children and youth. Heather is a former president of the Council of Canadian Child and Youth Care Associations and the Child and Youth Care Association of Newfoundland and Labrador, a founding board member of the Child and Youth Care Educational Accreditation Board of Canada, a board member of the Child and Youth Care Certification Board and the International Child and Youth Care Network, and an editorial board member of the *Relational Child and Youth Care*

Practice journal. Heather has an MSc in Child and Youth Care Administration from Nova Southeastern University and a PhD in Child and Youth Care from the University of Victoria. Correspondence can be directed to heather.modlin@ keyassetsnl.ca.

Janet Newbury is an adjunct professor in the School of Child and Youth Care at the University of Victoria, where she instructs and does research. Her focus has shifted from individual interventions to the value of community engagement when it comes to health and well-being, and to democracy in general terms. Her work experiences and research interests have led her to explore the connections between community-based approaches to economic and social development and the well-being of children, youth, and families. Through this work, she has participated as co-founding member of the Post-Growth Institute, an associate with the Canadian Centre for Policy Alternatives and the Taos Institute, and a member of the global Community Economies Collective. She lives on Tla'amin territory near Powell River, BC, where she is currently a member of the boards of directors for the Powell River Division of Family Practice, the Powell River Historical Museum and Archives, and the Sunshine Music Festival. Correspondence can be directed to janet.newbury@gmail.com.

Kelly C. Shaw is currently on faculty at the Nova Scotia Community College in the Child and Youth Care Diploma Program. She teaches in Truro and in the Nunatsiavut region. She has an MA in Child and Youth Study, holds certification from the CYC Certification Board, and is completing a PhD in Educational Studies at Brock University. For the past few years, she has also been working in Nunavut in adolescent group care environments. She is a believer in creative interactive programming with youth and with learners, and is interested in exploring further how creative programming can be used to build essential practice skills within a child and youth care educational setting. Correspondence can be directed to Kelly.Shaw@nscc.ca.

Heather Snell has been involved in child and youth care education and practice for over 30 years. Her work has enabled her to be with young people and families sharing a variety of settings including residential, community, and medical care. As an educator, Heather has coordinated and taught in CYC diploma, degree, and graduate programs at Humber College and Ryerson University in Canada, and the University of Strathclyde in Scotland. She is a board member of the

Child and Youth Care Education Accreditation Board of Canada, where she chairs the Education Day and the Research Committees. Heather is the author of several publications investigating field practicum models in CYC education. She is the editor of the international journal *Relational Child and Youth Care Practice*. Heather's approach to CYC education and practice is characterized by interdisciplinary and collaborative inquiry, and is always informed by her reflective arts-based lens. Correspondence can be directed to heather.snell@ryerson.ca.

Carol Stuart began her career in residential care in Ontario and has worked within residential and community-based child and youth care organizations. She has been a faculty member at Grant MacEwan Community College (now University), the University of Victoria, and Ryerson University, and maintains an adjunct professor position at University of Victoria and Ryerson University. She is currently the associate vice-president, Academic at Vancouver Island University. She has supported over 25 graduate students, including Aboriginal students, at the University of Victoria and Ryerson University. Carol has authored two editions of Foundations of Child and Youth Care and is the co-author of *Right Here, Right Now: Exploring Life-Space Intervention for Children and Youth*. She lives in Nanaimo with her husband and an assorted menagerie, and regularly appreciates the beautiful West Coast from the edge of the island, the middle of the rainforest, or the cockpit of a kayak. Correspondence can be directed to carol.stuart@viu.ca.

Wolfgang Vachon has been working with children and youth for close to three decades. Community-based arts practices have informed his work with diverse young people including those who are street involved, homeless, LGBTQ2S+, survivors of trauma, living in detention, and other forms of state care. Wolfgang is a full-time faculty member in the Child and Youth Care programs at Humber College in Toronto, Canada, and is the host of CYC Podcast: Discussions on Child and Youth Care (www.cycpodcast.org). Correspondence can be directed to wolfgang.vachon@humber.ca.